T0110450

PRAISE FOR
THE PIRATE'S DILEMMA

Best Pirate of 2008, *BusinessWeek*

"Reading *The Pirate's Dilemma* is like stepping into a parallel universe [that is] vast and deep. . . . Mason nimbly guides us through decades of the underground youth scene [in a] tour [that] is diverting and written in a pleasing patter. . . . Something more . . . than a business book [and] more satisfying—more authentic, as he might put it—than most books that rave about the Web 2.0."

—James Pressley, *Newsday*

"Through a tornado of hip-hop beats and remarkable stories, Matt Mason takes us on a riveting journey to the heart of innovation. In this explosive book, he shows us that companies face a stark choice: Will you allow yourself to be gutted by a pirate or will you actually become one?"

—Frans Johansson, author of *The Medici Effect: Breakthrough Insights at the Intersection of Ideas, Concepts, and Cultures*

"Smart and thought-provoking . . . Mason has crafted a fascinating primer on the intersection of piracy, youth culture, and business."

—*The Boston Phoenix*

"This thought-provoking book, which also argues that the globalization of hip-hop culture could save the world by keeping it real, is ready to blow your mind."

—*Zink* magazine

"Matt Mason free runs over a half century of global popular culture to describe the shape of our possible future. *The Pirate's Dilemma* is a series of leaps of imagination, and it always lands with style."

—Jeff Chang, author of *Can't Stop Won't Stop: A History of the Hip-Hop Generation* and editor of *Total Chaos: The Art and Aesthetics of Hip-Hop*

"An attractive argument . . . A theory that's pro-technology, pro-money, and pro-youth all at once [and Mason] does a good job of proving it. . . . For once, someone is telling young people that we have power, and that we're not selfish and apathetic but demanding 'a more democratic strain of capitalism' while still looking out for our enlightened self-interest."

—Nona Willis Aronowitz, *The New York Observer*

"Provocative stuff [with] a spooky prescience . . . A must-read for our legislators, who seem intent on stamping out youth's unruly practices—downloading and graffiti—with ever more draconian laws. . . . The idea of capitalism reclaimed and remixed, infused with an altruistic bent leading to a more engaged corporate mentality, has appeal."

—*The New Zealand Herald*

"In comparison with most other contemporary books that seek to educate corporate culture about what kids are doing, Mason exudes the authority, and sheer joyful fascination, of someone who is saturated in what he talks about. Book of the week."

—*The Guardian*

"Importantly accessible . . . [Mason has] insights that align him with the most sophisticated of academics in a style anyone can read."

—*Scotland on Sunday*

THE PIRATE'S DILEMMA

How Youth Culture
Is Reinventing Capitalism

MATT MASON

FREE PRESS

New York   London   Toronto   Sydney

*f*P

FREE PRESS
A Division of Simon & Schuster, Inc.
1230 Avenue of the Americas
New York, NY 10020

First Free Press hardcover edition May 2009

FREE PRESS and colophon are trademarks of Simon & Schuster, Inc.

For information about special discounts for bulk purchases,
please contact Simon & Schuster Special Sales at
1-866-506-1949 or business@simonandschuster.com.

The Simon & Schuster Speakers Bureau can bring authors to your live event. For more
information or to book an event, contact the Simon & Schuster Speakers Bureau at
1-866-248-3049 or visit our website at www.simonspeakers.com.

Designed by Kyoko Watanabe

Illustration by Ji Lee ⒸⒸ

Manufactured in the United States of America

1   3   5   7   9   10   8   6   4   2

Library of Congress Control Number: 2007023530

ISBN 978-1-416-53220-0

For Emily

CONTENTS

You are now about to witness the
strength of street knowledge.
— Dr. Dre, 1988

THE PIRATE'S DILEMMA

Enter the Lollipop

"Meter Pop" street installation by Mark Jenkins—
Independence Avenue, Washington, D.C., January 15, 2006
© *Mark Jenkins*

Imagine you're in your car, rolling down Independence Avenue in Washington, D.C. It's a cold, crisp January morning. You flick on the radio and rotate through the FM crackle until a song you like hacks its way through the static. You twist the tuner until you're locked in and the track floats from the speakers in clear stereo, filling the vehicle.

But not for long. Moments later, at the light, an SUV lurches to a stop beside you, blasting bass-heavy hip-hop beats. Your music instantly splinters as the low-end frequencies of the superior neighboring system rattle your windows. You glare at the guy reclining in the driver's seat, but his cap is pulled too low over his face to catch his eye, and the sunlight is catching on the expensive-looking watch on his left arm, stretched across the steering wheel. As the bass reverberates through the traffic, he nods in time with a stuttering snare drum. Gravelly lyrics make their way out into the winter air.

This guy, it strikes you, could be hip-hop's modern-day poster child. He exudes swagger, confidence, and aspiration. The penchant for heavyweight cars and luxury jewelry is obvious, yet the sound track suggests a deep-seated connection to the street and the perceived realities of poverty. He looks like an extra from a P. Diddy video, but he could be a college student, crack dealer, or quantum physicist. There is no way of telling.

He could be from any number of social or ethnic backgrounds. This guy is one of a hundred million people in the United States *alone* under hip-hop's influence, enchanted by one of the largest cultural movements on our planet today. To many, he represents the sum total of youth culture's progress.

But you're too busy admiring his watch and glaring at his obnoxious speakers to check your mirrors. If you had, you might have noticed that the future of youth culture is actually pulling up behind you.

What you *did* notice is your radio, which has just cut out. You lean forward and adjust the tuner. Nothing. In the SUV next to you, the radio has gone silent, too. You look across to see hip-hop's poster child banging his dashboard; he looks as frustrated as you are. You check the sunroof—the skies are clear, no aliens jamming your signal. Nothing in your rearview mirror either, except some kid in a Prius with a blank expression.

Of course, you can't see the iPod connected to a modified iTrip on his passenger seat. It's even less likely that you'd guess he's using these devices to broadcast silence across the entire FM band, transmitting tranquillity pirate-style in the thirty-foot radius around his car.

The unassuming face in the Prius is the latest in a long line of youth culture revolutionaries, a band of radio pirates who have manipulated media for decades. They founded Hollywood, reinvented many forms of broadcasting, and helped win the Cold War. While changing the face of media around the world, the guy in the Prius, like his many predecessors, has gone almost completely unnoticed by mainstream society.

The light turns green and you pull away, still puzzled about what just happened. You head straight on. As the SUV and the Prius hang a right onto Ninth Street toward the Southwest Freeway, your radio suddenly comes back to life. A few minutes later, you've almost forgotten the incident as you park farther down the avenue. But as you fumble for change for the meter, you are about to have an even stranger encounter with youth culture.

Instead of the parking meter you use every day, a four-foot-high lemon-yellow lollipop is sticking out of the ground, basking unapologetically in the morning sunshine. Did you accidentally park on the set of *Hansel & Gretel*?

On closer inspection, it becomes clear you didn't. The parking meter has been remixed into a piece of countercultural candy, its sugary facade made entirely of bright yellow Scotch tape. It is the calling card of another group of society's unsung heroes—a group of pirates who manipulate public space rather than the public airwaves. The lollipop is one of the many hallmarks of an invisible army who started a revolution with pens and spray cans. They have affected advertising, fashion, film, and design, among other industries. They have established billion-dollar brands, focused the media spotlight on controversial political issues, and changed the way we think about the world around us.

On our airwaves, in our public spaces, and through the new layers of digital information that envelop us, pirates are changing the way we use information, and in fact, the very nature of our economic system. From radio pirates to graffiti artists to open-source culture to the remix, the ideas behind youth cultures have evolved into powerful forces that are changing the world.

For the last sixty years, capitalism has run a pretty tight ship in the West. But in increasing numbers, pirates are hacking into the hull and holes are starting to appear. Privately owned property, ideas, and privileges are leaking out into the public domain beyond anyone's control.

Pirates are rocking the boat. As a result people, corporations, and governments across the planet are facing a new dilemma—the Pirate's

Dilemma: How should we react to the changing conditions on our ship? Are pirates here to scupper us, or save us? Are they a threat to be battled, or innovators we should compete with and learn from? To compete or not to compete—that is the question—perhaps the most important economic and cultural question of the twenty-first century.

A man at the intersection between youth culture and innovation named John Perry Barlow, the cofounder of the Electronic Frontier Foundation and former lyricist for the Grateful Dead, summarized the problem in 2003:

> Throughout the time I've been groping around cyberspace, an immense, unsolved conundrum has remained at the root of nearly every legal, ethical, governmental, and social vexation to be found in the Virtual World. I refer to the problem of digitized property. The enigma is this: If our property can be infinitely reproduced and instantaneously distributed all over the planet without cost, without our knowledge, without its even leaving our possession, how can we protect it? How are we going to get paid for the work we do with our minds? And, if we can't get paid, what will assure the continued creation and distribution of such work?
>
> Since we don't have a solution to what is a profoundly new kind of challenge, and are apparently unable to delay the galloping digitization of everything not obstinately physical, we are sailing into the future on a sinking ship.

This is the story of how pirates might save this sinking ship. Often pirates are the first to feel the winds of change blowing. The answer to the Pirate's Dilemma lies in the stories of pirates sailing into waters uncharted by society and the markets, spaces where traditional rules don't apply. The answers lie in the history of youth culture.

For more than sixty years, teenage rebels have been doing things differently and working out new ways to share information, intellectual property, and public space. Behind youth movements familiar to us are radical ideas about how we can compete, collaborate, and coexist in an environment where old assumptions about how we treat information do not hold.

The Pirate's Dilemma will chart the rise of these radical ideas—ideas that started with individual mavericks conducting crazy social experiments which eventually enter everything, influencing business, politics, and many other areas.

For the first time, the dots between our collective future and youth culture's checkered past will be connected, illustrating how a handful of seemingly random absurdities inspired some of our most important innovations. Right under our noses, the ripple effects of youth culture have been changing the way we live and work. But much of the time these effects have gone unnoticed.

Soon enough, though, everyone will notice. The Pirate's Dilemma is not just facing those who deal in digital information—it's escaping into the real world, too. As we shall see, new technologies could make it just as easy for us all to download physical products the way we download music, and we can already jam information being broadcast with a narrowcast signal of our own, signals that collectively have the power to overthrow presidents.

The Information Age has hit puberty and is experiencing growing pains. By remembering our own teenage years we can piece together the best way to ease this transition, searching out and understanding successful business models that entered society from the edges, many directly from youth cultures.

We rebel through youth movements because we recognize that things don't always work the way they should. They are a way of communicating alternatives without inciting bloody revolutions, a way to reorganize systems from the inside, which isn't easy to do. As rebel economist E. F. Schumacher observed of the damaging effects of the systems that govern us: "to deny them would be too obviously absurd, and to acknowledge them would condemn the central preoccupation of modern society as a crime against humanity." But as teenagers most of us aren't reading Schumacher. Instead we protest with youth culture, social experiments—informal studies in the art of doing things differently that have given us good music, bad haircuts, and new ways to operate.

The little-known eureka moments in youth culture documented in this book are rare and priceless. The big bang happens when a strange new idea suddenly makes sense to a handful of people, who then transmit it to others. Experiencing one is like a revelation, a glimpse into the future.

When we see superstars and brands emerge from these scenes years later, it becomes clear to us all what these radical ideas that start small can mushroom into. The story of youth culture's commercial success has been reenacted many times, performed by a variety of players against the backdrop of different genres across the globe. Rappers such as 50 Cent can make $50 million a year without even releasing a record; a graffiti artist such as Marc Ecko can develop his tag into a multinational brand worth more than $1 billion. "Today the most disruptive voices are no longer the artists' voices being piped over the corporate airwaves," Ecko told *Royal* magazine in 2006. "It's the voice of the pirate, the pirate has become the producer. The indy-punk 'f the man' message is no longer a hook in a song. It's scary. It's hungry. It's Godzilla. He's knocking on the door uninvited, ready for dessert."

And these new Godzillas aren't just graffiti artists or multimilliondollar MCs. The face under Godzilla's rubbery mask could be yours. I call this problem the "Pirate's Dilemma" and not the "Pirate Dilemma," because there is no difference between us and them. Illegal pirates, legitimate companies, and law-abiding citizens are now all in the same space, working out how to share and control information in new ways. The Pirate's Dilemma is not just about how we compete against pirates, and how we treat *them*, it's also about how we can become better by recognizing the pirate within ourselves.

How did we get here? What do the new conditions shaping our ship mean, and what do they tell us about where we are going next? To answer these questions, I've pulled together the work of leading academics, historians, innovators, and visionaries from a wide variety of disciplines, whose ideas and insights are illustrated with a cast of characters that includes such icons as Andy Warhol, the Ramones, Madonna, Pharrell, and 50 Cent. I've drawn on my own experiences growing up as a pirate DJ in London, at the flash point of emerging scenes, and my professional life immersed in the mainstream music, media, and advertising industries.

I've met with and interviewed legendary musicians, artists, entrepreneurs, and DJs who have changed things for the rest of us, often without us knowing. From hip-hop moguls such as Russell Simmons to media mavericks such as Wikipedia founder Jimmy Wales, I'll tell the story of a world ruled by the Pirate's Dilemma with the assistance of some of our best-known change agents.

But I'll also be introducing you to some extraordinary people who are telling their stories for the first time. You'll meet the nun who helped invent dance music, and learn how the ideas she promoted in a children's home in the 1940s are transforming the free market as we know it. You'll meet the three high school kids who remixed Nazis into Smurfs in the 1980s, and changed the future of the video game industry as a result.

We'll meet the professor who can tell us what will happen to Nike when it becomes possible for kids to download sneakers. We'll see how the hippie movement was responsible for the birth of the personal computer. We'll find out what graffiti artists, fashion designers, and French chefs can teach us about the future of copyright, and uncover how a male model, messing around with disco records in New York in the 1970s, changed the way Boeing designs airplanes. But before we do, we need to understand the thinking behind the business model that gave rise to the Pirate's Dilemma. This is a new version of the old system I refer to as "Punk Capitalism."

"This is Punk Capitalism," Bono proudly announced to the world, as a torrent of camera flashes ricocheted off his trademark tinted glasses at an October 2006 press conference. The rock star philanthropist was in Los Angeles to launch the Product Red campaign, backed by a phalanx of CEOs from companies such as Nike, American Express, Gap, Apple, Armani, and Motorola, all of whom had signed on to create a range of products whose profits are used to help fight AIDS in Africa.

But ten years before Bono's press conference, three Canadian punk rockers, who we'll hear from shortly, had been using the term to sum up their philosophy long before Product Red—a philosophy they used to grow a fanzine into a multimillion-dollar media empire.

I use the term Punk Capitalism to describe the new set of market conditions governing society. It's a society where piracy, as the cochair at Disney recently put it, is "just another business model." A society where the remix is changing the way production and consumption are structured, rendering the nineteenth-century copyright laws we use obsolete. A world where advertising no longer works quite the way it did. It's a place where open-source ways of working are generating a wealth of new public goods, niche markets, knowledge, and resources—free tools for the rest of us to build both commercial and noncommercial ventures. It's a place where creativity is our most valuable resource. It's a marketplace where things we used to pay for are free, and things that used to be free have to be paid for. It's a world where altruism is as powerful as competition, inhabited by a new breed of social entrepreneurs, a creative resistance who make money by putting as much emphasis on truly making a difference as they do on turning a profit.

The philosophies that underpin Punk Capitalism took shape in the roots of punk rock. But as we shall now see, the story of Punk Capitalism actually begins in the roots of a hairstyle, created in the 1960s by a runaway teenager from Kentucky—a hairstyle that would change the world.

CHAPTER 1

Punk Capitalism

From D.I.Y. to Downloading Sneakers

Illustration by Art Jaz

"I'd noticed that hair *mattered.*"

He's sitting across from me in the back of a café. You wouldn't think that hair mattered to look at him. His dark brown hair falls around his thick-rimmed glasses down to his jaw, casually framing his face. He has that relaxed, just-got-out-of-bed look. Not the on-purpose kind media types have, but as though he actually might have. It doesn't look as though he's given hair much thought at all, but the man I am talking with had one of the most important haircuts of the twentieth century.

This is Richard Meyers: writer, poet, artist, and former front man of bands the Neon Boys, Television, and the Voidoids. He is better known as Richard Hell, and the angular hairstyle and cut-up clothing he pioneered in the early 1970s would come to define a movement better known as punk.

Not far from where we're sitting on New York's Lower East Side was the club CBGB, where Hell's early performances inspired punk's first generation. A runaway from Kentucky, he arrived in the city an aspiring writer, affected by beat poets and writers such as Jack Kerouac and Allen Ginsberg, but quickly realized he could make a more powerful statement with music. "Part of what I liked about music was all these other means for communication," Hell told me. "In rock 'n' roll it's always been important how you looked. How you looked said something. And it was usually something about rejecting convention and the nine-to-five, and any kind of control, but you could get really elaborate with how you used the way you looked to communicate stuff. You're always being interviewed, your album covers, your live shows, it was so broad, the areas for getting your message across. I wanted to use all of them."

And use them he did. Inspired in part by the rebellious French poets Rimbaud and Artaud, who had sported spiky hair in the early nineteenth century, Hell chopped his mane into a short, aggressive style as a way of rejecting the hippie movement and the big-hair glamour of stadium rock. He looked at the Beatles' bowl haircuts and asked himself, what are they really saying? "Well," he explains, "they really say *five-year-old kid*. So I thought, 'What was my generation's haircut like when we were five years old?' Where I grew up, the most popular haircut was called the 'Butch.' Short all the way around, and you'd maybe wax up the front of it. But of course being kids, we wouldn't get to the barber that often, and we wouldn't keep it neat, it would just be kind of raggedy. . . . I wanted it to be do-it-yourself. I wanted it to *not* be something you'd go to the barber for."

Richard fused the Beatles, the "Butch," and two radical nineteenth-century French bohemians into his new do-it-yourself hairstyle, and hell literally broke loose. In 1974 Television took to the stage at CBGB on Sunday nights. Hell wore clothes slashed as aggressively as his hair, held together with safety pins and emblazoned with slogans such as

PLEASE KILL ME. "It was a rejection of having who you are imposed on you by corporations who were gonna profit from making you feel insecure about how you look," he says. "I've just always been really skeptical and suspicious and resentful of people who try to sell you stuff by intimidating you."

Hell's statements were a full-frontal assault on the senses, burning his ideas into the minds of his audience, who at the time happened to be some of the most influential people in New York City, and in pop culture period. After Television's success, CBGB (which stood for "Country Blue-Grass Blues") switched to a punk rock–only format every night, becoming a creative hotbed for artists and bands such as the Ramones, Patti Smith, Talking Heads, and Debbie Harry, all of whom cut their teeth on its stage. Malcolm McLaren, then manager of another influential group, the New York Dolls, was so stimulated by Hell's look he took it back to London and used it to create a new band: the Sex Pistols.

Punk exploded.

Thirty years after it first shook the world, punk is in a museum. A few miles uptown from where Hell and I are sitting, the Metropolitan Museum of Art is holding a punk exhibition sponsored by multinational luxury goods brand Burberry. Tourists are studying early British punk clothes—made by now world-famous fashion designers such as Vivienne Westwood—and listening to a podcast commentary by the world-famous Sex Pistol Johnny Rotten.

Punk is dead.

But Hell survived. Instead of becoming a parody of his former self, he moved on. He remains on the Lower East Side, under the mainstream's radar, but credible in many other circles, now the successful poet and published writer he always aspired to be. This new attitude, career, and his current, less threatening hairstyle are all part of a strategy. "The interesting thing is to not remain the same," he muses. "To me that's what's boring; I don't really care to see fifty-year-old people going around in punk leather jackets. The point is to stay unclassifiable. Then they don't own you."

When the hairstyle lost its meaning, Hell lost the hairstyle. But his statement and the do-it-yourself ideal he promoted affected the world. Today it is the driving force behind a new generation of D.I.Y. entrepreneurs who are raising hell once again. Disruptive new D.I.Y. technologies are causing unprecedented creative destruction. The history of punk offers us valuable insights into how this new world works. Punk was an angry outburst, a reaction to mass culture, but it offered new ideas about how mass culture could be replaced with a more personalized, less centralized worldview.

Punk has survived in many incarnations musically—it became new wave, influenced hip-hop, and conceived grunge and the notion of indie bands. But more important, its independent spirit also spurred a do-it-yourself revolution. D.I.Y. encourages us to reject authority and hierarchy, advocating that we can and should produce as much as we consume. Since punk, this idea has been quietly changing the very fabric of our economic system, replacing outdated ideas with the twenty-first-century upgrades of Punk Capitalism.

Suddenly like at a punk gig, today everybody is getting smashed together in a much more turbulent, concentrated environment that is constantly changing. There are fewer conventional "jobs," and increasingly complex relationships between those consuming and those producing. And changes in manufacturing mean soon all of us could have the means to create literally anything ourselves, from the comfort of our own homes.

As we shall now see, the possibilities of D.I.Y. are reaching new heights. Like a roomful of teenagers with green hair throwing bottles at one another, this new world can look frightening. But once you get it, it's obvious it's a better place to be. The end of top-down mass culture is creating opportunities and freedoms for us all.

Hell used the past to create a hairstyle that shaped the perspective of a generation. Generations since have grown up using ingenuity and creativity to do the things punk always promoted: tearing down hegemonies and hierarchies, starting over, and improving the way we operate as a society.

Hell is right. Hair *mattered.*

Long live punk.

"Where everything went wrong in the world. Previously."

When punk was born, polite society didn't think it was right about anything. Initially, punks were seen as threats, menaces, scum. "What is punk music? It's disgusting, degrading, ghastly, sleazy, prurient, voyeuristic, and nauseating. Most of these groups would be vastly improved by sudden death," remarked a member of the Greater London Council in 1976. But when Joe Strummer, lead singer of the legendary punk band the Clash passed away in 2002, the BBC described punks as "pioneers who kicked down musical and social barriers, making anything seem possible."

So what changed? Why does history remember them fondly? Because the punks had a point. Established ideas and outdated dogma create limitations. Limitations suck. As the Sex Pistols lead singer, Johnny Rotten, said in the documentary *The Filth and the Fury*, "All our first rehearsals were a nightmare. It would be constantly 'You know you gotta learn to sing' and it's a Why? Says who? Why are you accepting all these, like, boundaries? That's where everything went wrong in the world. Previously."

Youth cultures often embody some previously invisible, unacknowledged feeling in society and give it an identity. They are reactions or responses to other factors, and once a critical mass of people endorse such movements, they take on lives of their own. "I think it was in fact, inevitable in history," says Hell. "Western culture got homogenized and corporatized to an extent where it was inevitable that would come into existence a stratum under the radar, where people who saw the stupidity and boredom of the mass culture started doing things themselves and for each other, and opposing the standards and values of the false, mass way of doing things. . . . I don't think it was someone's brilliant idea, it just followed from the way things had become."

The urge to rebel and express oneself is clearly many moons older than punk, but its angry, loud, minimal sound concentrated this feeling and sent shock waves through society, demonstrating to a generation disenchanted with rock 'n' roll that once again, anything was possible. "We thought pop stars came from outer space and we couldn't do it," says Paul Cook in *Punk* by Colegrave and Sullivan. This is no surprise; at the time most aging rockers were hanging out in Monaco with supermodels (in fact, many still are) and had no idea about the predicament of Britain's underclass. But Cook soon found out he was wrong. He was the drummer for the Sex Pistols.

The Pistols, and punk, empowered ordinary people. Not only did they encourage others to start making music, but also to design their own clothes, start fanzines, and set up gigs, demonstrations, record stores, and record labels. As Hebdige points out in *Subculture: The Meaning of Style*, the punk fanzine *Sniffin' Glue* "contained perhaps the single most inspired item of propaganda produced by the subculture— the definitive statement of punk's do-it-yourself philosophy—a diagram showing three finger positions on the neck of a guitar over the caption:

"Here's one chord, here's two more, now form your own band."

In the 1970s punk was youth culture. In Britain it was a reaction to mass unemployment, boredom, and the lack of opportunity many young people saw in their future. Today we live in a world where doing-it-yourself doesn't seem that radical at all. We accept that anyone is capable of becoming a change agent.

Punk is the place where our story begins, because *all* the ideas in this book are underpinned by the punk perspective and the D.I.Y. philosophy it championed. The do-it-yourself movement of more than thirty years ago offered some suggestions as to how mass culture could be brought down. Today the ideas and technologies empowering us are underpinned by D.I.Y., and mass culture is beginning to falter.

Hurricane Punk

Economist Joseph Schumpeter once said economic development requires "gales of creative destruction." Punk was a category five hurricane.

This hurricane had been brewing since the nineteenth century at least, through a number of countercultural movements that sought to subvert the status quo. Realism, Impressionism, Dadaism, and surrealism all helped forge the spirit of punk, encouraging artists to break the rules and ignore traditions. But it was a gang of drunks from Paris's Left Bank who had the clearest idea where Hurricane Punk was heading.

The Situationists were a small group of radical artists who, during the 1950s and '60s, promoted their anarchic, antiestablishment worldview through art, film, graffiti, writing prose, and any other way they could think of. Their legacy includes not only a huge influence on punk, but also every modern form of activism, pop culture, and even the corporate marketing they despised. Their specialty was *détournement*, the act of taking an existing message, subverting its meaning, and turning it into a new one, as a way of rendering the original statement obsolete.*

Many movements that followed amplified these ideas, such as the beat poets and the Expressionists, but it was Andy Warhol above all others who became obsessed with subverting mass culture. And where better to subvert mass production than at a factory.

Manufacturing Meaning

Warhol churned out his silk screens, lithographs, and films between 1963 and 1968, mimicking mass culture by producing art in the same way.

Warhol also began managing his own band, the Velvet Underground, who encouraged people to question traditional forms of entertainment, placing the avant-garde movement firmly in the context of pop music. Another band that hung out at the Factory was a crossdressing street gang, the New York Dolls, who also promoted the D.I.Y. ethic and would have a huge influence on the Ramones, the Clash, and many others.

After the Factory, Hell and the Neon Boys hit the Lower East Side.

---

*This would later influence remix culture, as would some other important influences on punk, such as the German artist who invented montage, John Heartfield, and the author William S. Burroughs.

The Ramones, Blondie, and many other incredibly influential musicians followed soon after, playing for larger and larger audiences. These bands became the foundation of New York punk, inspiring the bohemians of the Bowery, not to mention a British guy named Malcolm McLaren.

McLaren was an art school dropout who ran the clothing shop Let It Rock on King's Road in London with his then girlfriend, the designer Vivienne Westwood. He was visiting New York in 1974 when he first saw Richard Hell and realized the potential of punk. McLaren wanted to strengthen the connection Hell had made to the Situationist movement, and as *The Rough Guide to Rock* tells it, "he saw the link between French anarchist theory and New York trash, and then turned it into hype for art's sake." After briefly managing the New York Dolls, he returned to London in May 1975 infused with these new ideas. The birth of British punk wasn't far behind him.

Pistol-Whipped

McLaren and Westwood rebranded their King's Road store with a new name, SEX, swapping the tired rock 'n' roll gear they previously peddled for more subversive S and M attire and Hell-inspired cut-up pieces. From the revitalized shop, McLaren began rounding up some of the more promising musicians who hung out there (although as legend has it, Johnny Rotten was recruited simply because he was wearing a Pink Floyd T-shirt, on top of which he had scrawled "I HATE").

The moment the Pistols came onstage was the moment punk became a political and ideological monster. Suddenly even fans who couldn't play an instrument were imbued with D.I.Y. confidence, because being able to play properly no longer mattered. "In England, it all erupted from the Sex Pistols," says Hell, not bitter that they totally jacked his swagger. "So it was all really consistent. Everybody was so outraged on one side—the adults, and turned on by them—the kids, so it was huge news. We in New York knew how much of that had come from New York via Malcolm, the Ramones, and the Dolls. But it hadn't been this consistent wave of activity, publicity, and hysteria until the Sex Pistols and all these other bands suddenly appeared. . . . I don't think they got lucky, they were spectacular, no question about that. They sounded great."

Their first single, "Anarchy in the U.K.," said it all. In three intense years, they were signed and dropped by three major labels. They made more headlines than records, but the one album they did produce, *Never Mind the Bollocks,* released by a young entrepreneur named Richard Branson, is one of the most important in rock 'n' roll history. Their single "God Save the Queen" was so offensive, when it hit number one in the British charts, the spot was left blank in many newspaper and magazine listings. Glen Matlock left the band in 1977 and was replaced by Sid Vicious, punk's most famous martyr. As their popularity grew, so did the national hatred of punk fueled by the press. Mass hysteria took hold of the entire country, with gigs ending in complete chaos, sometimes riots. They demanded anarchy, and they got it. Soon they themselves spun out of control.

The Pistols famously split in San Francisco in January 1978. "Ever get the feeling you've been cheated?" Rotten bitterly asked the crowd. Overtaken and consumed by their own image, the Pistols lost their grip. In a final, tragic blow, Sid Vicious died of a heroin overdose shortly after the breakup. Punk's first wave was too fast to live and too young to die.

Despite the short-lived nature of this subversive shake-up, Hurricane Punk was one of the most powerful youth cultures the world ever endured, leaving a deluge of sounds, scenes, and movements in its path. The innovative ideas that traveled through the prism of punk illuminated every subculture that followed, wiping the slate clean of perceived limitations and introducing a range of new possibilities. Punk presented us with a new perspective, a perspective we can apply virtually anywhere.

All the World's a Stage
(and It Just Got Rushed)

Fifty years ago the world operated like a conventional rock concert. Some of it still does, and many of us still view it that way. Picture yourself in the crowd at such a concert. The producers, bosses, and owners are the rock stars above, generating the goods, services, salaries, and content we the fans consume from below the inaccessible stage, singing along obediently with our lighters in the air.

Very occasionally a lucky fan is pulled up onstage to give the rest of us something to aspire to, but only very occasionally. You can see that the stage is surrounded by barriers to entry and mean-looking roadies, stopping us from climbing up. These barriers might be a lack of skills or technology; they could be financial. But often they're made of nothing more than our own perception of what's possible. The mean-looking roadies are the doubts society creates that tell us it'll never work, managing our ambitions, keeping our aspirations in check. Looking around the stadium, you see the thousands of others who would also like to get up on that stage, and it's painfully clear you're just another face in the crowd without a chance.

Under punk, the concept of a gig totally changed. Punk despised the one-way flow of information typically found at a rock show. At punk shows the band and the fans occupy the same space, as equals. There is no hierarchy. Everyone is part of the performance. Instead of worshiping a big-hair rock idol from the cheap seats at the back of the stadium, fans now found themselves crammed into smaller venues interacting with the band, shoving and pushing them like other fans. You got to chuck as many beer bottles at the band as they did at you; everyone was allowed to spit on everyone else; and at the end of the performance you all smashed stuff up together. It was often a violent hate/hate relationship, but it was fair.

Our world today is starting to look a lot more like a punk gig (okay, maybe with slightly less spitting). The barriers to entry are being kicked down, and this new breed of fans-turned-performers, including you, is rushing the world stage. Technology is cheap; information is everywhere; and the roadies are gone (who takes advice from *roadies* anyway?). The only thing left to do is to stop defining ourselves by the old hierarchy and run up onstage.

Think about something you have always wanted to do but haven't. You probably didn't do it for a good reason; maybe you didn't know how, couldn't afford it, or didn't think you could get your foot in the door. But with the wealth of information now available to us, we can easily find out how to give most things a try, for the price of access to a computer. And in fact, the less formal knowledge we have of an area, the better we may be at discovering new ways to innovate within it.

In his book *The Medici Effect*, innovation guru Frans Johansson asserts exactly that, putting forward the idea that our knowledge about an area can make us put up "associative barriers," or stifling assumptions we make can subconsciously influence us to do things a certain way. "Although chains of associations have huge benefits," he argues, "they also carry costs. They inhibit our ability to think broadly. We do not question assumptions as readily, we jump to conclusions faster and create barriers to alternate ways of thinking about a particular situation."

None of the punk bands could play very well to begin with (many never learned to play well at all), but they thought broadly about the possibilities of a band. Hell and the Pistols brought fresh ideas they had picked up from other places.

We don't always need to learn everything there is to know; the basics and our own experience and imagination can create far better results. It can make more sense to learn one chord, then maybe just two more.

Then form your own band.

Punk instilled these ideas in its fans from an early age; it is a great metaphor for a huge cultural shift taking place today. So it should come as no surprise that some of the punks who grew up under its influence are the entrepreneurs making this shift happen.

Punk Capitalists

Worldwide there are still many underground incarnations of the punk movement. But punk has also produced a number of movements and companies that work inside the system as much as outside. Gavin McInnes, Shane Smith, and Suroosh Alvi are three old punks who run such a business.

Shane and Gavin grew up in Ottawa listening to punk bands such as the Dead Kennedys and the Subhumans, heavily influenced by the possibilities of D.I.Y. They had to be, according to Smith, because "there were probably like eight punks in the city." They formed several bands from age thirteen, with eloquent names such as "Leather Ass Butt Fuck" and began putting on their own shows. "It wasn't like, oh, well we'll wait 'til the band comes," Smith recalls. "It was, we'll set up our own band, learn how to play, learn how to do it, find the pub to play in, and steal the beer to sell. To do whatever it takes, no matter what."

They did pretty well in Ottawa, until a disagreement with the management at a local punk club led them to leave town. After touring with a couple of bands, they found themselves in Montreal in 1994, where they met Suroosh Alvi. Suroosh had recently come out of rehab and had started a free magazine called the *Voice of Montreal* to keep himself occupied in a bid to stay clean. After he met Gavin and Shane, the title became *VICE*, and the magazine was run the same way as their bands, with an editorial policy just as colorful, violent, and controversial.

"When you start doing music for just you and your buddies, you don't care," Smith tells me. "You do it for you and a couple of your friends, and if some other people come then great, but you don't really give a shit, right? It's the same doing the mag. We don't do the mag for like an audience, it's not like 'what demographic are we gonna go for?' 'Should we put extreme sports in there?' Cos we don't actually care. We put in whatever we think is interesting."

VICE became famous for their often shocking and seemingly tasteless content. Examples range from the "Dos & Don'ts" fashion section, famous for its scathing yet hilarious evaluations of anyone unfortunate enough to be snapped by a *VICE* photographer, to beauty articles with titles such as "cum vs. moisturizer," reports on the urban foxhunting scene, and exposés on why it's getting harder for old folks to smoke crack in hospitals.* "We're not like *Details* or *GQ* where we have to do one certain kind of thing," explains Smith. "That definitely comes out of the old punk thing of we're just gonna play this small thing for ourselves and if it gets big, fine, but if it doesn't, it doesn't."

More than a decade later, *VICE* magazine is published in fourteen countries and counting, described by *BusinessWeek* as "the funniest

---

*In the interests of full disclosure, I should point out that I have written for *VICE* many times.

print publication in the world . . . the Martha Stewart of the cheap drugs and sex set." The *VICE* empire now includes a successful record label, film company, TV channel, a London pub/gig venue, and several book and merchandise deals. Operating like a punk band has turned *VICE* into a multimillion-dollar brand. So it's also become one of punk's archenemies: a multinational corporation.

From the Situationists to punk, style has long served as a weapon of the disenfranchised, and style magazines such as *VICE* have carried on that tradition, turning this subversive practice into a business plan. Like all successful youth cultures, punk has been co-opted by the establishment.

VICE is today a very credible franchise, used by many mainstream advertisers such as Nike, Levi's, and Absolut vodka. The Sex Pistols reunited for a tour in 1996 (original bassist, Glen Matlock, replaced the late Sid Vicious). "We have found a common cause, and it's your money," remarked Johnny Rotten. In 2004, Rotten starred in another credible franchise used by many mainstream advertisers, the U.K. reality show *I'm a Celebrity, Get Me Out of Here!*

Ever get the feeling you've been cheated?

Image Is Nothing

Despite their ideals, many old punks are kept in business by corporate advertisers, doing the very thing they once rebelled against. Advertising is a gargantuan, multibillion-dollar industry. We are exposed to more than three thousand advertising messages a day. Much of the time, we don't even realize it. The Situationist notion of making art indistinguishable from everyday life is now known as branding.

Punk spoke out against commercialization venomously,* but this unwittingly gave the enemy valuable new ammunition. When something becomes cool, it is more or less instantly consumed by the mainstream, and punk was no different. "I remember in 1977 seeing

---

*Though punk, in practice, was riddled with as many contradictions as the rest of society. Signing with a major label to reach more people is not seen as a justification for doing so by many contemporary punk bands that remain true to their roots. Yet nearly all the early successful bands did.

ripped-up clothes in Macy's windows," recalls Richard Hell. Punk was trying to give people a sense of purpose and freedom from capitalism. So capitalism responded by selling us punk, and mass-produced Ramones T-shirts for the whole family are now sold in shopping malls across the world.

Antiestablishment slogans became the hallmark of big businesses interested in promoting themselves by supposedly empowering us with the D.I.Y. ethic. "Image Is Nothing," says Sprite as it defiantly sells fizzy drinks. "Go Create," Sony urges us. "Don't Be Evil," Google advises. "Have It Your Way," cries Burger King. "Just Do It," bellows Nike. Apple tells the hoards that gather every time it opens a new store to "Think Different," holding D.I.Y. seminars for Mac users, teaching them how to get the most out of punk-branded music software such as GarageBand. "It's hard to spend your life working for peace, justice and a society rich with opportunities for all" wrote Lee Gomes in *The Wall Street Journal*. "It's pretty easy, though, to buy a computer and tell yourself that by doing so, you're somehow still helping to fight that good fight. Good deeds become equated with good shopping."

Purpose Is Everything

The values youth cultures promote often end up as empty gestures in corporate graveyards. Since capitalism emerged, culture has been rebelling against it and figuring out ways to improve it. For more than a hundred years, capitalists have been marketing youth culture back to people, attaching cultural significance to goods and services through advertising.

What is interesting is what else is happening; punk capitalists are starting to use the free-market system to their advantage, and are turning the tables by selling real issues back to us through the things we consume.

The fact that *VICE* has become a minimultinational conglomerate isn't a problem for cofounder Shane Smith, who argues that although they "sold out," their success has actually given them the freedom to be *more* subversive. "When we started out we were really idealistic, and we had a mission, we hated the baby boomers and we wanted to be anti-status quo and all this stuff. But the business of running a magazine, I mean most of my favorite magazines went out of business. It's really difficult. The creative side is one thing but the business side is quite another.

"We started to be in competition with bigger magazines. We were growing and doing different shit . . . concerned about building a brand and money and stuff. [But] now we have money in the bank we're like fuck it, we can do what we want to do and all of a sudden we're getting a lot more political." VICE has in recent years traded basic punk shock tactics to cover genuinely shocking and important stories, stories that often don't get relayed to VICE's young hip audience. When they published "The Special Issue" in 2005, edited by a team of people with various disabilities, featuring articles such as "The Totally Retarded Use of the Word Retard," critics feared they would overstep the line. Instead, the issue received praise for the heartwarming and original way it portrayed one of society's most marginalized groups of people. When Shane Smith and VICE contributing editor Jamie-James Medina traveled to Darfur in 2006 to shoot an extreme travel guide to Sudan, the documentary they came back with* was one of the first in the Western media to explicitly make the link between the actions of Western and Asian oil companies that operate in Sudan, and the genocide that has killed hundreds of thousands of people there and displaced millions more.

"In America there is no anti-status quo media," says Smith. "It's all the same four big companies, and they're all afraid of losing Budweiser so it's just like, there's no voice. The Daily Show with Jon Stewart is the most watched 'news' program by people under thirty-five and it's a spoof comedy show. There is a huge market out there of disenfranchised kids, and we do these political things which aren't Republican or Democrat, but more like how a punk would look at things, which is more like 'This is absurd. It's not right, left, center, whatever, it's just fucked.'"

The future belongs to a new breed of change agents—punk capital-

---

*The five-part documentary Inside Sudan can be seen for free at www.vbs.tv.

ists putting purpose next to profit. Abstract economic constructs have long told us that we are governed by nothing but self-interest, but reality has consistently proved this notion wrong.

These new ventures "leave the competition scratching their heads because they don't really aim to compete in the first place," wrote Richard Siklos in *The New York Times* in 2006. "They would certainly like to cover their costs and maybe make a buck or two, but really, they're not in it for the money. By purely commercial measures, they are illogical. If your name were, say, Rupert or Sumner, they would represent a kind of terror that might keep you up at night: death by smiley face."

Andy Warhol once said, "Good business is the best art." And punk capitalists are proving it by creating some masterpieces in factories of their own. Another teenager born in Montreal who grew up at the same time as the punks from *VICE* is Dov Charney, founder of clothing label American Apparel. Charney began hustling T-shirts while he was at school, and dropped out of Tufts to start his D.I.Y. garment business in 1989. He has grown his considerable aptitude for the fashion business into a hip brand, with fifty-three outlets and counting in five countries. The company's Manhattan store generates $1,800 worth of sales per square foot per year according to Charney, seven times the industry average. This seems unusual given that American Apparel sells only plain, logo-free clothes such as T-shirts and track suits that don't look particularly different to other plain T-shirts and track suits. What their fans buy into is the company's message.

Like Warhol, Charney manufactures meaning. All the garments American Apparel produces are sweatshop-free, manufactured in a factory in downtown Los Angeles that is now the single largest clothing manufacturing plant in the United States. American Apparel's forty-five hundred employees earn an average of $13 an hour, and receive benefits such as paid time leave, health insurance, subsidized lunches, bus passes, free bicycles, and free parking. The company also pursues progressive environmental policies: more than 20 percent of the cotton it uses is organic (plans are under way to get this figure up to 80 percent), and fabric scraps are recycled; 20 percent of the power the factory uses comes from solar panels on the roof.

It sounds idealistic, but companies such as American Apparel are far from flakey. Punk capitalists realize they have to compete on every level, not just ethically. "It is this system that allows us to stay competitive while paying the highest wages in the garment industry" reads American Apparel's mission statement. "Because we don't outsource to local or developing-nation sweatshops (or to ad agencies, for that matter) the entire process is time-efficient, and we can respond faster to market demand. . . . Not to suggest that we are more ethical than the next business. We're just out to try something different, to make a buck, to bring people the clothes they love, to be human, and have a good time in the process." The good times at American Apparel are reflected in the company's ads depicting hot young employees winning "unofficial wet T-shirt competitions," not to mention a bootylicious bottom line of $250 million per year and counting.

American Apparel may be the modern-day version of McLaren and Westwood's shop SEX. Not just because of the company's '70s porn-flick-obsessed branding and advertising campaigns, or the fact that Charney has been known to walk around the factory in nothing but his sweatshop-free underwear and encourages "freedom of expression" at work (or because of the very public relationships Mr. Charney has conducted with some of his female employees, something he has been criticized for), but also because of the subversive message the company pushes on the rest of the garment industry. By refusing to use sweatshop labor and producing all their products in the United States, American Apparel is making a statement to the rest of the fashion world about what is possible without using sweatshops.

Brands and products with a purpose are finally writing checks with their mouths that their wallets *can* cash. And because more people are being persuaded by these products, their checks are pretty good. Some other examples include the global market for fair-trade products, which increased in 2005 alone by 37 percent, and hybrid car sales, which doubled between January 2005 and January 2006 in the United States, while the rest of the car market stuttered off the starting grid, growing at just 3 percent.

We have absorbed so much spin and misleading advertising that we are slowly becoming immune to it (something we shall discuss more in chapter 4). Punk capitalists have responded to this by selling us both substance and style. Shane Smith of *VICE* agrees. "Punk was about not taking it, not believing what you see on TV or in the newspapers, and I think that definitely carried over, because people get their news from the Internet and don't believe any of the major networks. I don't know if it's necessarily anarchy, but it's definitely thinking for yourself."

Creative Destruction

Punk amplified the idea that nothing else mattered apart from the will to do it yourself. "We wanted to be amateurs," Johnny Rotten once said. Technology is helping the D.I.Y. mentality realize its full potential. On every continent, amateurs are now armed with easily (and sometimes freely) accessible state-of-the-art hardware and software, not to mention the open, global distribution channel that is the Internet. Doing it yourself has never been easier.

Jobs are radically changing because of this shift in the way the labor force is operating, and the idea of the work/life balance is being replaced by a new discussion on what work and life as separate entities actually means. A 2004 study for the U.S. Department of Labor on the future of work predicted, "Employees will work in more decentralized, specialized firms, and employer-employee relationships will become less standardized and more individualized. . . . We can expect a shift away from more permanent, lifetime jobs toward less permanent, even nonstandard employment relationships (e.g., self-employment)."

The exponential growth of self-employment isn't just about sticking it to the man on a global scale. It reflects a deeper change in our attitudes. Those of us with full-time jobs are becoming increasingly dissatisfied. In a survey carried out in the United States by the private research group the Conference Board in 2007, more than half of the respondents said they disliked their current jobs. In a similar survey conducted by the group twenty years ago in 1987, less than 40 percent of the respondents made this claim. Apparently even money isn't doing it for us as much as it used to, either. In 1989, 58 percent of the U.K. population claimed they were happy, but this figure had fallen to 45 percent by 2003, despite a 60 percent increase in average incomes.

In his book *The Rise of the Creative Class,* Richard Florida argues that across the West, we are being driven by creativity above all else. "We strive to work more independently and find it much harder to cope with incompetent managers and bullying bosses. . . . Whereas the lifestyle of the previous organizational age emphasized conformity, the new lifestyle favors individuality, self-statement, acceptance of difference and the desire for rich multidimensional experiences."

There is a misconception that all the changes we are experiencing as a society are the result of new technologies, but as Florida and others see it, the real changes are profoundly cultural. As we shift to a D.I.Y. culture that runs on creativity, the implications could be as profound as when society shifted from farming to manufacturing. Managers and CEOs are fast being usurped as the creative emerges as society's new rainmaker. "The creative individual is no longer viewed as an iconoclast," says Florida. "He—or she—is the new mainstream."

The New Mass Production

The punk ideal may be at long last getting close to subverting the rat race altogether. It's just as well that we are finding new ways to work, because the industries supplying the jobs are changing just as quickly.

Punks found their D.I.Y. inspiration in the beat poets of the '50s and '60s who found innovative ways to produce their literature. "The people that mattered to me in the world that I was operating in were all about doing it yourself," remembers Hell of the writers who influenced him. "They completely bypassed the establishment of outlets and manufacturers. They were coming from that tradition of making it new, keeping stuff fresh. You could write the book one day and publish it the next."

The printing presses and bookstores that allowed beat poets and punks to express themselves have evolved into new print-on-demand trade book ventures such as Xlibris, which prints more than seven thousand books a year and distributes them to major bookstores. Other print-on-demand companies, such as Lulu, take this idea even further, giving you the option to publish and distribute music, movies, and pictures, as well as the tens of thousands of books it publishes each month. Meanwhile the life expectancy of a blockbuster has halved in the past decade, according to a study done by Lulu. "The blockbuster novel is heading the way of the mayfly," announced Lulu's CEO, Bob Young. "The publishing revolution is nigh. . . . It's part of a cultural shift."

D.I.Y. is altering the traditional frameworks of many industries; this has already happened in music, movies, and video games. Anything and everything else could be next. As a result, many companies are now basing their entire operation around punk capitalists, pandering to their every need with ever more advanced technology.

It seems that ownership of the means of production—the backbone of capitalism—is falling into the hands of the masses. But soon the notion of "owning" the means of production may itself be redundant.

3-D.I.Y.

Anything that can be transmitted electronically and downloaded is being affected by the ever-increasing flurry of D.I.Y. activity. Because of downloading, the media and entertainment industries are becoming very different beasts. But the final frontier for punk capitalists, and possibly the final nail in the coffin for mass production, may be just around the corner. The Internet has changed the game for anything that could be transmitted electronically. Now it has the material world in its crosshairs, too. Soon we may be doing the manufacturing ourselves.

Thanks to a new breed of punks rocking lab coats rather than spiky hair, D.I.Y. is today more of a threat to the establishment than ever. Forget printing on demand, Adrian Bowyer and his team of engineers based at the University of Bath, in England, are embarking on what may be D.I.Y.'s ultimate power move.

Bowyer dreamed of taking apart the machine from a young age, dismantling washing machines and TVs in his room and building explosive devices large enough to take out cars. "I learnt that the only way to learn about anything is to break it thoughtfully, then to make it work again," he told me. Bowyer always had a problem with the way machines work, and imagined how they could be different. "I have been convinced that engineering has been making things wrongly since the industrial revolution. . . . The production methods used by biological organisms are so much more efficient and elegant. Specifically, biological organisms both self-assemble and self-reproduce, but no current engineering products do."

For twenty years, Bowyer has being applying Darwin's theory of evolution to engineering, creating design software that evolves "in the same way plants and animals grow." But it wasn't until he discovered something called 3-D printing that he truly awakened his inner punk.

3-D printing might sound like science fiction, but it is already here. In the same way an ordinary printer precisely sprays ink onto paper, a 3-D printer the size of a photocopier can spray powdered metals, ceramics, and other materials, fusing them together in layers to create *actual* 3-D objects.

Companies such as Adidas, BMW, Timberland, and Sony are already using 3-D printers to produce prototypes of new products in-house. 3-D printing helps keep new concepts under wraps, not to mention making the entire design process more efficient and responsive. "They are extremely useful in a research environment," explains Bowyer. "Whenever any of us needs to make a machine for an experiment we just design the parts in a CAD [computer-aided design] system; one of the 3-D printers then makes the parts automatically, and we put them together. A process that used to take months now takes a day or two."

Most 3-D printers are still pretty cumbersome, as are their price tags. But the technology is developing at speeds not unlike that of the PC. In the not too distant future, the 3-D printer could be a welcome addition to homes and offices around the world.

If this happens—or rather, *when* this happens—there will no longer be any boundaries left between producer and consumer. The only thing left will be the creativity and ingenuity of the design itself. A world where anything and everything could be printed out at home is a world full of questions. What would happen to Nike when kids start printing out Air Jordans at the rate at which they illegally download music? Will your new ride be printed down at the showroom? Would Christmas morning be ruined if the printer jammed and nobody's presents were printed?

D.I.Y. is about becoming more independent. The more independent we become as a society, the more industries become decentralized. Indeed, we may reach a point where there is no "industry" left at all, in its place many vibrant local markets producing value, but not controlled exclusively by big players. This is already happening to the music industry, and it's starting to happen with anything that can be transmitted electronically. But soon this may also happen in the world of physical goods. "We have reached a point in history where our most advanced technology is dirt cheap," Bowyer continues. "I want to make it an order of magnitude cheaper yet so that poor people can exploit rich people's toys to raise themselves up." If we learn to copy everything like we did with MP3 files, the fate of the music industry may have been the canary in the coal mine, an omen for the end of mass production as we know it.

Like any technology still in it prototype stage, the RepRap may not live up to its creator's expectations, but the implications are pretty insane. 3-D printers could mean the end of the world's current manufacturing system and the beginning of a new, localized process where individuals have as much control over production as they do over consumption. This would, as Bowyer explains, "allow the world's poorest people easily to put a foot on the first rung of the manufacturing ladder that has made the rest of us rich."

When it started, D.I.Y. was chords printed in fanzines that allowed you to form your own band. Soon it could be designs transmitted electronically that will allow us not just to download sneakers, but also to design and build anything we want, including a better, more efficient world.

Here's One Idea, Here's Two More . . .
Now Form Your Own Future

The punk perspective is a subversive mind-set we can all use, especially now that we have equally subversive technologies. Punk didn't take old assumptions for granted, and didn't assume self-interest was the only thing that motivates us, the way neoclassical economics does. It found new ways of doing things as a result.

Punk Capitalists are creating change using three separate ideas that came directly from the philosophy of punk rock:

1. Do It Yourself

Punk refused to take its cues from the mass market, and created a vibrant cultural movement as a result. Now a critical mass of punk capitalists is removing the associative barriers that held them back. They are working for themselves, setting up businesses, and finding ways to produce as much as they consume, laying the foundations for a wealth of new markets and business models. D.I.Y. is changing our labor markets, and creativity is becoming our most valuable currency.

2. Resist Authority

Punk resisted authority and saw anarchy as the path to a brighter future. Punk capitalists are resisting authority, too—by leveraging new D.I.Y. technologies and the power of individuals connecting and working together as equals. This twin engine of the new economy is creating new ways all of us can live and work, leaving old systems for dust. Technology + Democracy = Punk Capitalism.

3. Combine Altruism with Self-Interest

Punk had high ideals—it looked aggressive and scary, but through its angry critique of society and subversion of it, it sought to change the world for the better. Punk capitalists are using the same techniques, subverting a world full of empty corporate gestures, manufacturing businesses and products with meanings that attempt to inject substance back into style. Punk injected altruism into entrepreneurship, a motivator of people long overlooked by neoclassical economics. Not only that, punk made the idea of putting purpose before profit seem cool to an entire generation. It manufactured new meaning in an area where it was really needed.

Everywhere we look, the traces of these three ideas can be seen in the things we consume. The corporate world that punk rejected mimics it, talking the antiestablishment talk. But this is no longer working as well as it once did, and instead new generations of punk capitalists are making a mark by walking the purpose-driven walk.

The ideas punk amplified are reaching fever pitch. Today we can see the aftereffects of punk everywhere if we look hard enough. But this short, sharp, violent jab at society could have been forgotten entirely had it not been for another group of radicals, illegally broadcasting the D.I.Y. message. As music historian Clinton Heylin suggests in *Bootleg: The Secret History of the Other Recording Industry*, "It could be argued that the influence and impact of the original punk bands lingered on only because their music was bootlegged." Punk changed the world, but none of it would have been possible without a little help from another dedicated group of innovators: pirates.

CHAPTER 2

The Tao of Pirates

Sea Forts, Patent Trolls, and Why We Need Piracy

The Principality of Sealand
© *Bobleroi.co.uk*

Drift a few miles east from Harwich, a town on the southeastern coast of England, into the murky salt waters of the English Channel, and you'll see two hulking concrete towers jutting out of the briny deep. At the base of these columns, the wreckage of a sunken ship languishes on the seabed like some drowning Atlas supporting their weight. Eighty-five feet above, on the towers' twin summits, rests a gigantic rusting platform lashed by decades of wind and rain. It was built during World War II, complete with living quarters that housed hundreds of British troops and an arsenal of antiaircraft guns that picked off the Luftwaffe descending on London. This embattled structure was known as Fort Roughs before it was decommissioned in 1946 and left to rot on the high seas by the British government. Nobody predicted the coming of Major Paddy Roy Bates.

Former army man Bates happened upon Fort Roughs when he was running Radio Essex, a pirate station broadcasting rock 'n' roll to the United Kingdom from another one of four identical sea forts in the area. But the problem was that this particular fort stood less than three miles off the mainland, still within the United Kingdom's jurisdiction. Her Majesty's government was not amused. They ordered the station to close.

Bates realized that these rules didn't apply farther out to sea, at Fort Roughs. In fact, he realized that *no* rules applied farther out to sea. On Christmas Eve 1966, Bates stormed the sea fort, evicted with brute force a pirate station already there, and seized control. But this time he was thinking bigger than just running a radio station. The self-appointed Prince Roy; his wife, Princess Joan; and their son, Prince Michael, declared their decaying bounty an independent sovereign nation in accordance with international law, and the Principality of Sealand was born.

Prince Roy set about transforming the crumbling fort into the world's smallest state, hoisting a flag and adding a helipad. The British did nothing to prevent the population of Sealand (at the time, three, and since then, rarely north of five) from minting their own coins and stamps, issuing passports, and handing out regal titles. In fact, you can become a lord or a lady of Sealand via eBay for £18.95 plus postage.

"Sealand was founded on the principle that any group of people dissatisfied with the oppressive laws and restrictions of existing nation-states may declare independence in any place not claimed to be under the jurisdiction of another sovereign entity," the Bates family proclaimed. And so began one of the most bizarre stories in British (or Sealandish) history.

Strange tales from Sealand regularly made headlines over the years. In 1968, shots were fired at a passing navy vessel (that may or may not have been trying to invade). Bates landed in court, but the English judge took the position that Sealand was indeed outside the United Kingdom's territorial waters. In 1977 it *was* invaded by a posse of German and Danish conspirators, but the Bates family regained control and fended them off in a war the size of a large bar fight. Sealand has long attracted legions of shady characters looking to set up casinos, brothels, and other such illicit enterprises safe from national laws. Sealand passports (many of them forgeries) have turned up in the possession of unsavory characters around the world; one was found with the body of Gianni Versace's assassin in Miami.

The micronation made international headlines in 2000 when a company called HavenCo struck a deal with the "royal family" to build a heavily armed offshore data sanctuary to house "sensitive" information anonymously, outside the reaches of governments, lawyers, ex-wives, and other prying eyes. Gambling sites, file-sharing networks—really, anyone trying to escape state surveillance or the tax man—were welcome. The only data HavenCo won't house is anything to do with child porn, spamming, or terrorism.

Sealand wasn't just the world's first man-made sovereign state, but also the first global capital of Internet anarchy. The second-craziest Bates family in the world turned a pirate station into a renegade, pirate nation.

Sealand may be the first and only sovereign territory founded by a pirate DJ, but it's far from being the only country built on pirate culture. In fact, pirates have been the architects of new societies for centuries: they have established new genres of film and music and created new types of media, often operating anonymously and always—initially, at least—outside the law. They overthrow governments, birth new industries, and win wars. Pirates create positive social and economic changes, and understanding piracy today is more important than ever, because now that we all can copy and broadcast whatever we want; we can all become pirates.

No sea fort required.

Copyrights and Wrongs

So who exactly is a pirate?

A. That guy who sells bootleg DVDs on the corner;

B. Some dude with a beard and a parrot who might mug you if you go boating;

C. A guardian of free speech who promotes efficiency, innovation, and creativity, and who has been doing so for centuries.

The correct answer is all of the above. A pirate is essentially anyone who broadcasts or copies someone else's creative property without paying for it or obtaining permission.

First things first: some acts of piracy are quite simply theft. Every year industry loses billions to piracy. Companies suffer, artists and creators lose earnings, and people lose their jobs.

But although intellectual property rights seem right and piracy clearly seems wrong, the opposite also can be true. One man's copyright terrorist is another's creative freedom fighter: many forms of piracy transform society for the better.

Another pirate nation that began in a fashion similar to Sealand is the United States of America. During the nineteenth-century Industrial Revolution, the Founding Fathers pursued a policy of counterfeiting European inventions, ignoring global patents, and stealing intellectual property wholesale. "Lax enforcement of the intellectual property laws was the primary engine of the American economic miracle," writes Doron S. Ben-Atar in *Trade Secrets*. "The United States employed pirated know-how to industrialize." Americans were so well known as bootleggers, Europeans began referring to them with the Dutch word "Janke," then slang for pirate, which is today pronounced "Yankee."*

Trace the origins of recorded music, radio, film, cable TV, and almost any industry where intellectual property is involved, and you will invariably find pirates at its beginnings. When Edison invented the

---

*This was a little unfair, as every major European country was also heavily engaged in piracy and industrial espionage at some point in the eighteenth century. Piracy was the only way the United States could keep up.

phonographic record, musicians branded him a pirate out to steal their work, until a system was created for paying them royalties. Edison, in turn, went on to invent filmmaking, and demanded a licensing fee from those making movies with his technology. This caused a band of filmmaking pirates, among them a man named William, to flee New York for the then still wild West, where they thrived, unlicensed, until Edison's patents expired. These pirates continue to operate there, albeit legally now, in the town they founded: Hollywood. William's last name? Fox.

When cable TV first came about, in 1948, the cable companies refused to pay the networks for broadcasting their content, and for more than thirty years operated like a primitive illegal file-sharing network, until Congress decided that they, too, should pay up, and a balance was struck between copyright holders and the pirate TV broadcasters.

If copyright laws had stopped these pirates in their tracks, today we might live in a world where America looked more like a giant Amish farm. We would have no recorded music, no cable TV, and a selection of films on a par with an economy airline seat. The pirates were on the wrong side of the law, but as Lawrence Lessig expounds upon in his book *Free Culture*, in hindsight it's clear their acts were important. By refusing to conform to regulations they deemed unfair, pirates have created industries from nothing. Because traditionally society has cut these pirates some slack and accepted that they were adding value to our lives, compromises were reached and enshrined in law, and as a result new industries blossomed.

Could it be that the guy bootlegging DVDs on the corner is still forcing the film industry to become more efficient, even today? HDTV billionaire Mark Cuban seems to think so, arguing that consumers *should* be able to view a film "how they want it, when they want it, where they want it." His company chose to simultaneously release Oscar-winning director Steven Soderbergh's film *Bubble* in cinemas, on DVD, and on HDTV on the same day in 2006. "Name any big-title movie that's come out in the last four years. It has been available in all formats on the day of release," Soderbergh told *Wired*. "It's called piracy. Peter Jackson's *Lord of the Rings*, *Ocean's Eleven*, and *Ocean's Twelve*—I saw them on Canal Street* on opening day. Simultaneous release is already here. We're just trying to gain control over it."

The history of piracy repeats itself. By short-circuiting conventional channels and red tape, pirates can deliver new materials, formats, and business models to audiences who want them. Canal Street moves faster than Wall Street. Piracy transforms the markets it operates in, changing the way distribution works and forcing companies to be more competitive and innovative. Pirates don't just defend the public domain from corporate control; they also force big business and government to deliver what we want, when we want it.

Pirates for the People

More often than commandeering sea platforms, pirates invade media platforms. Who do you think is fighting back against government censorship in China? That guy from the corner again. When Beijing banned the film *Memoirs of a Geisha* in 2006 for being "socially unhealthy," pirates stepped in, selling millions of copies and punching through the great wall of propaganda with the invisible hand of the free market. The $565 million market† motivates the pirates who produce 95 percent of all Chinese DVDs sold, but the side effect is free speech on a scale that renders movie censorship irrelevant. "Forbidden things are always attractive," subversive Chinese blogger Muzimei‡ later said. "The politicians at the top introduce policies. The people at the bottom find a way around them."

Thanks to advances in technology, people everywhere are running rings around censors and regulators. From citizen journalists to bloggers and those producing and broadcasting their own online con-

---

*For those unfamiliar with New York, the Canal Street area in Manhattan's Chinatown is one of piracy's main hubs, where vast numbers of knocked-off DVDs, handbags, and fragrances are traded daily.

†The value of the pirate DVD market in China, according to a 2006 study released by the Motion Picture Association of America, is $565 million. This figure represents losses to U.S. movie studios.

‡Muzimei is seen as being so radical and outspoken by the Chinese government, his name was once on their list of words banned from the Internet.

tent, we are being persuaded away from conventional channels* by a generation of broadcasters with the pirate mentality. Pirate culture is the backbone of the public domain, and the media is just one of many areas being claimed by pirates, for the good of the people—and themselves.

Like many other nouns polite society is fighting against, the war on piracy will rumble on for years to come. But this is a war that will be difficult to win, not just because warring with nouns is ridiculous, but also because history shows, time and again, that society benefits from the work of pirates.

As more of us become them, often just because the entertainment industry is trying to make the recording of anything it can illegal (if you've downloaded something without paying for it, or photocopied pages from a book, the entertainment industry thinks you're a pirate), it's important to understand the pirate mentality.

So here's the story of an industry built on pirate culture that wasn't just born out of piracy, it even grew up on real live pirate ships. It's a business that still hasn't found the balance between regulation and creative freedom. It probably never will. But this industry has illegally beamed the work of others all over the world for a century, often giving that work valuable exposure by broadcasting it somewhere it wouldn't otherwise be heard or seen, increasing its value and opening up entirely new markets. This is the tale of pirate radio.

The Legend of DJ Fezzy

DJ Fezzy is getting ready for his set. It's a cold, dark Christmas Eve in his studio, and the time is coming up to 9:00 P.M. Fezzy has come prepared for a crazy-hot show, packing an arsenal of scripted material, instruments, and records, set to deliver a sonic blast of talk radio and live music. Then he'll throw down on the wheels of steel.

At nine o'clock, it's on. Fezzy grabs the mike, introduces himself,

---

*A survey conducted by Google in the United Kingdom in 2005 found that people spend an average of 164 minutes online every day, compared with just 148 minutes watching television.

and explains the evening's program. He then hits the ones and twos, dropping straight into an extra fly new phonograph recording of Handel's "Largo," sung by fresh-to-death vocalist of the moment, Dame Clara Butt. Once the record has done its thing, DJ Fezzy draws for his Bible, reading from the Christmas story in the Book of Luke, before picking up his violin and hitting off the audience with a killer solo from Gounod's "O Holy Night." And just to prove how versatile he is, Fezzy even sings over it himself.

The man is on fire.

Fezzy's variety show may not sound too controversial, but it shocked his audience in a way Howard Stern could only dream of.

It was 1906, and DJ Fezzy is broadcasting the first radio show ever.

From the coastal village of Brant Rock, Massachusetts, forty-year-old Canadian professor Reginald Fessenden ("Fezzy" was a nickname given to him by Thomas Edison) was transmitting to an audience of several United Fruit Company ships bobbing up and down in the Atlantic and a smattering of New England ham radio enthusiasts. People were dumbfounded by what they were hearing. Used to receiving only the blips and bleeps of Morse code through the static, they were being subjected to the first ever broadcast of music and the human voice using radio waves, and a technique known as amplitude modulation, which would later be renamed AM radio.

Fessenden is better known as a brilliant inventor on a par with Tesla, Marconi, or Edison, with more than five hundred patents to his name. But he is also technically the first pirate radio DJ. Not only because he didn't have a license (they didn't exist yet) but also because he went against the grain, manipulating an existing media format to create what he wanted, regardless of the conventional wisdom. Marconi and Edison laughed and scoffed at Fessenden's theories about sound waves at first, but those two losers were still messing around with Morse code when DJ Fezzy hit the airwaves.

The New York Herald Tribune later wrote, "It sometimes happens, even in science, that one man can be right against the world. Professor Fessenden was that man. He fought bitterly and alone to prove his theories . . . against the stormy protests of every recognized authority. . . . The progress of radio was retarded a decade by this error."

Fessenden was quickly followed onto the airwaves by other scientists and hordes of ham radio nerds across America. The United States understood the potential of radio from the get-go,* using it to boost troop morale in World War I and launching the first commercial station, KDKA in Pittsburgh, in 1920. Soon, there were more than five hundred commercial stations across the country. But outside of the United States, radio was initially thought of as nothing more than another tentacle of the state, good for broadcasting information and educational programs, too powerful to be turned over to the people. This situation set the scene for one of pirate radio's most monumental achievements: bringing rock 'n' roll to Europe.

Rock the Boat

The gap between pirate radio stations in the United States and Europe is almost as wide as the Atlantic itself. In the United States most pirates have traditionally been fun, quirky operations run by hobbyists, who come on air for a few hours at a time and close down after a few days or weeks.† But in Europe, pirate radio is big business. Stations operate around the clock, generating new strains of music and occasionally boatloads of money. Many pirates have even become brands in their own right, selling merchandise and setting up spin-off ventures.

This difference was a result of Europe's failure to catch on to the potential of commercial radio. And this failure forced Europeans to take to the seas, taking advantage of the fact that it was perfectly legal to broadcast from international waters.

---

*U.S. radio didn't start to become heavily regulated until after the *Titanic* sank in 1912, when a separate frequency for distress calls, a twenty-four-hour shipping service, and licenses for radio operators were introduced. Before 1912 many feared the freedom of American radio would be derailed entirely and the whole radio spectrum turned over to the military, which did happen temporarily during World War I.

†That's not to say there isn't a rich, weird, and wonderful history of pirates in the United States. Stations that stand out include CSIC, which made a name for itself by mailing rubber chickens to its listeners, and Radio Cell, a pirate that exclusively broadcasts snippets of other people's telephone conversations (mostly of lovers and spouses arguing), eavesdropping on the people since 1996. Larger stations such as The Voice of Laryngitis and Radio Free Harlem did attract many listeners, and pirate radio even upstaged Christian Slater in the 1990 brat-pack flick *Pump Up the Volume*.

The first legendary European stations weren't on ships at all. In 1929 Radio Normandie began broadcasting to northwestern France and southern England from an opulent villa in the French town of Fécamp. Radio Paris transmitted from an antenna hoisted atop the Eiffel Tower,* and in 1933, from a country so small the letters of its name won't fit inside it on most maps, came Radio Luxembourg. Radio Luxembourg boasted what was the world's single most powerful radio transmitter, which not only allowed it to legally blanket its own tiny homeland but also to reach out to the United Kingdom, France, Germany, and many other parts of Europe where commercial radio was contraband, and where pop music couldn't be heard on the radio. It was the largest commercial station in Europe by the 1950s, with millions of listeners. Some Europeans claim they learned to speak English just by listening to Radio Luxembourg, but the station's first language was rock 'n' roll, and soon enough the whole continent would be fluent.

The legal loophole highlighted by Radio Luxembourg was the gateway to a lucrative new radio market. Quickly others realized that if they were transmitting from outside of nation-states where commercial radio was illegal, they could still legally broadcast to European audiences and sell commercials. The pull of this new rock 'n' roll music and the potential revenue to be made from advertising were like buried treasure to entrepreneurs around the world, who quickly found their sea legs and began to take to the waters in droves.

Offshore radio exploded in the 1960s, with stations such as Radio Caroline (started by a young Irishman named Ronan O'Rahilly, who for a time also managed some band called the Rolling Stones), Radio Sutch (founded by British pop star/politician Screaming Lord Sutch, operating from another disused sea fort), Radio London (housed on a secondhand U.S. minesweeper and funded by a consortium of Texas businessmen), and at least thirty others patrolling the English Channel transmitting the latest hits to millions of listeners in London and beyond. The rock group the Who even recorded their 1967 album *The*

---

*Perhaps even more unusual than transmitting from France's most famous landmark was the fact that only three people ever wrote in to the station to say they had heard it.

Who Sell Out as if it were transmitted live from Radio London. But despite what the Who thought, the British government had decided that these particular kids weren't all right, and legislated heavily against the pirates the same year, making offshore broadcasting illegal and scuppering almost all of them.*

The BBC launched a pirate copy of Radio London, called Radio 1, whose mission, according to Bill Brewster and Frank Broughton in *Last Night a DJ Saved My Life*, was "to take the last breath of wind out of the pirates' sails." Some of the original pirates, including Caroline, continue to fight on, many now reincarnated on digital and satellite frequencies. For the most part, the English Channel was returned to the relative calm of ferries, fishing boats, and our friends on Sealand. But although the pirates had lost this particular naval battle, it turned out they'd already won the war.

Coming Up from the Streets

Rather than stopping the pirates, legislation forced them back onto land, where they hit the ground running. This community of pirate entrepreneurs and DJs had revolutionized radio and European society, helping to bring rock 'n' roll, the top-forty charts, and the very idea of pop music to the people. The British music industry recognized this as commercial radio took off in the 1970s, and rewarded many of them handsomely for their services. Former Radio London and Caroline DJs such as Jimmy Savile, John Peel, and Tony Blackburn were hired by BBC Radio 1, and went on to become household names in the United Kingdom. And as the first generation crossed over and went legit, a new underground was forming in cities across the Continent.

Instead of exposing themselves on the open seas, this new breed of pirates began to operate cloaked in the anonymity of urban sprawl. Switching over to the FM band, pirates in the 1980s and '90s serviced a new generation of radio listeners in London, Paris, and beyond, lis-

---

*There were worse repercussions than legislation. Radio Nordsee, a pirate transmitting to the Netherlands, was closed down by *air and sea attack* from the Dutch armed forces in 1964. Not to be discouraged, the pirate became TROS, now one of the Netherlands's largest broadcasting corporations.

teners more interested in sounds such as soul, hip-hop, house, garage, and techno drifting over from the United States. The powers that be can detect a pirate's homemade antenna, usually tacked to the top of a tower block, but the studio connected to this antenna by a less powerful (and undetectable) microwave signal, hidden in the concrete labyrinth of a city grid, is difficult to track down. Transmitters are found and confiscated, but studios are harder to find, and stations earning revenue from putting on raves and selling advertising* can afford to replace lost antennae, sometimes within hours. This game of cat and mouse continues to keep pirates operating across the planet today.

The estimated 150 pirate stations on the FM dial in the United Kingdom† act as musical petri dishes—they have spawned new genres and cultures for decades, and attract as much as 10 percent of London's radio audience. Acid house, hard-core, drum 'n' bass, U.K. garage, grime, and dubstep are just a handful of now worldwide underground movements that developed in this way. Pirate radio is an incubator where new music can mutate. Initially, the new strains of music it produces are seen as too risqué for the mainstream to touch, but once this music reaches a critical mass in popularity, anthems from the pirates start hitting the pop charts, pirate DJs become crossover celebrities, and the scenes created by these stations grow into cottage industries and worldwide exports.

Brand of Pirates

Kiss FM was one such incubator. Beginning in 1985, it broadcast hip-hop and house to the capital from the suburb of Crystal Palace in South London, one of the highest points in the city. The site gave the station a huge reach over the region, and its roster of incredible DJs‡ kept the

---

*Many major record labels, promoters, and legitimate blue-chip businesses advertise on pirate stations, looking to tap into their taste-making audience, even though it is illegal.

†According to OFCOM estimates made in 2007. More than half of these pirates operate in London.

‡Many of the original Kiss crew, such as Tim Westwood, Pete Tong, Trevor Nelson, Danny Rampling, Norman Jay, and Paul Oakenfold, are now among the world's most famous DJs and some of the most influential people in dance music.

listeners locked. By 1990 it was so popular it was granted a license. Kiss went from being a band of pirates to a *brand* of pirates, and today, as part of the company Emap Performance, it is a multimillion-pound media franchise with spin-off ventures ranging from digital TV channels to package vacations and club tours, which turned over £161 million in 2005. But the execs in charge still recognize where Kiss's kudos come from, and the station still recruits the hottest pirate DJs directly from the underground frequencies, giving many pirates their big break in the world of legal radio.

"With a pirate, none of the pressures we have are there," programming director Simon Long told me in 2003. "You can play what you want to smaller groups of people and you have complete freedom; that's why pirates will always be the breeding ground for new talent. . . . That's why at Kiss we're determined to make sure talented and passionate young DJs have a chance to make it onto legal airwaves." The BBC and the United Kingdom's many commercial stations also recruit directly from urban pirates today, which act as a minor league, feeding the major corporate stations the hottest DJs and sounds, already tried, tested, and approved by the pirate listeners. Piracy is tolerated by the radio industry because pirate stations make our music better.

These radio outlaws still exist all over Britain, and continue to be hounded by the authorities. But the music the pirates forge and support is the lifeblood of many of their corporate counterparts. Pirates continue to invigorate communities with new sounds and styles around the clock, generating creativity, innovation, and revenue. And as radio pirates go digital, sounds from the London streets are spilling onto the Internet, attracting global audiences, and building interest in new genres and scenes in faraway places.

Of course, this story of radio piracy is just one frequency in a wider spectrum. Tune the dial out a little farther, and we could listen to pirates generating change in a host of other areas. We would hear how military forces used pirate radio to keep troops' spirits up in both World Wars, Vietnam, and Iraq. We'd eavesdrop on armies using pirates as tactical weapons, as the United States did when it created Radio Swan, a pirate broadcasting anti-Castro programming into

Cuba from Swan Island in the Gulf of Mexico in 1960, and which also was used to send coded messages in the Bay of Pigs invasion.* We'd catch transmissions from the Cold War, when Russia and America continuously broadcast propaganda at one another pirate-style.

If we twist the dial in the other direction, we also would hear pirates working for peace, such as activists who underpinned the draft resistance movement taking to the airwaves in 1970s Australia. We might pick up a new breed of offshore pirates opposed to the Chinese government's oppressive regime, operating throughout the 1990s from the South China Sea and the Formosa Strait, while another fleet was busy broadcasting peace to the Middle East off the coast of Israel.

If we were to tune out far enough, we would hear the collective buzz of more than two thousand pirate stations that have been operating in the shantytowns of Argentina since 1986, and countless others transmitting from Brazil, Haiti, Mexico City, El Salvador, and across South America. In fact, we would hear pirates on seven continents, giving a voice to those who aren't being represented, growing new music into flourishing movements, turning the tide of public opinion, and forcing laws and societies to respond more effectively to the wants and needs of their citizens. For some it's a way to promote a musical freedom of choice not offered by commercial, playlist-driven radio. For others it's a way to promote freedom, period.

The Tao of Pirates

Pirates highlight areas where choice doesn't exist and demand that it does. And this mentality transcends media formats, technological changes, and business models. It is a powerful tool that once understood, can be applied anywhere.

Successful pirates adapt quickly to social and technological changes, but this is true of all entrepreneurs. What pirates do differently is create new spaces where different ideas and methods run the show. Some create their own media formats, as DJ Fezzy did with AM radio. Others

---

*The CIA later admitted to owning the pirate station.

manipulate formats that already exist to create new choices, as Hollywood did when it created an alternative unlicensed film industry, or as the pirates today bootlegging Hollywood are doing, giving you the option of watching new movies at home (albeit filmed secondhand on a camera phone).

Thinking like a bootlegger can take you in new directions. If you have an idea, but the infrastructure to get it out there does not exist, you may have an opportunity to create your own. Finding a space to get your idea across is as important as having the idea itself. If the idea is good, growing an audience won't be difficult. It's this audience that gives pirates their power.

Lao-Tzu, the founder of Taoism, famously said that when leaders lead well, people feel that they did it themselves and that it happened naturally. Pirates are experts at leading communities in this way, bringing people products, services, and sounds they didn't know they couldn't live without. Once these new ideas are broadcast, they unavoidably create a Pirate's Dilemma for others in that market. Should they fight these pirates, or accept that there is some value in what they are doing, and compete with them?

On one side, regulators may argue that pirate stations are illegal and damaging to holders of radio licenses. But radio listeners may ask "Why isn't there a legal station playing music like this when so many people clearly want to hear it?" Artists may protest that "the pirates play and support my records, when the mainstream stations and stores won't, and as a result I actually sell more."

The actions of pirates raise questions, and when they do something society finds useful, it creates productive discussions that often lead to changes in the law, which result in social and economic progress. If democracy is about creating processes that allow people to empower themselves, then pirates are clearly the perfect catalysts for such processes.

Pirate stations in London create this momentum by empowering the DJs who play the music. These DJs are so passionate about the music they play, most pay a monthly subscription fee to the station owner just to play on the radio at all, not to mention risking their liberty for the privilege of creating shows and content that give them and the station credibility. When they strike a chord with their audience, the community spirit of the listeners is also harnessed. This community intimidated the British government so much that they didn't start trying to close down the offshore stations until they had created the state-sponsored pirate Radio 1 to appease the millions of music fans they knew they would anger. It was the listeners who stood behind Kiss and drummed up enough support for the station, until the buzz reached fever pitch and the authorities had to grant them a license. The Internet community that believes file-sharing networks are vitally important to culture and innovation have never stopped opening new p2p networks as fast as the authorities try to close them down. A good idea is powerful only if people are willing to get behind it. By giving a community a new space that was not previously available to them, you can empower them, and they in turn will propel your idea forward.

In the cases of piracy we have looked at so far, there are two ways in which they win. Either the laws prohibiting them change, or the pirates become so popular the laws are effectively ignored. But the pirate mentality has now been taken on by many who weren't breaking the law in the first place.

Pirates 2.0

Today every man and his blog are celebrating the power of "Web 2.0." The idea of a living, breathing Web constantly improving itself is a great one, but it's underpinned by an old one. On the Web, anyone can broadcast whatever he or she likes to anyone else, the way pirates have for decades. Web 2.0 is all about the pirate mentality.

Pirate radio gave citizens the chance to become DJs, but today a connection to the Internet is all you need to broadcast to the entire world. Individuals with the pirate mentality are using the Web to become journalists, comedians, porn stars, prophets, TV producers, and many other things besides, and it is quite conceivable that the media may one day be conquered by pirates altogether. The big boys know it, and they're quaking in their corner offices. "Societies or companies that expect a glorious past to shield them from the forces of change driven by advancing technology will fail and fall," said Rupert Murdoch in a speech in March 2006. "That applies as much to my own, the media industry, as it does every other business on the planet. Power is moving away from the old elite in our industry, the editors, the chief executives, and let's face it, the proprietors. A new generation of media consumers has risen demanding content delivered when they want it, how they want it, and very much as they want it."

The difference is that this generation is not a posse of outlaws on the run from the authorities, but normal people who would never think of themselves as pirates in the first place. But without realizing it, when society went online, it became dominated by the pirate mentality. And nothing illustrates this better than the rise of the blog.

Blogger, Please

In the early 1990s the creation of a new Web page was a rare and wonderful thing. That all changed in 1994 with the arrival of the first bloggers. One of the best known was Swarthmore student Justin Hall and his creation Justin's Home Page, later renamed links.net. At first he posted some basic information about himself and how to start a blog, some links to other sites, and a picture he found of Cary Grant dropping acid. "Howdy," Justin wrote, "this is twenty-first century computing. . . . (Is it worth our patience?) I'm publishing this, and I guess you're readin' this, in part to figure that out, huh?"

These days, everyone has pretty much figured out it was. Blogs have gone mainstream, with tens of millions and counting,* providing information on anything and everything. Today there are political blogs left, right, and center, sports blogs, pet blogs, makeup blogs, gadget blogs, shopping blogs, and even blog blogs.†

The mainstream news media are being undermined by bloggers and citizen journalists offering a wider variety of local and niche cov-

---

*At a rate of seventy thousand new blogs created every day, according to Technorati.

†The aforementioned Technorati is the biggest blog blog of them all, reporting on what the rest of the blogosphere is talking about. It saw its readership increase by more than 700 percent in 2005.

erage. But they also are regularly beating the pros at the networks to some of the world's biggest stories. This is happening because journalism doesn't work quite as it should anymore. As bloggers dig deeper and wider, the mainstream news networks are becoming increasingly shallow.

In June 2005, the major U.S. network and cable television stations ran 6,248 segments on the Michael Jackson child molestation trial. There were 1,534 segments discussing Tom Cruise, and 405 on a runaway bride from Georgia. Dramatic fighting broke out in eastern Sudan that June, an intensely newsworthy event, especially when one takes into account the largely ignored steady-state genocide in Darfur, which had killed more than four hundred thousand people in the previous two years. A total of 126 segments ran mentioning Sudan. Michael Jackson got fifty times more coverage than what was fast becoming one of the largest humanitarian crises of the decade.

The same way concerns about ratings keep the same selection of playlisted songs rotating on legal radio stations all day, commercial and political pressures have taken a heavy toll on quality news reporting. As legendary U.S. TV news anchorman Dan Rather put it, "It is an obscene comparison . . . but you know there was a time in South Africa that people would put flaming tires around people's necks if they dissented. And in some ways the fear is that you will be necklaced here, you will have a flaming tire of lack of patriotism put around your neck. Now it is that fear that keeps journalists from asking the toughest of the tough questions, and to continue to bore in on the tough questions so often. And again, I am humbled to say, I do not except myself from this criticism."

The Pentagon denied that the United States military was using white phosphorus as a weapon in Iraq, until Iraqi bloggers went public with the evidence that they were. The mainstream only picked the story up afterward. Hours after the London 7/7 bombings in 2005, survivors and witnesses were posting firsthand accounts, helping the rest of the world make sense of what had happened, backed up with videos and pictures shot on camera phones. "Increasingly, bloggers are penetrating the preserves of the mainstream news media," wrote *The New York Times*. "They have secured seats on campaign planes, at political conventions and in presidential debates, and have become a driving force in news events themselves." In fact, they now have so much power around the world, they are deciding who gets to run the place.

Citizens on Patrol

Citizen journalists are countering the homogenization of the news media the same way pirate DJs counter bland radio playlists. The online newspaper *OhmyNews* was established in South Korea in 2000, with a full-time staff of seven people. Today it has a team of thirty-five thousand citizen journalists who provide 80 percent of its content,* which makes it one of the nation's most powerful media platforms. The *OhmyNews* motto is "Every Citizen Is a Reporter," but as founder Oh Yeon Ho says, "The slogan is not only about changing journalism, but about changing all of society." The organization has gone on to do exactly that. *OhmyNews* has become so influential, it can and has swung South Korean presidential elections.

When Roh Moo-hyun decided to run in the 2002 presidential race, many South Koreans thought it was a joke. Hailing from a poor farming family, he had escaped poverty through a high school scholarship. He went on to study law by himself, passing the bar exam on his fourth attempt. Moo-hyun became a do-it-yourself success story—a first-rate punk capitalist, making headlines as a human rights lawyer.

But when he ran for president, he found himself without the strong ties to the traditional political elites that other candidates enjoyed. In fact, he had the support of just one congressman. Most of Korea's conservative newspapers ignored him completely. The odds were not in his favor, but these are exactly the kind of odds the pirate mentality can overcome.

The story of this self-made man inspired hope in many young South

---

*Citizen journalists for *OhmyNews* get paid if their story makes the front page of the site. Readers can also make voluntary payments to reporters. One article by a philosophy professor struck such a chord with readers, six thousand people decided to contribute between $1 and $10 (the maximum), earning the professor more than $24,000, which is roughly the average annual wage in South Korea.

Koreans, disillusioned with dirty politics and sick of corruption. In Roh Moo-hyun, they saw a chance to clean things up, and as a result he was able to build a strong grassroots campaign online. His supporters "mobilized the power of the Internet to disseminate information about him faster than traditional media platforms, and encouraged others to participate in the election," *OhmyNews* reporter Victor Foo later noted. Soon enough, even without the aid of the mainstream political and media players backing him, Roh Moo-hyun became a contender.

But on Election Day, disaster struck. Just eight hours before voting began, Roh Moo-hyun's campaign partner, Chung Mong Joon, suddenly withdrew his support, shocking the nation. The mainstream media waded in to deliver Moo-hyun's campaign the knockout blow. The *Chosun Daily* newspaper posed this question: "Mr. Chung withdrew his support for Roh. Will you?"

Unfortunately for the old guard, Moo-hyun and his supporters weren't on the ropes quite yet. Election night saw two worlds colliding. As old media's printing presses ground to a halt, the new media pirates who supported Moo-hyun jumped into the ring, blindsiding the unsuspecting opposition with a new technique. "They visited many Internet bulletin boards and posted urgent messages such as 'Mr. Chung betrayed his party, Roh Moo-hyun is in danger. Save the country, please vote for Roh,'" *OhmyNews* founder Oh Yeon Ho remembers. "They even called their conservative parents to persuade them, crying, 'If Roh Moo-hyun fails, I will die.'"

OhmyNews updated the story every thirty minutes throughout the long night as thousands pitched in and voiced support. By daybreak, Roh Moo-hyun had emerged victorious, defeating his opponent by a narrow margin, something no one would have predicted just hours earlier.

He gave his first interview as president to *OhmyNews*.

When Europe wanted to hear rock 'n' roll, pirates stepped into the breach. Today a new generation is demanding more choice once again, getting their information in new ways. Bloggers are stealing the mainstream media's thunder, and the mainstream media have responded by trying to buy it back.

Some of the most successful blogs have changed hands for hundreds of millions of dollars, and plenty of bloggers are also cashing in without selling out to the big players. Bloggers (for now at least) don't face the same commercial pressures that the mainstream media do, but many earn tens of thousands of dollars a week in advertising revenue by offering highly focused niche audiences that the scattergun of big media cannot target. "You wanna reach New York, you buy on Gothamist. You want to reach mommies, you buy on Busy Mom," Brian Clark, an ad buyer for Audi, told *New York* magazine. "How does traditional media match that?"

More important, how can traditional media even think about clawing back power from bloggers when pirates are busy seizing the rest of traditional media's assets?

"Well, if You're Wondering What Happened . . . So Am I"

These were the first words uttered by flustered sports reporter Dan Roan on WGN-TV on November 22, 1987, after a TV pirate dressed as 1980s TV icon Max Headroom hijacked the station's signal. The pirate's silent transmission jammed the nightly news for twenty seconds, which was transmitting from the top of the Sears Tower in Chicago.* This was a pretty unusual event. It's incredibly expensive and difficult to jam a TV frequency (the Max Headroom incident remains the most recent in U.S. history), so pirates were never much of a threat to television—until the advent of online video sharing. Today a host of services such as YouTube allow anyone to upload content, both self-made and material ripped from other sources. Pirates are taking over TV the way they took over music, and the networks seem as confused as Mr. Roan about how they should respond.

Some media owners are responding with lawsuits, suing sites such as YouTube for copyright infringement. But just like the smart guys in the commercial radio industry hire pirate DJs, so savvy network bosses

---

*The pirate in question was never caught, or even identified.

are giving pirate TV personalities the chance to take over our living rooms, too. When Andy Milonakis began releasing Webcam recordings of his home-brewed comedy hip-hop freestyles, a body of work with titles such as "Crispy New Freestyle" and "The Super Bowl Is Gay," he didn't expect to be recruited to the *Jimmy Kimmel Live* show in 2003, and he certainly didn't expect MTV to give him his *own* show in 2005. "It doesn't seem real," he told *USA Today.* "It's weird when I'm watching MTV and I hear my own disgusting voice."

Meanwhile, back on the Web, Amanda Congdon notched up hundreds of thousands of viewers per day with her video podcast Rocketboom. The struggling actress started cowriting and starring in the two-minute broadcasts in 2004, and her popularity as the presenter soon had book and TV agents knocking at her door. She left Rocketboom in July 2006 to develop a TV show for HBO, as well as producing new video podcasts for DuPont and also U.S. media network ABC. "One of the best pieces of advice I ever received from an acting coach was to go out there and create your own vehicle," she told *Newsweek.* "The Internet allows you to do that."

The guy in the Prius we met in the introduction is the latest incarnation of the pirate radio DJ. Using an iPod connected to a hacked iTrip, it's possible to transmit pirate radio podcasts over the FM band in the vicinity around your home or car (even if you're just broadcasting silence to mute neighboring bass tubes).

Pirates like our friend in the Prius are creating new vehicles such as podcast radio shows, blazing new trails across the mainstream radio landscape. According to Irish technology site Silicon Republic, there are now more podcasts than radio stations, with hundreds more podcasts springing up every day. Some London pirates are now beginning to turn away from pirate radio in favor of podcasts, with several grime MCs and DJs, tired of petty pirate station politics, releasing Internet-only shows for free download (one 2006 offering was imaginatively titled "Fuck Radio"). From the top to the bottom, pirates force the media (and other pirates) to keep up with technological changes, or get left behind.

In the same way that pirate DJs are only as hot as their last show, bloggers are only as hot as their last post, and podcasters are only as cool as their last viral video. With pirates knocking down all barriers to entry, the only way to stay on top is to offer the best content, the most variety, and the latest, most entertaining, and accurate information. Even though anyone can say anything online, with millions of bloggers vetting each other, inaccuracies in stories on the most popular blogs are usually pointed out quickly. Pirates are cracking the whip, and the media is getting leaner and moving faster as a result.

But not everyone using the pirate mentality is a starry-eyed celebrity hopeful looking to break into the tough worlds of media and showbiz. Others are using it for the sake of piracy and piracy alone, and some are gaining so much support, they're not just electing presidents but also taking over governments themselves.

P for Vendetta

One of the most notorious and widely used Web portals for downloading music, movies, and pirate media of all types is the Swedish site the Pirate Bay. Its Googleesque layout makes it easier to use than an IKEA instruction manual, and it receives more than one million unique users every day. But what long kept the Pirate Bay afloat while many other sites were boarded by saber-rattling copyright lawyers were Swedish laws that permitted such tracker sites to operate.*

"Until the law is changed so that it is clear that the trackers are illegal, or until the Swedish Supreme Court rules that current Swedish copyright law actually outlaws trackers, we'll continue our activities," the Pirate Bay's legal adviser, law student Mikael Viborg, told *Wired* in March 2006. "Relentlessly."

The Pirate Bay is a militant file-sharing space powered by its founders' desire to defend free culture. Their actions were reactions to the fact that many regulators are arguing that the only way to defend copyright law is to invade and infringe upon people's rights and privacies. This is already happening—some entertainment companies, for

---

*A tracker site is one that doesn't contain any pirate data, but torrent files that point to other places where content is available. Kind of like a map to shoplifters' homes.

example, have embedded spyware in hardware and software such as DVD players or CD albums that note everything you record. Like all successful pirates, the Pirate Bay's actions created fierce debate.

On one side is the entertainment industry, scared for its future, as it was in the 1980s, when cassette tapes and video recorders were introduced. Cassette tapes and video recorders both brought the film and recording industries hugely lucrative new revenue streams once they had stopped fighting the new formats and started figuring out how to make money from them.

On the other side of the debate are people eager to consume media in new ways, enjoying the freedom to make back-up copies they always have, who are being threatened with million-dollar fines and prison sentences for what is essentially no different from home taping. The debate over the Pirate Bay's legality escalated into an international wrangle involving Hollywood, the White House, the World Trade Organization, and the Swedish government. The wrangle became so heated it sparked a new political movement: the Pirate Party.

"Copyright has been said to be necessary for the creation of culture, and patents have been said to be necessary for innovation to happen," declares the Pirate Party's website. "This has been repeated so often, that nobody questions it. We do, and we say that it's just a myth, perpetuated by those who have something to gain from preventing new culture and technology. When push comes to shove, copyright PREVENTS a lot of new culture, and patents PREVENT a lot of innovation. Above all, today's copyright laws has [sic] no balance at all between the creator's economic interests and society's cultural interests."

The party's position may seem extreme, but given the history of pirates we've taken in, they have a point. Piracy has generated innovation throughout its history. In a world where a paranoid entertainment industry is criminalizing citizens even for legal file-sharing, spying on people through their PCs and forcing them to pay fines far higher than if they actually *were* stealing CDs or DVDs from a store, some might say it was about time governments pushed back on behalf of their people—the people copyright laws and patents were initially designed to protect.

The Pirate Bay was raided by the Swedish authorities in May 2006, after the White House threatened the Swedish government with trade sanctions, and the laws there pertaining to tracker sites were changed. But this was not a good idea. The site was back up in just three days, and the raid catapulted support for the Pirate Party to new heights, so much so that the Swedish government is now planning to repeal its laws against tracker sites. The Pirate Party now has close to ten thousand members, lobbying for free culture on a global scale. Outside of Sweden, officially registered Pirate Parties have been started in Spain, Austria, and Germany, while unregistered but active branches exist in the United States, France, Poland, Italy, and Belgium, with more forming in the Netherlands, Brazil, the United Kingdom, Australia, Canada, Switzerland, New Zealand, and Norway. The Pirate Party is showing the world that piracy is one of the most effective forms of civil disobedience. "File-sharing is not a problem, it's an opportunity," says Rick Falkvinge of the Pirate Party in the documentary *Steal This Film*. "There's a Chinese proverb saying that 'When the winds of change are blowing, some people are building shelters, and others are building windmills.'"

But the Pirate Bay isn't just building windmills, it's also taking over sea forts. In perhaps the most bizarre twist in this story, the Pirate Bay announced it was attempting to buy Sealand* from the Bates family in January 2007, in an international power move that would unite the world's foremost pirate nation with some of Earth's most fearsome political pirates. But while pirates took over the media and became a geopolitical force to be reckoned with, the powers that be were already hatching a plan to defeat them.

Fighting the Net

"Net neutrality" is why the Internet is a level playing field. This is the principle that everyone using the Internet has an equal amount of access to everyone else. As inventor of the Web, Tim Berners-Lee, defines it:

---

*Sealand was put on the market by the Bates family for £500,000 after being badly damaged by a fire in July 2006.

"If I pay to connect to the Net with a certain quality of service, and you pay to connect with that or greater quality of service, then we can communicate at that level." Telephone and telegraph networks were both successful because they were network-neutral, and it is why the Web has become such a world-changing force, both economically and socially. This principle has allowed citizens and consumers to seize a great deal of power. Because of Net neutrality, it's as easy (in most Western countries, at least) to access any blog as it is to access any mainstream news website. When we are given the choice between global mass media and local, homemade varieties, many of us, as we have seen, are choosing the latter. And not everyone is happy about that.

In the United States, some (although by no means all) big media and telecommunications companies are lobbying Congress heavily to overturn Net neutrality. They want to replace it with an undemocratic system, where instead of the Internet just sending you the data you ask for, when you ask for it, websites would have to pay an extra fee to communications companies to guarantee that the data you asked for would be delivered. This would allow Internet service providers to prioritize the data you saw, and even decide whether you should see it at all.

As Craig Newmark, founder of Craigslist described it, this would be like trying to order a pizza and being told by the phone company, "AT&T's preferred pizza vendor is Domino's. Press one to connect to Domino's now. If you would still like to order from your neighborhood pizzeria, please hold for three minutes while Domino's guaranteed orders are placed."

Other influential voices think it's already too late for the old establishment to turn back the clock. "It all seems to come down to paranoia vs. opportunity," commented HDTV magnate Mark Cuban. "Some are paranoid that the telcos will use this to destroy the openness of the Net. The telcos don't have that kind of leverage anymore."

While a handful of media and telco companies try to wipe out Net neutrality to serve their short-term interests, their concerns aren't shared by everyone. As some corporate behemoths gradually, begrudgingly get used to the most recent wave of pirates, many are starting to accept that this is not a battle, but a form of competition—one that is driving them to innovate. "Pirates compete the same way we do—

through quality, price, and availability," said Disney's cochair Anne Sweeney in a 2006 keynote address. "We understand now that piracy is a business model.* . . . The digital revolution has unleashed a consumer coup. We have to not only make in-demand content but make it on-demand. This power shift changes the way we think about our business, industry, and our viewers. We have to build our businesses around their behavior and their interests," she said. "All of us have to continually renew our business in order to renew our brands because audiences have the upper hand and show no sign of giving it back." Steve Jobs of Apple backed up Disney's sentiment, telling *Newsweek*, "If you want to stop piracy, the way to stop it is by competing with it."

Trolling Deep

If suing customers for consuming pirate copies becomes central to a company or industry's business model, then the truth is that that company or industry no longer has a competitive business model. A company's or individual's ability to make money should be based on their ability to innovate and create value, not file lawsuits. But for some, frivolous lawsuits are the entire business plan.

These companies sometimes get called patent trolls: they don't invent or make anything themselves, they just buy patents that already exist—or register patents for good ideas already in the public domain. They then track down businesses and individuals already using those ideas, and extort money from them either by suing or threatening to sue. These companies create no value for society at all. The only purpose they serve is to make money by suing other people who are.

Forgent Networks was a company accused by critics of patent trolling when they purchased a patent to JPEG digital image compression in 1997, a widely used technology that had been freely available since 1987. In 2004 Forgent threw lawsuits at forty-four businesses

---

*Piracy, one could argue, was at the birth of Disney, too. Disney was built on fairy tales originally written by the Brothers Grimm, which had fallen into the public domain. Yet today it is companies such as Disney who have successfully lobbied Congress to keep their trademark characters such as Mickey Mouse from entering the public domain as quickly as the fairy tales of the Brothers Grimm did.

using the JPEG technology, settled out of court with another fifty, and went after more than a thousand others. "It's the American way," Dick Snyder, CEO of Forgent, told the Associated Press in March 2006. "We're just doing what we believe is the right thing to gain value from what we own."

Microsoft and twenty-one other companies disagreed with Mr. Snyder's interpretation of the American way, and filed countersuits against Forgent. In May 2006, the U.S. Patent and Trademarks Office reinvestigated Forgent's claim and found the patent to be invalid, because the technology was previously in the public domain. The company abandoned all claims on the patent and walked away, keeping the $90 million it had made licensing the rights to JPEGs to thirty companies.

The negative effect this is having has not gone unnoticed, and laws are being proposed in the United States and many other countries that will make patent trolling of this kind much more difficult in the future. But patent trolls aren't just going after private businesses; they also have their sights set on our most priceless assets. Our attitude to piracy is important, because what is happening to our freedoms in the world is a troubling sign of things to come elsewhere. There is a race on to patent and control the building blocks of life itself.

Biotech companies are patenting the genetic codes of crops, animals, and even human tissues. The multinational biotechnology corporation Monsanto, for example, has patented a number of seeds, some of which are its own genetically modified mutations, albeit of seeds that took thousands of years to develop naturally before they were patented. The biotech giant has sued farmers for saving, reusing, and sharing these seeds, even though many who have been sued claim they didn't even know they were using them (it's common for seeds to blow into fields from neighboring farms). Monsanto and other biotech firms have also developed seeds with "terminator technology," new strains of sterilized seeds that will not reproduce, like copy-protected MP3 files. Organizations all over the world, from farmers' unions to human rights and environmental groups such as Greenpeace, are protesting this.

Sharing seeds with family and friends and reusing them for the next year's harvest is clearly not the same as ripping albums from the Pirate Bay. If you copy a music file illegally, you haven't taken a material object and deprived someone else from using it. If you stop people from producing food efficiently, on a planet where environmental scientists are warning us that grain stocks are shrinking, our aquifers are drying up, and every living system and life support mechanism Earth has is in decline, you are depriving society of something priceless. And yet it is perfectly legal to patent anything alive (apart from a full-birth human being) and claim ownership of it, from a single strand of DNA to entire species of animals.*

It seems that our economic system is broken. For it to work, we need to be able to trust that corporations and the market will do the right thing and work in the interest of the public good as well as the private. But we are losing our rights and innovation is being stifled because companies using outdated business models and inefficient distribution systems don't want to switch to the new formats people are being criminalized for using. Meanwhile, economic development is being hampered because of trolls hiding behind and abusing the patent system. When the trust is gone, the system stops working properly. But this in turn produces new breeds of pirates, pushing back in the name of a fairer society when no one else will. Perhaps the noblest pirates out there today are those tackling an issue that literally means life or death for millions of people.

Pirates Without Borders

When regulations and patents are stifling our economies, our environment, and even human life itself, individuals and entire nations have responded with the pirate mentality, raising the stakes with world-changing consequences. And nowhere are the stakes currently higher than in medicine.

Patent trolls going after human gene sequences have already cost us lives. "Companies raced to beat the Human Genome Project in order to patent genes such as that associated with breast cancer," writes Nobel Prize–winning economist Joseph E. Stiglitz. "The value of these

---

*In August 2005 Monsanto filed patents in 160 countries, claiming ownership of the rights to pigs, and any and all future offspring those pigs may produce.

efforts was minimal: the knowledge was produced just a little sooner than it would have been otherwise. But the cost to society was enormous: the high price that Myriad, the patent holder, places on genetic tests (between $3,000 and $4,000) may well mean that thousands of women who would otherwise have been tested, discovered that they were at risk, and taken appropriate remediation, will die instead."

There are more than 40 million people around the world living with HIV/AIDS, including 640,000 children under age fifteen. Because patents allow drug companies to maintain a monopoly on new medicines they develop, and charge highly inflated prices, the pharmaceutical industry is one of the most profitable industries in the world. Billions of dollars are spent developing new drugs, including those that fight HIV/AIDS. With that level of investment, there need to be incentives and protections in place so companies will continue to develop new medicines that benefit society. This is fair. But in practice it doesn't work very well.

Western drug companies don't sell many AIDS drugs in developing countries because more than 90 percent of the people in the world suffering from HIV/AIDS can't afford to pay inflated Western prices. And because these companies make a profit only when they have the monopoly, measures are taken by drug companies to extend the life of these patents for as long as possible, preventing cheap generic drugs from entering their foreign or domestic markets. The drugs do work, but the patents don't. As a result, according to the World Health Organization, some three million people die every year.

Never before has an industry needed piracy so badly. And one such pirate who is making major waves is Dr. Yusef Hamied of the Mumbai pharmaceutical company Cipla. When his company produces generic drugs for the West, they are thought of as a legitimate and well-respected organization. But when Dr. Hamied began producing anti-HIV drugs for the developing world in the year 2000 for as little as $1 a day* compared to Western prices of more than $27 a day, he was branded by the former head of GlaxoSmithKline as a "pirate and a thief."

---

*This may not sound like a lot, but in India alone there are more than four hundred million people who make less than $1 a day.

"We have offered to pay royalties," Dr. Hamied told *Positive Nation* magazine in 2003. "Nobody denies that patents are valuable and that the person who invents a drug should be adequately rewarded. But not obscenely rewarded. We believe in patents but we don't believe in a monopoly."

Shannon Herzfeld, a spokeswoman for the Pharmaceutical Research and Manufacturers of America, or PhRMA, disagrees with his position. "We object to their premise that intellectual property rights are a barrier to access to good medicine," she told *The New York Times*. "Anyone who says, 'We have to steal' is wrong. Stealing ideas is not how one provides good health care."

The World Trade Organization (WTO) voted on the issue of countries deciding for themselves if they could import cheap generic drugs in a national health crisis at its 2001 meeting in Dohar. A total of 143 countries voted in favor of this. One, the United States, voted against it. The United States won.

When the market fails and democracy is ignored, pirates should step into the breach. In this case, it was governments in the developing world who became pill pirates, providing better health care *precisely* by stealing ideas. In India, Brazil, Argentina, Thailand, Egypt, and China, private and state-run enterprises are ignoring international patent laws written in the interests of profit, churning out generic versions of vital drugs at a fraction of the cost, saving and improving millions of lives as a result.

Because India didn't recognize intellectual property rights in medicine or agriculture since 1970,* pharmaceutical companies there were able to reverse-engineer cheap drugs and pesticides based on Western formulas, and life expectancy in India has gone up from forty years in 1970 to sixty-four years today.

The pill pirates put an international spotlight on the issue, and although there is a long way to go, some Western drug companies have now cut the prices of AIDS drugs to Africa by 80 percent, and the pressure is on for other pharmaceutical giants to do the same. But

---

*Under pressure from the West, these laws are now starting to change.

as Dr. Javid A. Chowdhury, the Indian minister of health, noted in *The New York Times*, "If they can offer an 80 percent discount, there was something wrong with the price they started off with."

Losing Patents

The WTO wouldn't grant developing nations patent relief instead of drug discounts, even though the majority of its members voted in favor of doing so. So those nations became pirates, and fought back against the WTO's cheap imitation democracy. Now that nations of pirates are challenging patent laws head-on, some are saying that in the case of health care, it is time these laws changed. The pharmaceutical industry is a perfect example of the system gone wrong. Drug companies make much bigger profits from selling Viagra or Botox to rich people than they can from developing AIDS or malaria drugs for poor people. Patents are not helping drug companies to break this bad habit. The debate created by the pill pirates just might.

Former chief economist of the World Bank Joseph E. Stiglitz is one of many who think there is another solution. Patents protect ideas, but they are ultimately inefficient because they restrict the use of knowledge, something that in this case clearly benefits us all. Instead, Stiglitz and others have put forward the idea of a medical prize fund, which would reward those who discover cures and vaccines. Governments, alongside pharmaceutical giants, already foot the bill for a great deal of pharmaceutical research.* If governments are funding research already, Stiglitz argues, they could finance a prize fund that rewards drug companies for developing treatments or preventions for diseases affecting hundreds of millions of poor people, something patents do not do efficiently. He suggests:

---

*As Noam Chomsky points out in "Unsustainable Non Development," "the pharmaceutical corporations and others claim they need this (protection via patents and intellectual property rights) so they can recoup the costs of research and development. But have a close look. A very substantial part of the research and development is paid for by the public anyway. In a narrow sense, it's on the order of 40–50%. But that's an underestimate, because it doesn't count the basic biology and the basic science, which is all publicly funded."

When it comes to diseases in developing countries, it would make sense for some of the prize money to come from foreign assistance budgets, as few contributions could do more to improve the quality of life, and even productivity, than attacking the debilitating diseases that are so prevalent. . . . The type of prize system I have in mind would rely on competitive markets to lower prices and make the fruits of the knowledge available as widely as possible. With better-directed incentives (more research dollars spent on more important diseases, less money spent on wasteful and distorted marketing), we could have better health at lower cost.

Pirates are forcing decision makers to reconsider the use of patents, and now the idea of a prize system is getting support, not just for developing countries, but also for Western markets. "Under a drug prize system," wrote *Forbes* magazine in April 2006, "the U.S. government would simply pay cash for the rights to any drug that wins FDA approval, then put the U.S. rights in the public domain. Voilà! a free market in the manufacture and sale of new drugs. Generic drugs ("generic" being another way of saying the rights are in the public domain) already do a wonderful job of keeping prices down. While the price of patent-protected drugs has been rising at roughly twice the rate of inflation, the real price of generics has fallen in four of the last five years."

Medicine is an industry where the social benefits of piracy are clear, and the social costs of putting profit and intellectual property rights before people are horrifying. Yet the needless death of millions of people every year, in the name of economic growth, is the still the status quo. Patents are important, but in cases where they shut out the positive forces of the free market *and* have a negative effect on society, it's clear they need to be replaced.

Many such patents are actually owned by the U.S. taxpayers, and could easily be turned over to the World Health Organization, the United Nations, or the developing world. Will the United States, a nation built on piracy itself, ever allow this to happen? That all depends on whether there is still honor among thieves.

The Three Habits of Highly Effective Pirates

From the birth of America to the birth of the Internet, it is often left to pirates to chart the winds of change and plot better courses for the future. When pirates start to appear in a market, it's usually an indication that it isn't working properly. When governments and markets recognize the legitimacy of what these pirates are doing, their activities are enshrined in new laws, creating a new order that serves society better.

We live in a new world where things we used to pay for, such as music, movies, and newspapers, are now available for free. But things that used to reproduce for free, such as seeds and pigs, have to be paid for. This is a world where we all need to understand the finer points of the pirate mentality:

1. **Look Outside of the Market**

    Entrepreneurs look for gaps in the market. Pirates look for gaps *outside of* the market. There was no market for Hollywood films before William Fox and friends. There was no market for commercial radio in Europe before pirate DJs. Pirates have proved that just because the market won't do something, it doesn't mean it's a bad idea.

2. **Create a Vehicle**

    Once pirates find a space the market has ignored, they park a new vehicle in it and begin transmitting. Sometimes this new vehicle becomes more important, or as Marshall McLuhan put it, the medium becomes the message. The platform that pirate DJs created was more important than rock 'n' roll. The idea of the "blog" had a much greater impact than the picture of Cary Grant dropping acid on Justin's Home Page.

3. **Harness Your Audience**

    When pirates do something valuable in society, citizens support them, discussion starts, and laws change. It is the supporters that pirates attract that enable them and their ideas to go legit. Kiss FM got a license thanks to its listeners. Roh Moo-hyun became president thanks to citizens using the pirate mentality on his behalf. Entire nation-states are supporting pill pirates to save lives.

Power to the Pirates

Piracy has gone on throughout history, and we should encourage it. It's how inefficient systems are replaced.

Wherever you tune in, somewhere you will find a pirate pushing back against authority, decentralizing monopolies, and promoting the rule of the people: the very nature of democracy itself. The pirate mentality is a way to mobilize communities, drive innovation, and create social change. By thinking like pirates, people grow niche audiences to a critical mass and change the mainstream from the bottom up. They've toppled more inefficient corporate pyramids than they've invented styles of music, and as long as there are people or choices not being represented in the marketplace, there will always be pirates pushing the envelope. Margaret Mead famously said, "Never doubt that a small group of thoughtful, committed citizens can change the world. Indeed, it's the only thing that ever has." Pirates are some of the most committed citizens we've got.

Many pirates aren't just copying the work of others. Some give this work new meaning by broadcasting it somewhere else. But as we shall now see, there are pirates reinventing the work of others entirely, using a process that gives them a unique perspective, a powerful tool we can all use to create change.

CHAPTER 3

We Invented the Remix

Cut-'n'-Paste Culture Creates
Some New Common Ground

"One is a groundbreaking consumer electronics device released in a range of catchy colors, enabling a hugely addictive portable listening experience—the other is the iPod mini."—John Ousby
© *John Ousby*

"What the fuck do you think you're doing?" Madonna snaps, making you jump as her voice reverberates around the bedroom. This wasn't the reaction you were expecting; far from it. You wanted to kick back, relax, and listen to some new music. But Madonna's not having it. She repeats the question again and again, her voice growing louder in your head.

It's April 2003, and you, along with Madonna fans worldwide, hit KaZaA to download some tracks from her latest album, *American Life*. Instead, you get spoof MP3 files: the material girl verbally bitch-slapping the file-sharing community. It's her and Warner Bros.' latest bid to thwart Internet piracy by fighting fire with fire, acting like a pirate herself. Madonna flooded peer-to-peer networks with digital decoys that appeared to be tracks from the new album but were actually recordings of her cursing and snarling at would-be illegal downloaders everywhere.

Intended as another genius publicity stunt by one of the smartest women in music, this turned out to be one of the biggest blunders of her career, right up there with *Evita*, Sean Penn, and *Shanghai Surprise*.

Madonna is the fourth-bestselling recording artist *in history*, worth hundreds of millions of dollars. When she started screaming at ordinary people worldwide through their computers, she was bound to upset a few of them. Many of her fans viewed the stunt as Madonna's response not just to file-sharing, but also against the very notion of free culture. Frustrated by a globalized music industry force-feeding them plastic pop music, hackers, remixers, and activists began to mobilize within hours against Madonna, who had just reinvented herself yet again, this time as the poster child for the music industry's war on downloading music. Big mistake, Madge.

Madonna hadn't anticipated how the pirates and hacktivists she lashed out against might manipulate her message. Pirates create their own media and push out their own content, as we have seen. They also have at their disposal a powerful creative tool: the remix.

Days after the decoy files were released, new versions of Madonna's a cappella outburst started springing up with new backing tracks underneath. Soon clubs and radio stations around the world were spinning the many remixes of this new Madonna single, now known as "WTF," a song that had been created, adapted, and distributed completely outside of Madonna's control. Dmusic.com launched a competition to find the best one (the prize was a "Boycott RIAA"* T-shirt).

---

*The Recording Industry Association of America (RIAA) is the trade group that represents the U.S. recording industry. In recent years the association has come under heavy fire from free culture advocates who claim the RIAA is aggressively trying to stifle innovation in the music business and is unfairly penalizing music consumers. In 1998 the RIAA filed a lawsuit that, if it had been a success, would have outlawed MP3 players. It also supported 1999 legislation stripping artists of their copyright interests and transferring those interests to their record labels, and has sued mothers and children for astronomical sums for downloading music. In 2007 the RIAA won the *Consumerist*'s "Worst Company in America" reader poll, narrowly beating Halliburton.

Fifteen of the best "WTF" remixes were compiled in an album and released by an independent label. "HACKERS HAVE FIELD DAY WITH MADONNA DECOY," exclaimed the *Hollywood Reporter*'s headline as media outlets around the globe jumped on the story.

The final blow came on Saturday, April 19, 2003, when Madonna's official site was hacked and every track from her new album, the real tracks, were pinned to the home page free for anyone to download. Across the top of the page, the remixer posted a response to Madonna, the music industry, and everyone else threatening to stand in free culture's way:

THIS IS WHAT THE FUCK I THINK I'M DOING.

The remix is of the most powerful forces in pop culture today. There are many ideas we consider original innovations which are actually versions of someone else's idea. The Old Testament (Ecclesiastes) said it best: *"The thing that hath been, it is that which shall be: And that which is done is that which shall be done: And there is no new thing under the sun."* And hey, even the Old Testament is no exception. Many scholars believe its stories (and for that matter, the similar stories that appear in the Torah and the Qur'an as well) are rooted in pagan myths of ancient Mesopotamian cultures, based in a land we now call Iraq.

Rip. Mix. Burn.

The iPod has become a modern-day cultural icon. Its slick marketing, hi-gloss colors, and impeccable design have made it a huge success; but MP3 players were old news when Apple released them in 2001. Sony developed the iPod's long-life battery; Toshiba perfected the hard drive, and its operating system was originally created by a company named Pixo. Its "groundbreaking" design has even been attributed to the Regency TR-1 transistor radio, released in 1954. The TR-1 was the world's first commercially sold battery-powered pocket radio. It was small enough to hold in your hand, had a single circular dial, and came in a variety of cool colorways, delivered with the marketing slogan "See it! Hear it! Get it!" In fact, in response to iPod mania, BBC News commented in 2005, "Hi-tech, trendy colors, rock music, punchy slogans . . . remind anyone of anything?"

Original ideas are often historical concepts mashed up and served as something new. If you flip to the notes at the back of this book, you can clearly see where many of the ideas discussed here came from, and if you check those sources, you'll find the source's sources, and so on. But as the Old Testament, the iPod, and a million other innovations have already proved, a great remix is much more than the sum of its parts.

More Than Music

Humans have always created new things by repurposing old ones. Like when some New England college kids began playing catch with empty cake tins in the late nineteenth century and invented a new sport (the tins all came from the Frisbie Baking Company of Bridgeport, Connecticut). But this doesn't mean that remix culture is just pie in the sky.

The phenomenon known as "the remix" is different. It is a conscious process used to innovate and create. In fact, it's no exaggeration to say that the cut-'n'-paste culture born out of sampling and remixing has revolutionized the way we interpret the world. As Nelson George said in *Hip Hop America*, the remix "raises questions about the nature of creativity and originality . . . it changes the relationship of the past to the present in ways conventional historians might take notice of. What is the past now?"

The past is now public property for us to do with as we see fit. It has been said that "history is written by the winners"*—but these days, we all can have a shot. Remixing is about taking something that already exists and redefining it in your own personal creative space, reinterpreting someone else's work your way. The remix started as a happy accident in music, evolved into a controversial idea, then became a mass movement that straddled several music genres. Today it's an industry standard in hundreds of industries.

---

*Ironically enough, no one knows who first said this. Alex Haley and Winston Churchill are just two of the many of people this quote has been credited to, but nobody is completely sure of its origin.

But despite its success, the remix is still sending mixed messages. Lawsuits rage across the world as artists struggle to prove they aren't simply plagiarizing someone else's concept by remixing it, but changing it; putting it in a different context, amplifying part of an idea, emitting another, or making it palatable to a whole new audience. Today, the ethos behind the remix is so pervasive in pop culture, so engrained in everyday life that chances are you probably didn't notice it was there at all. But in a world governed by Punk Capitalism, where our creativity is our most important asset, we need to understand how this process works and where it came from.

Its story is an unholy trinity, spanning reggae, disco, and hip-hop, that crosses decades, continents, generations, and three very different (yet in many ways very similar) music scenes. The long version would require a whole book. To do this in a handful of pages is a problem, but not a problem that can't be fixed with a remix. To break this three-part history down and to understand the phenomenon fully, let's remix the story of the remix and look at it from the point of view of another huge, influential pop-culture trilogy.

(Cue *Star Wars* music.)

EPISODE 1:
VERSION EXCURSIONS

Our story begins not in a galaxy far, far away, but in 1950s Jamaica. Here a battle has been raging for many years between an evil empire and a rebel alliance. The empire is British, and the rebels are the people, who will come to form a movement born out of R&B, ska, and a deep desire for political change, later known as reggae. The dark forces of colonization and commonwealth that have suppressed the country for decades are slowly being pushed back by a small army of heroes, including our Jedi knights in this epic saga, the deejays.*

---

*The term "deejay" is not the same as the modern definition of the DJ. The deejay in Jamaica was the DJ in the conventional sense—the guy playing the records—but also the compère, toaster, and MC, rapping over the top of the music he was playing. To confuse

The deejay did not need a phallic symbol like a light saber to make him feel like a man; he had something way more powerful: the sound system. Sound systems evolved from mobile record stores into trucks loaded with huge bass bins and earsplitting amplifiers, endlessly touring Jamaican towns and cities battling one another sonically through another great Jamaican innovation, the soundclash.*

Soundclashes were to 1950s Jamaica what gladiator fighting was to ancient Rome, but the sound system's real power was its political muscle, and the real fight was with the establishment. As hip-hop historian Jeff Chang points out in his book *Can't Stop Won't Stop*, "All any [Jamaican] prime minister had to do to gauge the winds was listen closely to the week's 45 rpm single releases; they were like political polls set to melody and riddim."

Our Han Solo in this epic story is Arthur "Duke" Reid. When he and his wife, Lucille, won some money in the Jamaican national lottery, the Reids spent their winnings on a Kingston liquor store, the Treasure Isle. Reid installed his own sound system in the store to entice customers (the two industries have long been linked, most sound systems made their money by selling alcohol at clashes). The sound system came to be known as the Trojan. If the average sound system was better than a light saber, then the Trojan was the Millennium Falcon. Duke loaded his system onto a Bedford "Trojan" truck and began to dominate soundclashes across Jamaica. Like Solo, Reid always had his blaster on show (two handguns, a belt of cartridges, and a shotgun, to be precise) and would never hesitate to put some shots in the air if a clash became unruly. Flying through the countryside with the war cry of "Here comes the Trojan!," he was a sound system crusader, taking the highly prized "King of Sound & Blues" title in 1956, 1957, and 1958. Even before he invented the remix, Duke Reid was the stuff of legend.

When the rebel alliance overthrew the empire in 1962, the sound systems became more powerful than ever. Not only did Jamaica gain

---

things even more, later the two roles split and the "selector" stuck to playing the tunes, while modern deejays such as Sean Paul and Beenie Man stick to MCing.

*The soundclash is a musical competition in which rival sound systems pit their deejay and selecting skills against one another in a test of sonic strength.

some independence from the British, but also Jamaican music was becoming independent of America. As cheaper vinyl 45 rpm records started to replace 78s, Reid realized he could now afford to record and press his own homegrown music. In 1964 he built a recording studio above the Treasure Isle's new Kingston premises, 33 Bond Street, and here the foundations for the remix were laid.

It happened in 1967. Duke was now fifty-two; the rocksteady genre he pioneered was dominant; and a new breed of sound systems was emerging from the old capital, Spanish Town. One afternoon, Reid's associate, Ruddy Redwood, was cutting some tunes at his studio, one of which was an already popular track, "On the Beach" by The Paragons. And that's when it happened. Studio engineer Byron Smith forgot to pan up the vocals on the mixing desk, and by doing so accidentally recorded the first "dub version," an instrumental of a song minus the vocals, perfect for MCing over.

Redwood was intrigued by the mistake, and took the instrumental with him to a soundclash he was playing at that night. Using two turntables, he switched between the original mix and the vocal-less version, giving the master of ceremonies a lot more room to maneuver on the microphone and giving the crowd the space to sing along between verses, sending the whole dance crazy in the process. That night he rewound the dubplate so many times, by the next morning it was completely worn out.

Use the Force, Duke . . .

Right away, Redwood knew something special had happened. "Everybody was singing. It was very happy, an' I get a vibe," he told Steve Barrow and Peter Dalton in *The Rough Guide to Reggae*. And Reid saw the beauty of the idea immediately. He also realized he could eliminate the B side of a single by including an instrumental rather than a second original track, cutting his costs in half. He took the concept and ran with it. By 1968 Reid had hit light speed, releasing a slew of versions through his labels. In a few months, the mixing desk and turntable became instruments, studio engineers became performers, and the rules of standard song structures were suddenly obsolete.

"Dub" became a style of music in its own right. Artists such as Lee "Scratch" Perry and King Tubby pushed the idea further, deliberately accentuating the drums and bass lines of tracks as well as stripping out the vocals, and liberally scattering primitive sound effects such as vocal snippets, echo, and reverb throughout. A dub version takes the core elements of a song, throws out the vocals, and turns up all the parts that sound great on a huge, bottom-heavy sound system. This was the first evolution of the remix.

By the time Duke passed away in 1975 at sixty, he had secured his place in music history, and the Jamaican sound system giants of that era continue to inspire people around the world. But as Reid's revolutionary reign in Jamaica was ending, another was beginning, in America. This particular revolution would end badly, but inflict its glitzy vengeance on dance music forever.

EPISODE 2:
DISCO'S REVENGE

Our second act opens on a huge synthetic, silver orb floating in a cavernous black space. The orb is immensely powerful, the tool of a new world order sworn to wreak havoc across the galaxy, hell-bent on destroying ancient preconceptions pertaining to class, race, economic group, and sexual orientation, mercilessly tearing down any and all social barriers in its path.

That's no moon . . .

This orb is a mirror ball. It's floating not in deep space, but in several hundred square feet of loft space, in an old garment factory on Broadway in New York City. The year is 1972, and the loft is filled with bodies writhing to a new sound, a strange type of psychedelic R&B—a bass-heavy concoction of countless genres, mixed into a new all-inclusive message of love, the product of newly liberated sections of American society high on the fallout of flower power and a deep-rooted faith in equality. This loft is known simply as "the Loft," owned by a young Italian American DJ named David Mancuso. What's going on there will come to be known as disco.

Disco doesn't mean a lot to most people these days. To say that *Saturday Night Fever* misrepresented disco is something of an understatement. Although many of the DJ pioneers behind the scene were Italian Americans, if the film were more accurate, Travolta would have probably been black or Latino—and as gay as a hat stand.

Disco is now mostly memorialized by Afro wigs and polyester flares, but its origins are rooted, like reggae, in a story of liberation. As music historians Bill Brewster and Frank Broughton tell it in *Last Night a DJ Saved My Life*, "The last days of disco might have recalled the decadent fall of Rome, but the first days were filled with hope." As the sixties ended, so did the dominance of rock 'n' roll. The Beatles split, Hendrix passed, and Elvis was experimenting with ballads and sleeping pills. The victories of the civil rights movement and the Stonewall rebellion were fresh in people's minds, and Vietnam would soon be over. It was a time of optimism for many American people, so they decided to party.

Once again, our brave heroes the DJs made that party happen, with a whole new batch of sick Jedi skills. They turned empty lofts, garages, and disused churches into mini-utopias governed by nothing but peace, love, and unity (and some uppers, downers, cocaine, tranquilizers, acid, heroin, and orgies).

However, disco's biggest contribution to the remix came not from a DJ but a male model. His story begins on a remote sandy outpost one weekend in the summer of 1972. Tom Moulton, our twentysomething it-boy hero, headed out to Fire Island, a secluded beachfront community carved into the side of the narrow sandbar that underscores Long Island. Fire Island was the weekend home of New York City's gay glitterati in the 1970s, and disco music pumped out of every club, ramshackle bar, and house party. At the Botel club, Tom noticed that the crowd was frustrated with three-minute singles. "People were getting excited, then this change would happen and they would be walking off the floor. . . . It was a shame," he told radio station WFMU. "So I thought, gee, let me try something."

Moulton took his findings, a tape recorder, a huge pile of tapes, and a razor blade to cut songs up and paste them back together the way he wanted to hear them. Eighty hours later, he emerged triumphantly with a forty-five-minute tape of reedited disco tracks. This was the second evolution of the remix: the edit. By dropping out parts of the songs that he noticed weren't working on the floor, and looping the sections that were, he built a sonic time bomb he was sure would ignite the clubs in a way the DJs couldn't.

Unfortunately, it took a little while to go off. Upon hearing the tape, the owner of the Botel told Tom "not to give up the day job." But give our hot model some credit: Tom passed the tape on to another club, the Sandpiper. Tom's remix detonated there the following night; his phone woke him at 2:30 A.M., but all he could make out was a huge screaming commotion on the other end of the line. Bewildered, he took the receiver off the hook. The next morning, the owner of the Sandpiper finally got hold of him. The noise had been the crowd at the club going crazy to Tom's tape. The Sandpiper offered Tom $500 a week to make a new mix tape every week.

Tom's mixes ruled the Sandpiper for two seasons, and the young pinup went from unknown audio activist to New York City disco darling, remixing for Gloria Gaynor (transforming an entire side of her album *Never Can Say Goodbye* into one seamless eighteen-minute mix), Grace Jones (who at the time was showing up at Studio 54 completely naked on a regular basis), and everyone who was anyone in disco. The male model had become a grandmaster without ever setting foot behind the turntables.

Tom took the idea of the version, remixed it, and dropped it into the American consciousness. Soon the rest of the disco DJs found their way into the recording studio, and the remix emerged as a canon of dance music. To some artists the idea of a reedit was sacrilegious, a notion the remix hasn't stopped fighting since. But like the reggae movement that birthed it, it was "the people's choice," and commercial success only continued to push it forward.

If disco made the remix a musical institution, it was hip-hop that hammered the idea home. As disco's breaks and beats spread to New York City's outer boroughs, a new audience would switch them up to create a new movement that would go on to become the largest-selling form of music in history.

EPISODE 3:
THE RETURN OF THE SOUNDCLASH

We'll cast Robert Moses as the evil emperor in Episode 3. "When you operate in an overbuilt metropolis," he once said, "you have to hack your way through with a meat ax." This is a great quote to explain how people use the remix to redefine their world in a world of infinite influences and combinations, as an antidote to information overload. But it sucks in context—Moses was the unelected city planner responsible for chopping the Bronx to bits in the late 1950s.

While the wealthier white populace headed to the 'burbs, those who couldn't afford to, predominantly poor black and Latino families, were forced into the newly built housing projects of the South Bronx. Slumlords torched the old neighborhoods in an epidemic of insurance arson, and many neighborhoods deteriorated in the face of gang violence, fires, race riots, and heroin. But even in these darkest of times, the rebel alliance would once again mobilize.

A new hope rose as the fires raged and gangs clashed. Among the chaos, four disciplines of self expression (DJing, MCing, B-boying, and graffiti) fused into hip-hop. And like the other episodes, it started with a battle for dance-floor supremacy.

The territorial markings of the gangs morphed into a powerful new medium that would be known as graffiti. In 1967, the same year Reid had pioneered the remix, a twelve-year-old named Clive Campbell, inspired by Duke and the other sound system giants of the time, left Jamaican shores with his family to start a new life in the Bronx. He was one of thousands of kids also inspired by the first graffiti writers, and he starts writing KOOL HERC on walls. This is the name he is still known by, as the DJ who created hip-hop.

Like Tom Moulton, Herc had a deep understanding of the dance floor. As a young DJ coming up, playing disco and funk at block parties (where the decks were often powered by hacking the electricity supply of a nearby lamppost), he began noticing groups of kids waiting specifically for the "break" section of the record, where the vocals dropped out and the drums and bass took the track back to its raw components. These dancers would then hit the floor just for these fifteen-to-thirty-second intervals with fierce, competitive energy, contorting their bodies in sync with the drum patterns, changing shape with every beat, inspired by the acrobatic moves of James Brown and a young Michael Jackson. This later became known as "breaking."

Herc liked what he saw. He wanted to maintain this level of energy for an entire performance, so he extended these breaks from fifteen-second snippets to new five-minute pieces by playing two copies of the same record into one another and isolating the break beat as the focal point of his performance.

Herc's innovations took the ideas of Reid and Moulton to a new level. Remixing records together in real time, he was able to respond to the ever-changing conditions on the dance floor in a split second. But hip-hop was far from done with the remix. Enter stage left, hip-hop's Anakin Skywalker and Obi Wan Kenobi. Anakin will be played by a prodigal young electronics whiz kid and regular at Herc's parties, Joseph Saddler. Obsessed with the idea that these new break beats could be even better, Saddler honed mixing and scratching into a fine art he called "quick mix theory." He was hip-hop's first mad scientist, and way before he was involved in this particular cheesy *Star Wars* metaphoric montage, he was referred to as "the Darth Vader of the sliding fader." But the world would come to know him by another name: Grandmaster Flash.

Hip-hop's Obi Wan was Afrika Bambaataa. The former leader of the notorious Black Spades gang, Bam would go from Sith Lord to peace-loving Jedi after seeing the Michael Caine classic *Zulu*. Watching the Zulu warriors fighting the British, Bambaataa had an epiphany. He saw what was happening around him and realized the fight was not with other people in the Bronx, but the imperial powers that be. He was the first politically charged force in hip-hop, taking his sound system all over the borough, breaking down the former gangland borders without violence, and uniting people with music. While today hip-hop is constantly blamed for inciting trouble and negativity, at its inception it was a force for peace.

Bam and Flash would be the artists to crystallize the next mutation of the remix process on vinyl. Inspired by the success of the first hip-hop hit, the Sugarhill Gang's "Rapper's Delight" (in which the Sugarhill Gang rapped over an edit of the disco hit "Good Times" by Chic), Flash and his Furious Five crew began putting out singles, and in 1981 released "The Adventures of Grandmaster Flash on the Wheels of Steel." This record would show the world this new remix music undiluted. A seven-minute-long lesson in quick mix theory, it was the first record ever made with turntables. Flash linked up three decks, two mixers, and fused together parts from Queen's "Another One Bites the Dust," Blondie's "Rapture," Chic's "Good Times," a mock children's story, and many more aural oddities and tracks besides. The result was the remix's manifesto, a blueprint for creativity.

A year later, Afrika Bambaataa refined this blueprint. Working with legendary producer Arthur Baker, their track "Planet Rock" was aimed squarely at both the hip-hop and punk rock markets. Ripping out the guts of Kraftwerk's "Numbers" and "Tran Europe Express," a track called "Super Sperm" by Captain Sky and Babe Ruth's "The Mexican," they wrapped them around a new beat from a Roland TR-808 drum machine and overlaid original lyrics. These two records were revolutionary. Flash and Bam's adventures would change the entire world of entertainment.

As the sampler* became widely used in studios, there was no turning back. Hip-hop, dance music, and reggae continue to evolve worldwide, but the remix saga remains their most important contribution to youth culture. Thanks to these three scenes and countless cultures and businesses that have since adopted the ideals behind the remix, it's now inspiring innovation everywhere you look, as the saga continues.

To Reid it was the version, to Moulton the reedit, and to Flash quick mix theory. By 2005, *Wired* magazine was calling the remix "the dominant art of the decade." When it hit the world, it was seen as a radical new sound. But we can also think of it as a radical new language. The remix is nothing less than a new way to communicate.

---

*For the uninitiated, a sampler is a musical instrument that records or samples different sounds that can then be reconfigured in a variety of ways to make new sounds.

In essence the remix is a creative mental process. It requires you to do nothing more than change the way you look at something. Albert Einstein once said, "No problem can be solved from the same consciousness that created it"; the remix is that mind-set crystallized. It's about shifting your perception of something and taking in other elements and influences. It requires you to think of chunks of the past as building blocks for the future. *Scarface*'s Tony Montana summed this sentiment up with his mantra "The World Is Yours," and his world has now been sampled to bits on records, T-shirts, sneakers, video games, and in other movies. Maybe if Tony were still around today, he'd be saying "The World Is Everybody's."

Remixing is easy. It's often the first place producers and sound engineers get started, and today filmmakers, game developers, and everyone else are using it as a base to jump off from as well. To prove how easy and how amazingly useful this can be, you and I are going to remix something right now.

Quick Mix Theory 101

The remix is a recipe for creativity that can make any idea into a mouthwatering concept. For this recipe you will need the following ingredients:

- a big idea (this doesn't have to be your own; a borrowed one will do);
- an idea of who is on your dance floor;
- a handful of other people's ideas (chopped up);
- a pinch of originality.

Directions

1. Take your big idea. This can be something you're working on, thinking about, have, or want. If you are on a train, it could be the seat under you, or the girl opposite's earrings. It could be your screenplay or Grandma's tiramisu recipe. It really doesn't matter; literally anything will do. This is your base, the subject you're going to remix.

2. Break this idea down into its component parts. In a song that would mean the drums, bass line, strings, vocals, etc. Separate out the things that work and don't work. If this was a dub version of a record, we'd lose the vocals and turn up the drums and bass. If it's the seat on the train, is it comfy? Aesthetically pleasing? What is it made of? How are the parts joined together? Pare it down—look at what's good and what's deadwood.

3. Next, think about the end users, your dance floor, the people consuming your remix. Who are they? What do they want? How can you reedit the base, the way Tom Moulton did, to better suit their needs? If the seat on the train, what would you need to do to it to put it in a trendy bar? How could you repurpose it so it was right for an old folks' home? Who are the people on your dance floor? What keeps them moving? What causes them to walk away? How are you going to make them go crazy?

4. Now look at your base again. Maybe there was an element you missed that would work really well, or something that, on second thought, you overestimated. If it's a record, a producer might think he needs louder bass, less treble, or more cowbell. DJ Kool Herc focused solely on using the break beats in disco and funk records, because this was the only part of the record his audience of break-dancers was interested in. If it's the train seat for the old folks' home, maybe you need to think about that lower back support. The remix is about taking an idea and making it suitable for a whole new audience.

5. The idea should already look very different, but we're just getting started. What you've done so far is a simple reedit. Now it's time to apply some quick mix theory. Go back to your dance floor, look at the other ideas out there that get it moving, and sample them. Line up your idea next to other things your audience seems to be into. When Afrika Bambaataa and Arthur Baker made "Planet Rock," their base was two records by the German group Kraftwerk, which were popular in New York at the time. But they also knew the punks and disco kids downtown liked hip-hop and the uptown hip-hop heads were feeling disco breaks, so they sampled elements from records that

already had these ingredients, and reused them to hook in these two different crowds.

Look at your new samples the same way you looked at your base, cherry-pick the best elements, and discard the rest. Once you have them distilled, work out how you can apply these new ingredients. Our old folks' train seat hybrid might benefit from a set of wheels, so why not mix it up with a golf cart? Or mash it up with a La-Z-Boy to make it more comfy, or even add some hopped-up hydraulics from a muscle car to help people get in and out of it more easily, controlled with technology our audience is already used to, swiped straight from a Craftmatic adjustable bed. Where will these new samples all sit in the mix? Once they're in and it's working, stand back and take another look.

6. The idea you are now looking at can be considered a remix, a new original arrangement that contains elements from previous original work or works. Through good reediting of samples, great new original material can be produced from unoriginal parts. But just like Bam and Arthur added rapping and a drum machine to their samples, throwing in something completely original isn't a bad idea. A good remix is defined by its signature original elements. It might be composing a new bass line, playing in some extra keys, or adding a new kick drum. You may decide the originality is already there; an original process or take on sampled material counts. Or you may end up with one tiny piece of the original mixed with an entirely new score of your own. Either way, your originality should outshine the borrowed elements, or at the very least, present them in a new light. A good remix adds value to something. If everything has gone right, you should now have a new idea that contains elements from, but is independent of, the original. This new idea is a remix. Garnish and serve.

Just like it is with Kevin Bacon, the distance between you and a great remix is just six steps or less. If the concept is still not clear, think about the story I just told. "The History of the Remix (Matt Mason's *Star*

Wars Remix)" was one I took from a number of other books, articles, radio programs, documentaries, and websites that were already out there. I sampled them all and mashed up what I thought was the best version for my dance floor, a broad group of people you are part of, with varying degrees of knowledge of music history and youth culture, interested in how it has produced innovation and changed things. I then overdubbed this version with elements of a popular story nearly everybody knows, which I thought would work on my particular dance floor. None of the elements in the story was original, but the way they were rewritten means that the finished product is. I hope George Lucas's lawyers see it like that anyway.

It Ain't All Good

Remixing something doesn't necessarily make it better; just ask anyone who's watched the remake of *The Italian Job*, listened to *Christmas Pan Pipe Moods,* or woken up after a night drinking vodka and Red Bull.

In fact, the remix can and has *devalued* the idea of the original idea. Hollywood studios now rely on big brand remixes, sequels, and remakes, while original ideas take a backseat at smaller development houses such as Fox Searchlight and Miramax.* Meanwhile, the "director's cut" is the remix du jour that helps sell the DVD a few months after its cinema release. The same thing is happening to video games, sneakers, magazines, automobiles, and pretty much any other industry where risk-averse decision makers are leading the way. Rather than taking big gambles on new, unproven ideas, hit concepts are repackaged, repositioned, and sold again, to both the original and new audiences alike, stifling creativity, homogenizing society, and keeping the same ten damn songs on the radio all day, every day.† The remix has evolved, on one level, into the bland mainstream franchise. Film direc-

---

*In 2001 the big Hollywood studios released a total of nine sequels and remakes. By 2003 this figure had hit a record high of twenty-five, and this was up to forty-four by 2005. By 2006, more than fifty were in production.

†Corporate consolidation can be blamed for this. More than 80 percent of the $12 billion in annual music sales is controlled by the four largest labels in the United States, and more than 75 percent of the radio market is controlled by a handful of giant companies, who each

tor Spike Lee complained at the 2005 Venice Film Festival, "There's no originality . . . it's the worst it's ever been."

But if you apply the science behind the remix properly, it is possible to create a remix so good that people forget about the original. Now that we have the basics down, let's take in some advanced quick mix theory and the people putting it into practice.

Vision Mixers

When the DJ evolved into the VJ (video jockey), the remix broke the sound barrier, and it became clear that this new phenomenon was actually the evolution of the patchwork quilt. MTV launched on August 1, 1981, with the Buggles' hit "Video Killed the Radio Star." As it turned out, video would empower the radio star as VJs kicked down doors for the remix, allowing it to grow into an amazing new visual performance art.

The technologies behind the DJ and VJ disciplines are remarkably similar. As samplers, synthesizers, software, and mixers shaped music, tools have developed in tandem that let you sample, cut up, and overdub film footage in the same way. When video found itself at the mercy of two turntables and a crossfader, the way film was both produced and consumed was revolutionized.

Today we have countless movies and TV shows centered around the remix. Hit shows such as *Pimp My Ride* and *Queer Eye for the Straight Guy* remix people's cars and closets, while fans illicitly remix and repost TV clips online daily. Meanwhile, the sampler has evolved into digital video recorders such as the TiVo, and the entire TV schedule has suddenly become remixable.

In 1992, Quentin Tarantino's *Reservoir Dogs* brought the remix to the big screen. By sampling elements from films such as Stanley Kubrick's *A Clockwork Orange* and Ringo Lam's Hong Kong action

---

own more than forty radio stations (Clear Channel currently owns twelve hundred). The flow of money and other payola-type perks from labels to stations create record sales for the major labels, but this closed loop drowns out diversity, new talent, and listener preferences. In a 2002 survey by the Future of Music Coalition, 78 percent of respondents said they wanted more variety on the air.

classic *City on Fire*, Tarantino added new flavors and made them his own, inspiring a new scene-stealing generation in Hollywood. But when fans began remixing films on the QT and distributing them via the Internet, movies suddenly became a two-way confabulation. One of the first examples of this is another *Star Wars* remix. When *Episode 1: The Phantom Menace* disappointed many original *Star Wars* fans, one decided to take things into their own hands. *Episode 1.1: The Phantom Edit* began to circulate online in early 2001, a new unofficial version that severed more than twenty minutes of the original, leaving the elements that had bugged many fans—namely the character Jar Jar Binks and young Anakin's childish dialogue—on the cutting-room floor. The infamous yellow intro text that scrolls into the cosmos was replaced with the phantom editor's mission statement:

Anticipating
the arrival of the newest
Star Wars film, some fans, like myself,
were extremely disappointed with the final product.
Being someone of the "George Lucas Generation,"
I have re-edited a standard VHS version of "The Phantom
Menace" into what I believe is a much stronger film by relieving
the viewer of as much story redundancy, pointless Anakin
actions and dialog, and Jar Jar Binks as possible. I created
this version to bring new hope to a large group of Star Wars
fans that felt unsatisfied by the seemingly misguided theatrical
release of "The Phantom Menace."
To Mr. Lucas and those that I may offend with this
re-edit, I am sorry:
—THE PHANTOM EDITOR

The implications of the phantom editor's actions were huge.* By creating this new edit, he had put the audience on a level playing field with the filmmaker. And with that, the games began. The next few years

---

*Though perhaps the greatest *Star Wars* remix of all time is the original 1970s set George Lucas built for the desert planet of Tatooine, which still exists, hidden in the desert in the

saw myriad movies get makeovers from disgruntled fans. When director Stanley Kubrick died, many were disappointed by the way Steven Spielberg handled Kubrick's unfinished film, *A.I.* Fans felt Kubrick's last melancholy daydream had been turned into a production-line blockbuster, and in 2002, the "Kubrick edit" appeared. The work of an independent filmmaker from Sacramento, DJ Hupp, the new version was cut on Hupp's home computer, omitting Spielberg's feel-good moments in an effort to exude Kubrick's darker, brooding signature style. Since then *The Lord of the Rings* trilogy has been remixed by purists to be more in line with Tolkien's original vision; *The Matrix: Dezionized* rid the series of the underground city of Zion plot string that many fans found a snooze; and *Star Trek: Kirkless Generations* is pretty much self-explanatory.

Underground "fan-tom" edits have exploded into a new genre of film, and even a new type of film store. CleanFlicks was a Utah-based chain of video stores, which offered more than seven hundred movies that had been remixed to appeal to Utah's religious family audience, cleansed of sex, violence, and profanities. Quite how some films on their list of titles, such as *Alien,* the *Scream* series, and *Saw* didn't bleed to death on the operating table after being hacked to pieces and restitched into fun family frolics is beyond me, but they must have been doing something right. CleanFlicks's edited movie business was operating in more than seventy stores across eighteen states, before a federal court judge ruled their remixes illegal in 2006. "We're disappointed," CleanFlicks CEO Ray Lines told the *Deseret Morning News* that July. "This is a typical case of David vs. Goliath, but in this case, Hollywood rewrote the ending."

Hollywood's lawyers have also gnashed their teeth at the community of fan-tom editors on more than one occasion. But some more enlightened movie execs see this practice as a new form of social innovation, because as journalist and filmmaker Danile Kraus put it, "If the filmmakers themselves can't cut it, the fans will."

North African nation of Tunisia. It is today a full-fledged town inhabited by Tunisian people. The house where Luke Skywalker grew up is now a hotel where tourists can stay for $10 a night.

Film remixing officially gained some acceptance from Hollywood in 2004, when Robert Greenwald's Fox News–bashing documentary *Outfoxed* was released, enjoying widespread critical acclaim and box-office success. Greenwald announced that he was making all his raw, unedited footage for *Outfoxed* available for third parties to download and remix. "One thing I've learned the last year and a half working on documentaries, is that it's all about the footage, and who controls access to that footage," says *Outfoxed* producer Jim Gilliam, "so we're walking the talk, and giving away the interviews to anyone who might want to use them."

Meanwhile, over at DreamWorks, Spielberg seemed to have gotten his head around the concept, too. In 2004, comic Mike Myers was signed to become a new kind of celebrity VJ, sampling and remixing old films into new creations. "Rap artists have been doing this for years with music," Myers told Reuters, "now we are able to take that same concept and apply it to film." "As an innovator, he is virtually unparalleled," added Spielberg. "If anyone can create a way to bring old films to new audiences, it is Mike." Four years later, however, the project is yet to bear fruit, and it would seem that the first film-sampling blockbuster is still a little way off. Maybe Spielberg should give Kool Herc or Tom Moulton a call.

The DreamWorks case is interesting, because as Lawrence Lessig points out in his excellent book on copyright *Free Culture*, "It is Mike Myers and only Mike Myers who is free to sample. Any general freedom to build upon the film archive of our culture, a freedom in other contexts presumed for us all, is now a privilege reserved for the funny and famous—and presumably rich." But history, as we saw in chapter 2, suggests that pirates will continue pushing the copyright envelope until these laws are changed.

Mods Rock

The remix proved highly contagious. Once it got inside the computer, it combined with the ideals of the open-source movement (a movement we'll examine in chapter 5). One result of this was the remixing and modifying of software—most noticeably the hacking and remixing of computer and video games, or "modding," which had some incredible effects on the mainstream.

The story of modding started in 1981, as the cut-'n'-paste worlds of hip-hop and MTV entered the mainstream consciousness. That year *Castle Wolfenstein*, an action game in which you play a World War II–era Allied spy shooting it out with the Nazis in a German castle, was released for the Apple 2. Three high school kids—Andrew Johnson, Preston Nevins, and Rob Romanchuk—were hooked, but something was missing. "Nazis just didn't seem that threatening to a suburban high school kid in the early '80s," they later posted on their fan site. "Smurfs. That was the real threat now."

In 1983, under the alias Dead Smurf Software, they remixed the game (a process now known as modding) into *Castle Smurfenstein*, replacing the Nazis with Smurfs and weaving in an entirely new Smurf-tastic plot inspired by *Monty Python* sketches. "I guess we were just interested in finding out how games were being created and this one happened to leave itself open to being explored more than others," says Andrew Johnson. "Once we started making a change or two and seeing the immediate results, it generated its own feedback loop to keep going further and further . . . and probably too far."

Rather than SS soldiers screaming at you in German before attempting to riddle you with bullets, in *Smurfenstein* you were confronted by psychotic little blue-and-white killing machines who garbled at you in unintelligible Smurf talk before opening fire as you traversed the levels of their Canadian castle.* The remix was created using nothing more than the Apple 2 and an original copy of *Castle Wolfenstein*. The sound effects and Smurfs theme tune were ripped directly from a VCR copy of the cartoon, and the game was copied via computer bulletin boards (early prototypes of what would become the Internet) and floppy disks and widely distributed for free. Copies spread like wildfire; it was an instant underground hit. But what started out as a harmless prank was to become the lifeblood of the

---

*To this day, even though they have thought about it for many years and are all highly intelligent people, the creators of *Smurfenstein* have no logical explanation as to why they thought Smurfs lived in Canada.

gaming industry. "I for one was totally oblivious to its effects for years. We just made it, released it into the wild, and forgot about it," Preston Nevins tells me. "About the only social implication I recall consider- ing at the time we did *Smurfenstein* was the public service of allowing many Smurfs to die. . . . I guess it spread far enough to become 'that weird thing we used to play' for a fair number of people." This is some- thing of an understatement. By remixing a game, the Dead Smurf Soft- ware crew changed the game entirely.

Ten years later, in the 1990s, fans weren't just redesigning games, they also were redesigning the tools that made them, adding new fea- tures, fixing software bugs, and improving upon products as they con- sumed them. Some of the kids who grew up under *Smurfenstein*'s influence had even become game developers, and completely under- stood the value of fan interaction in extending product life span and customer loyalty, as well as in generating creativity.

One of these kids was John Carmack, now the cofounder of game developer ID Software. ID acquired the rights to the original *Castle Wolfenstein* game and in 1992 unleashed *Castle Wolfenstein*'s sequel, *Wolfenstein 3-D.* Not only was this the original "first-person shooter,"* itself a revolutionary step for gaming, it also was the first game to encourage players to remix its code into new content. Car- mack pioneered subsequent successful games that embraced remix cul- ture such as blockbuster titles *Doom* and *Quake,* which owe not just their success but also the way they were built, to their remixability. In 1999 Carmack made the number ten spot in *Time*'s list of the fifty most influential people in technology. ID Software is now reported to be worth more than $105 million.

Mods of games have even become huge games in their own right. And the same way kids who make successful bootleg remixes of music often end up doing legitimate production for record companies, the game industry now recruits directly from the huge new labor pool of modders and hard-core gamers it has intentionally generated.

---

*A first-person shooter is a game where you view the action from a first-person perspective, staring down the barrel of some type of weapon that you invariably aim at some type of bad guy. They are now so popular that playing them has become a huge international sport, with professional cyber athletes competing for purses worth more than $400,000.

A mod for the popular game *Half Life** known as *Counter-Strike* became the number one online action game in the world, with an average number of a hundred thousand players battling it out simultaneously at any given time of day. *Counter-Strike* creators Jess Cliffe and Minh Le were still in high school when they finished their masterful *Half Life* remix. After *Counter-Strike*'s success, both Cliffe and Le were hired by *Half Life* creator *Valve Software*, where they remain highly successful and respected members of the industry. Another modder-turned-pro, Stevie "KillCreek" Case, is one of the most famous women in gaming.† After beating John Romero, Carmack's business partner and cocreator of *Doom* and *Quake*, in a virtual death match, Stevie made the jump from amateur-level designer to professional cyberathlete, writer, game creator, and designer. She even went on to cofound her own game development studio.

This is one reason why the industry has evolved and grown so quickly. By hiring the best amateur modders, who have trained themselves using all the software the pros have, the gaming industry has managed to keep its training costs low. And as so much innovation is coming directly from the consumers, R&D costs are kept down, too. Game development has become dominated by remix culture, and as a result is now one of the most dynamic industries in the world, which, according to Nielsen/NetRatings figures for 2007, is worth more than $30 billion.

But the remix has found even more interesting ways to bend video games into something new. When *Doom*, the follow-up to *Wolfenstein 3-D*, was released in 1993, it came with a function that let players record action replays of the combat as it happens. Modders began using this tool to make not just action replays, but also entirely new movie shorts and music videos, casting characters from games as programmable actors, using the backdrop scenery from video game levels as their sets.

**Half Life itself is also a mod, originally based on the *Quake* game engine.

†Contrary to popular belief, women are no longer such a rarity in gaming. The Interactive Digital Software Association (IDSA) estimates that women now account for 43 percent of all computer gamers. About half of all game purchases are made by women.

Modders now reprogram video game characters and levels into feature-length movies. The code for *Grand Theft Auto, Unreal Tournament,* and *Second Life* game engines are popular tools used for this weird new form of remixing, known as "Machinima." Entire series of Machinima, such as *Red vs. Blue,* made with the game engine from *Halo,* have proved to be incredibly popular and highly watchable. Scenes from *Monty Python and the Holy Grail* were re-created using the video game *The Dark Ages of Camelot.* Machinima hit the mainstream when MTV began using video games to kill the video star; its show *Video Mods* features popular computer game characters and set designs remixed into alternative music videos for the latest hits. The result is Sonic the Hedgehog, the Sims, and Crash Bandicoot singing all the latest hits, using the set of *Mortal Kombat* and other gaming classics as the stage. Elsewhere, politically motivated films are being made with Machinima to further important causes. Machinima is already a home-brewed industry with film festivals and online communities, another innovation that sprang from the font of violent games such as *Doom.* "There is little evidence that this controversial first-person shooter generated school shooters," writes Henry Jenkins in *Convergence Culture,* "but there is plenty of evidence that it inspired a generation of animators."

The implications of this approach to making videos, movies, and games are staggering. With current copyright laws being what they are, only companies with the muscle of MTV can do this on a grand scale without being litigated into oblivion, but anyone with the know-how and a decent PC can have a go.

In a few years' time, a teenage fan with an overactive imagination could be standing on the podium accepting the "Best Remixed Picture" Oscar for his outstanding version of *Ben-Hur,* which casts Will Ferrell as the leading man, using samples from *Anchorman,* filmed entirely on location in *Super Mario World.* Bestselling video games made of nothing but sampled film footage are a possibility. DVDs packaged with several remixable story lines, characters, and locations are not far off. The possibilities of this approach to creating new content are literally endless. This could lead to an unimaginably accessible new chapter in culture as we know it, with, as journalist Wagner James Au puts it, "no real barriers between creator and audience, or producer and consumer. They would be collaborators in the same imaginative space, and working as equals, they'd create a new medium, together."

DJ Frankie Knuckles once famously described house music as "disco's revenge." Forget house music. Disco's revenge is a new social democracy.

Aping an Idea

"If I'd suddenly had a mild desire to make music back when we were making *Smurfenstein* in the early '80s, I'd have probably wandered over to some music store, looked at the price of a guitar, then given up and wandered home again," says Preston Nevins of Dead Smurf Software. "The technology has advanced so much on us now, that that same mild desire would have a real outlet. Being a professional used to be the only way to go. Now that's just one nice option you can choose. That's a huge difference that I think is going to inevitably modify the way society structures itself."

What Preston did to video games and a generation did to music has evolved into a tool all of society is using. All of us can turn our mild desires into remixes if we choose to—and some have turned their remixes into new products and even new brands.

Consider Nike's Air Force One sneaker—a shoe that has been customized and rereleased thousands of times since its launch in 1982. The Air Force One's original audience was basketball players, but it was kept alive by the hip-hop generation's love for its simple, iconic design. Thanks to the remix technique, Nike has been able to keep the hip-hop generation interested by releasing new limited-edition versions, and the Air Force One is still the world's most popular basketball shoe franchise more than twenty-five years later. But even that didn't stop one hip-hop fan, a twenty-two-year-old designer named Tomoaki Nagao from Tokyo, from creating his own version.

Nagao knew the dance floor his remix was designed for inside and out. He made a remix of the Air Force One *specifically* for hip-hop heads, never intended to be used as a basketball shoe. From all appearances, he took the Air Force One design as his base, ripped off the

Swoosh logo, and stitched on his own shooting-star–like emblem. He used materials and colorway combinations even Nike hadn't experimented with at the time. He made his shoes using patent leather, each version comprising at least two or three garish colors, from loud, luminous yellows to muted, pastel pinks. Nagao gave the classic shoe a new high-gloss feel and a high-gloss price tag—many retail for upward of $300. Through his store, he then released very-limited-edition runs, usually of two hundred or less, compared to Nike's limited-edition runs of several thousand.

The ostentatious colors and the exclusive nature of the sneakers were even more appealing to the hip-hop market, who loved the originals. It surprised many people when his shoes, known as the "Bape Stas" or "Bapes," part of his A Bathing Ape clothing line, became a multimillion-dollar brand, with twenty-two stores in Japan, London, and New York under its customized belt. But it should come as no surprise to anyone that Nagao, better known as Nigo, is a former hip-hop DJ. "The thing I love about hip-hop is that it is constantly evolving," he told *The New York Times* at his SoHo store opening in 2004. "It's so free."

Bape consider their remix of the Air Force One to be an original in its own right. And Nike, instead of suing Nigo for aping their banana, used the new materials Bape introduced to create their own updated remixes of the Air Force One, releasing even more versions using similar materials and colors. Instead of viewing Bape as pirates, Nike realized they were the competition, and both brands have grown as a result.

Like music, fashion is an industry perpetuated by ideas that come up from youth cultures and are shared and remixed. As Coco Chanel once put it, "A fashion that does not reach the streets is not a fashion." Most major record labels and movie studios don't much like unofficial mixes of their products, but the fashion business is cut from an entirely different cloth.

Pirate-à-Porter

Intellectual property works very differently in fashion than it does in the world of entertainment. The 2-D design of a garment is protected, but the 3-D physical object is not, so copying is, and always has been, rife.

Freedom to copy other people's designs is taken for granted in the world of fashion, which makes it unusual, but it's also the reason it's so successful. Haute couture designs are copied, sampled, and modified, gradually trickling down until there are versions of last season's catwalk designs in bargain basements everywhere. The view that remixing or sampling a design is a serious threat to business is not one held by the fashion industry.* There are rarely objections from design houses when an idea is copied; in fact, it's almost encouraged. This is an industry where as soon as a high-priced designer garment becomes a trend, there are factories full of copies and knockoff designs competing at lower prices.

This approach seems counterintuitive. But as Professors Kal Raustiala and Chris Sprigman observed in a 2006 *Virginia Law Review* article, this approach, in the case of the fashion industry, actually encourages innovation.

In "The Piracy Paradox: Innovation and Intellectual Property in Fashion Design," Raustiala and Sprigman make the case that the remix stimulates growth in the industry. Because designs are copied quickly and styles diffuse down to the mass market, the original luxury items lose their allure, creating demand for new trends, and this pirate-induced demand drives the entire business forward. Raustiala and Sprigman call this process "induced obsolescence," arguing that copying in fashion is "paradoxically advantageous for the industry. IP [intellectual property] rules providing for free appropriation of fashion designs accelerate the diffusion of designs and styles. . . . If copying were illegal, the fashion cycle would occur very slowly."

Instead, they argue, appropriation speeds diffusion. The article quotes Miuccia Prada: "We let others copy us. And when they do, we drop it." Fashion trends are driven faster by widespread design copy-

---

*It's worth pointing out, as Raustiala and Sprigman do, that there is a difference between copying a design and copying a trademark or a logo to produce a fake. The latter is something the fashion industry takes seriously, and there can be some overlap here; for example, the Louis Vuitton monogram is a trademark that becomes part of the design, as is the trademarked Burberry check pattern.

ing "because copying erodes the positional qualities of fashion goods. Designers in turn respond to this obsolescence with new designs. In short, piracy paradoxically benefits designers by inducing more rapid turnover and additional sales. . . . What was elite quickly becomes mass."

But these copies are not just copies, as the article claims, they are also remixes. Designers sample one another, add original elements, and rarely infringe on others' trademarks. The speed at which this happens creates trends, which determine the fabrics, colors, and styles, that may or may not be hot that season, in a process Raustiala and Sprigman call "anchoring." These trends are copied as they trickle down fashion's corporate pyramid, disseminating quickly at various price points before they eventually die, as they become so popular they are no longer perceived to be cool by anyone, creating the necessary space for a new trend to emerge.

Anchoring makes old designs obsolete and helps new ones become relevant. It is the industry's way of communicating to the consumer when it's time to swap flares for drainpipes, all-over prints for pre-washed denim, and so on. Without the freedom to sample and remix designs, this couldn't happen. The fashion press wouldn't have a range of similar products to reference in order to prove a trend's existence, and consensus on what was hot would not be reached as quickly. "Thus anchoring helps fashion-conscious consumers understand (1) when the mode has shifted (2) what defines the new mode and (3) what to buy to remain within it."

New trends are just as likely to come from a street corner in Congo as they are from the mind of Karl Lagerfeld or Donatella Versace. But the effect of induced obsolescence and anchoring remains the same: widespread remixing leads to more innovation. Fashion houses even pirate their own designs, remixing new versions through "bridge lines"—less-exclusive labels such as Giorgio Armani's lowlier cousins: Armani Exchange and Emporio Armani, for example, which sell similar designs at lower prices without compromising the flagship brand. Without any intellectual property protection, a ferocious multibillion-dollar industry thrives and survives because designers share ideas and are free to remix the work of others.

The success of the fashion industry makes it clear that strict copyright laws aren't always necessary to protect the incentive to innovate. In fact, it turns this notion on its head. Without the freedom to copy, fashion trends would occur very slowly.

A Legal Grey Area

The way to apply the remix effectively and fairly for producers and remixers alike is a Pirate's Dilemma. Sometimes it can work very well when a brand gives outsiders the opportunity to deconstruct, analyze, and remix their new products. Outsiders bring a fresh pair of eyes and a new perspective that those inside the company cannot provide. Consider the case of Boeing, an organization sampling directly from their customers, with more than 120,000 members signed up to their online World Design Team, who worked with the company's aviation experts on the blueprint for the new 787 Dreamliner.

Another high flier partial to a good remix is rapper Jay-Z. When Def Jam Records released his LP *The Black Album* late in 2003, he insisted they make the a cappella versions of every track available on vinyl, sparking a host of fans and other artists to remix the entire project. The most notable was DJ/producer Danger Mouse's *The Grey Album*, which threw Jay's lyrics over samples from the Beatles' *The White Album*. This may seem crazy, but the stunt hyped Jay-Z's album to new levels, broadening his appeal as it introduced new fans to his lyrics. Unfortunately, EMI, which owned the master rights to *The White Album*, wasn't so pleased, and served Danger Mouse a cease-and-desist order. Danger Mouse cooperated with EMI, but Sony, which owns the Beatles' composition rights, also threatened legal action. Soon online activists got wind of this, and very publicly started fighting the case in the name of free culture. Sony, which has long championed the remix in various marketing campaigns, eventually backed off, and *The Grey Album* is still freely available online to this day.

This brings us to the remix's archenemy. As many artists and companies embrace this new culture, others are fighting its rise to protect their intellectual property rights. But as is true with piracy, rights should undoubtedly be protected, but so should the right to create new culture from old. The way the remix is currently being fought could extinguish it altogether. If the remix is to thrive and achieve its full potential, it has one last hurdle to overcome: outdated copyright laws.

Other People's Property?

Some still view the remix as nothing more than plagiarism. Hip-hop has never stopped coming up against this notion as lawyers, politicians, and other barbarians continue to gather at its iced-out gates. Rap group Stetsasonic hit back on their 1988 single "Talkin' All That Jazz," saying, "Tell the truth, James Brown was old, 'til Eric and Rakim came out with 'I Got Soul,' rap brings back old R&B, and if we would not, people could've forgot."

This is a good point. Mr. Brown is the most sampled man in the history of music. But as talented as the godfather of soul clearly was, his creativity was waning in the early 1970s. His career was undoubtedly boosted by the hip-hop generation's obsession with sampling him.

Copyright laws have expanded dramatically in the past few years, partly as a defensive reaction to illegal downloading, and partly because of corporations having an increasing influence on political decision making. While file-sharing and piracy clearly need to be regulated, copyright laws, like patent laws, are becoming so overbearing they now stifle the creative processes they were initially designed to protect.

Copyright periods are being extended by governments, and the entertainment industry continues to push that they be extended even further. Like the patent trolls fighting with pirates, there are also sample trolls out there, acquiring the copyrights to old songs (often very dubiously) and suing artists who have sampled them. Jay-Z is one of many artists who have been sued by sample trolls for millions of dollars. In 2005, a company named Bridgeport Music won a case in the federal appellate court in Nashville against defendant Dimension Films, who had sampled one single chord from George Clinton's "Get

Off Your Ass and Jam,"* then altered the pitch, and looped the now unrecognizable sound in the background of a new record. That court created a rule that *any* sampling, no matter how minimal or undetectable, is a copyright infringement. "Get a license or do not sample," the court said. "We do not see this as stifling creativity in any significant way." But as Tim Wu commented in *Slate:*

> Early rap, like Public Enemy, combined and mixed thousands of sounds in a single album. That makes sense musically, but it doesn't make sense legally. Thousands or even hundreds of samples, under the Bridgeport theory, mean thousands of copyright clearances and licenses. Today, Public Enemy's album, *It Takes a Nation of Millions to Hold Us Back*, would cost millions to produce or, more likely, would never have been made at all.
>
> The kicker is that while sample trolls are bad for artists, they're also bad for mainstream record labels. Record labels want to get out new music at minimum cost. But if clearing rights in the Bridgeport world costs a fortune, production becomes that much more expensive, and innovative music that much riskier a bet.

From Underground to Common Ground

Copyright laws are encroaching on the public domain, but if the history of pirates is anything to go by, such laws are not often observed, become impossible to enforce, and eventually change.

Thankfully, it seems this change is already happening, and slowly but surely consumers, corporations, and artists are working toward striking a balance between copyright protection and the freedom to build on the past.

Consumers are changing their attitudes to the products they value. The legal music download market grew by 187 percent in 2005, and

---

*George Clinton, who has voiced strong support for rappers sampling his records, will not receive a single dollar from Bridgeport as a result of the case.

part of the reason why illegal downloading became so prevalent, as we shall see, was because the music industry failed to respond to this new technology and offer legal alternatives quickly enough. More than one million games of the *Half Life* mod *Counter-Strike* are played each day online, but you can play it only if you have a legal copy of the original *Half Life* game. This system is policed by modders and players alike, who respect the rights of the game's designers to earn money from their original creation.

Producers and even politicians are slowly changing their attitudes, too. In the United Kingdom, the BBC has introduced the Creative Archive, a copyright-free library of video and audio available for any-one to use for noncommercial purposes. In 2006 the United Kingdom's (then) chancellor of the exchequer, Gordon Brown, recognizing the value of the remix as a tool of innovation, proposed new U.K. copyright laws that would give artists more creative freedom to remix the material of others while protecting everybody's rights as well.

In the United States in March 2007, Congressman Mike Doyle made a speech defending remix culture in the House, schooling his fellow politicians on the new rules of twenty-first-century creativity. He said at a hearing discussing the future of music:

> I hope that everyone involved will take a step back and ask themselves if mash-ups and mixtapes are really different or if it's the same as Paul McCartney admitting that he nicked the Chuck Berry bass-riff and used it on the Beatles' hit "I Saw Her Standing There."
>
> Maybe it is . . . or maybe mixtapes are a powerful tool. And maybe mash-ups are transformative new art that expands the consumers' experience and doesn't compete with what an artist has made available on iTunes or at the CD store. And I don't think Sir Paul asked for permission to borrow that bass line, but every time I listen to that song, I'm a little better off for him having done so.

The speech was inspiring. It seems the powers that be are beginning to get to grips with the Pirate's Dilemma. But to illustrate how much work needs to be done before politicians everywhere understand how valuable the remix can be, consider the opening remarks of congressman John Shimkus of Illinois who spoke after Mr. Doyle. He said: "Hey, Mr. Chairman, I was just trying to figure out half of the words that Mike Doyle just mentioned. I am clueless."

Perhaps the biggest changes in the law are coming from artists themselves, using a new type of remix-friendly copyright license known as Creative Commons. Creative Commons presents itself as the happy medium between total anarchy and total control, creating new, remixed copyright licenses that allow artists to grant some rights to the public without being exploited. Their "some rights reserved" model is becoming increasingly popular, with forty-six countries and counting now part of the initiative. Creative Commons doesn't do anything to roll back existing copyright periods or change the unlimited, unconstitutional powers being exerted on the public domain, but it does let creators legally share their work with others in a variety of ways, and indirectly it's attracting attention to the issue.

Because of cut-'n'-paste culture, the mainstream has shifted paradigms. The remix has altered music, games, movies, fashion, and many other industries besides. Now it's up to copyright owners, lawyers, and politicians to keep up. It's too late to protest. The remix has already been here for decades, and those not yet using it soon will be. If Creative Commons doesn't work, common sense will. The remix is gradually winning the war with a paranoid entertainment industry, proving itself to be a valuable form of expression, leveling playing fields for artists and entrepreneurs, and constructing new meaning from old material. The last battle is in sight. It is the future of the past, and perhaps the ultimate democracy, open to infinite criticism, reinterpretation, and improvement.

It is a creative tool that's providing us with new music, movies, sneakers, and clothes, but more important, it provides us with a simple, effective way to reinterpret established ideas into exciting new ones. If you let others remix your own ideas, like Boeing, Jay-Z, and the video game industry, you will unleash creativity in new ways.

Like piracy, it's controversial. But it is not piracy. The remix is a legitimate way to create new art, culture, products, and ideas from old ones. The only thing that's left to remix is our outdated copyright laws.

But as we shall now see, while the remix is being used to generate creativity and defend creative space, another youth culture phenomenon has been remixing public space for many years, redefining the world around us, right under our noses.

CHAPTER 4

The Art of War

Street Art, Branding, and the Battle for Public Space

© Droga5

The CIA calls it "blowback." Blowback refers to the unintended consequences of, or reactions to, covert government operations around the world. Of course, civilian populations are often kept in the dark about their government's murkier maneuvers, so when blowback happens, it's hard to put it in context. This is a story of blowback we see every day, the hallmark of a turf war that has raged for centuries between the establishment and a secretive, loose-knit network that doesn't like the top-down, one-way flow of information in public places.

This blowback goes down, hidden in plain sight. Its fighters step up for a variety of reasons. Here's one, for example. A young man with dark hair, moving through the bustle of the city streets, which are more crowded than usual because of a parade currently in full swing. His target is dead ahead, the Secret Service car he has been following. He's disguised as a messenger, so nobody notices as he slips through the revelers and approaches the motorcade. The car is a sitting duck.

His weapon, concealed in his hand, is highly specialized: all-plastic, compact, and accurate to thirty millimeters. Until now you would never have thought of this item as a weapon at all. But this man will soon become a martyr, and thanks to his efforts, the device he's holding will become considered so dangerous, the police will immediately arrest anyone caught buying, selling, or carrying one. But at this particular moment, the city has no idea what's about to hit it.

Sometime later, in Maryland, a second operative and his team move into position under cover of night. He turns and looks at his men, shrouded in hooded clothing and armed with night vision. "This never happened," he whispers. They scale a fence and begin to move across a golf course just south of Andrews Air Force Base. They strafe through the shadows toward a landing strip where the team abruptly skids to a halt, ducking into the darkness. Through the barbed wire, on the floodlit tarmac, they can see their target: *Air Force One*, the president of the United States's private jet and mobile White House.

A soldier with a sniffer dog patrols the perimeter of the base, heading back to the main hangar. Two more soldiers chat at a sentry post nearby. All the while, the hooded agents lurk undetected. Their cameras scan across the base, capturing every movement. In their backpacks are their own highly pressurized weapons—aluminum-encased tools similar to the one held by the operative in the city. These, however, are ten times more powerful.

They wait.

Meanwhile, back in the city, the messenger marksman is bearing down on his prey. He doesn't hear the crowd around him; his blood is pumping too loudly to notice the flags, the bright colors, the children yelling for cotton candy.

He draws his weapon, carves mercilessly into the side of the Secret

Service car, and in a flash, he's done. He's already melted back into the crowd when the first of the bystanders notices the damage. Unable to make sense of the event, no one yet sees the coded message scrawled on the side of the car as blowback, a declaration of war that will consume first the city, then the planet. All they see is four letters and three numbers. What the hell is "TAKI 183"?

It's 1971. The city is New York. The graffiti war has just begun.

Fast-forward thirty-five years and we're again at the air force base, where the coast is now clear. The second unit springs into action. Two of the men dash forward, tearing across the green, heading for the twin perimeter fences. The third, the eyes and ears of the operation, holds position. He watches as the others lacerate an entry point in the outer fence and pull themselves onto the roof of an outhouse next to the inner security fence at the edge of the golf course.

A military police car rolls by. The agents freeze.

It trundles past slowly and moves on. They breathe out.

Once the car is out of sight, they launch themselves into the air, clearing the razor wire and tumbling onto the tarmac. Darting across the landing strip unobserved by the guards, they split in different directions. One ducks behind the aircraft's landing gear, his heart racing as he keeps watch on the sentries in the distance, his head-mounted camera filming the whole thing. The other assailant slides into position, crouching below the huge twin turbines hanging from the vessel's left wing. Reaching into his backpack, he grabs the pressurized canister and takes aim. The silhouette of his arm reaches up from the darkness toward the plane. He pulls the trigger: black paint hisses from the cylinder and hits the jet engine's bodywork, transforming the ultimate symbol of presidential power into yet another vandalized government vehicle.

The agent stationed back on the golf course moves closer, crouching on the grass, zooming in on the ink meandering across the plane's box-fresh exterior. Later the film will fly around the Internet, downloaded countless times, along with a videotaped speech made by the guerrilla artist with the spray can currently defacing *Air Force One*.

"The president can't fly around the world like a rock star, talking about how America is the greatest country in the world, but ignore what makes it great," the tagger explains in the tape. "There are thousands of kids like me whose voices are being illegally suppressed. . . . Ignorant politicians continue to enact laws targeted at one of the most recognized art forms. . . . I'm advocating everyone's right to free speech. . . . I also refuse to live in fear; I have a different view of the American dream."

Graffiti is the blowback from centuries of advertising and the privatization of common spaces, which has armed corporations with new branding tools as much as it encouraged people to counteract these intrusions. This blowback inspired amazing new technologies, caused us to rethink how the organizations and public spaces we create should best serve us, as opposed to us serving them, pointing us in the direction of a revitalized dream that is no longer just American but truly global.

Mission accomplished, the taggers escape into the night, leaving their message, the blowback from three decades of war over public space, sprayed across the jet engine's hull. Some call it vandalism, but at its heart there is art, making sure we are, as the statement dripping down the fuselage of the president's plane reads:

STILL FREE

So What Was TAKI 183?

This question played on the minds of many New Yorkers when these strange markings began to appear in 1970, until *The New York Times* on July 21, 1971, uncovered the mystery with this headline: "TAKI 183 SPAWNS PEN PALS." The paper exposed TAKI 183 as a seventeen-year-old kid named Demetrius from 183rd Street. Inspired by a Puerto Rican gang member who scribbled JULIO 204 (guess which street JULIO lived on?) a few blocks away, TAKI began hitting up lampposts, ice cream trucks, and everything else in his neighborhood with a marker pen.

TAKI became famous not because he was a graffiti writer—he was far from the first—but because he was one of the first to go "all city."

When TAKI took a job as a messenger, he found himself traveling all over the five boroughs of the city, sometimes even to New Jersey, Connecticut, and upstate New York, and he began scribbling his tag everywhere he went. And as TAKI was "bombing" the city, people were noticing. In the following years, legions of kids hungry for fame armed themselves with paint and pens. They tagged their names and street numbers the way we now write hotmail addresses, coloring in the entire metropolis in a bid for status.

TAKI thought he and his new followers had the same right to use public space as politicians and private companies. When the backlash from city officials against the graffiti epidemic started, he pointed out the hypocrisy of those chasing him, saying in *The New York Times*, "Why do they go after the little guy? Why not the campaign organizations that put stickers all over the subway at election time?"

TAKI was an innovative radical. He knew he could gain even more exposure by harnessing the power of the media, pirate-style. It was no accident that he was the first person *The New York Times* spotted. "TAKI concentrated his work on the Upper East Side and the business districts of Manhattan, the stomping grounds of novelists, journalists, television executives, and other media brokers who might see his tag and mention it in one of the media . . ." writes Joe Austin in *Taking the Train*. "Using this method, TAKI added to his already mythic status when an actor in a frequently aired, nationally televised antismoking commercial paused and wheezed emphatically as he climbed the stairs of the Statue of Liberty; TAKI's name was clearly visible on the wall behind him."

TAKI's fame made him a target,* so he disappeared. In so doing, he became one of graffiti's most fabled deities. He has resurfaced a few times since, most recently with a phone call to *The New York Times* in 2000. These days TAKI is supposedly a family man working in the auto industry, residing somewhere in Westchester County. "Sometimes I see a wall and say, it would be nice there," he told the paper in 2000,

---

*He did get caught a couple of times at least, according to *The New York Times*. He was even apprehended after the parade by an angry Secret Serviceman, who apparently gave him "a stern lecture."

reflecting on his past. "I guess I'm a dangerous guy to carry around a marker, still. But that's something you do when you're sixteen. It's not something you make a career out of."

The second operative in our story is living proof that TAKI couldn't have been more wrong about the career part. The guy who marauded across the putting green and tagged *Air Force One* was Marc Milecofsky, a Jewish kid from New Jersey. Inspired by the graffiti on New York's subways, he began writing his own "Ecko" tag on T-shirts as a teenager and selling them from his parents' garage in the mid-1980s. When hip-hop luminaries such as Public Enemy's Chuck D and film director Spike Lee began rocking Marc's shirts, the tag became a brand. Marc Ecko Enterprises today grosses more than $1 billion a year, with twelve apparel and accessory lines, including Ecko Unlimited, 50 Cent's G-Unit Clothing, skate brand Zoo York, men's magazine *Complex*, and a graffiti-based video game franchise. For Marc and for many others, the business of bombing is booming.

Still, how did a fashion billionaire manage to spray-paint the president's plane without being shot to pieces, or even worse, shipped off to Guantánamo Bay? Simple: he faked it. Ecko didn't create a piece of graffiti—he created an advert.

Ecko commissioned advertising agency Droga5 to make the film, which was to be a branding exercise for his company, but also "a pop culture moment," as Ecko puts it. Droga5 hired a 747 cargo jet, painted the left side to look exactly like *Air Force One* (the fake was actually based at the San Bernardino Airport in California). The hired graffiti artists (none of whom was actually Marc Ecko) were told to say "this never happened" at the beginning of the clip by Droga5's lawyers, which they thought might help if they did land in court for violating the Patriot Act. They sprayed a couple of cars to look like military police vehicles, and re-created the layout of the fences exactly as they were at Andrews Air Force Base, even going so far as to add a computer-generated copy of the plane's hangar, using postproduction special effects. "All the detail was there," Duncan Marshall told me, the partner at Droga5 responsible for the ad. "We knew it needed to seem real for as long as possible, and all the nerds notice things like that. The brief was really to create a buzz about Ecko's interest in urban culture. He does have his views and he's quite outspoken about graffiti. We were just trying to create some chat about it online. We weren't really sure what would happen." The grainy video clip was posted on the Internet, and the result was mass hysteria. *Nobody* was really sure what had happened. First the message boards, blogs, and e-mail forwards circulated the story. Finally, hours later, the mainstream media around the world caught wind and went nuts. To date, 115 million people have seen the video clip. Ecko and Droga5 even fooled the U.S. Air Force, which double-checked the genuine presidential jet after seeing the video. "It looks very real," one bewildered lieutenant colonel remarked to the Associated Press afterward. The Pentagon had to officially deny it was a real event on three separate occasions.

"To reach 115 million people with traditional media would have cost an awesome amount," Marshall told me. "Ecko obviously wanted people to know about the Ecko brand, and he wants people to buy his T-shirts and his sneakers and all that kind of stuff, but at the same time there is a legitimacy about this piece of film I think—it promotes debate. It truly wanted to, that was our brief, and it did. Is it any worse to graffiti a wall than to put a poster up on it for a big brand? When I walk down the street, and I say this as an advertiser, and I see a poster for something that has nothing to do with me, is that better or worse than seeing a piece of graffiti I don't understand? That's a good debate. It was engaging."

TAKI and Ecko are polar opposites in graffiti's colorful spectrum. At one end is the originator who never made a penny but became a myth. Many view TAKI 183 as a legend. Others see a pest who started a plague. At the other is the imitator who never tagged much more than a T-shirt* and yet the tag became a billion-dollar brand. Ecko's

---

*Marc Ecko is the first to admit that he "never really got much higher than the eight-foot ceiling of [his] parents' garage" when it came to *actually* being a graffiti writer, but Ecko has remained committed to the cause that inspired him. In May 2006 he financed a lawsuit that overturned New York legislation that banned anyone age eighteen to twenty from buying or carrying spray paint or broad-tipped marker pens, which effectively prohibited many art students from buying supplies for school, or even carrying them to class. Judge George B. Daniels granted a temporary injunction against the law, arguing, "That's like telling me I can eat an apple, but I can't buy an apple, no one can sell me an apple and I can't bring it to work for lunch."

hoax was spectacular* and his ongoing defense of street art and free speech is admirable, but some critics see nothing more than thinly veiled PR stunts for his multinational corporation. The one thing both artists proved for certain is that the media afterlife of a piece of graffiti can be way more powerful than its temporary terrestrial body.

The Painter's Paradox

TAKI and Ecko highlight the conflicting ideals in graffiti. Like punk, graffiti was always regarded as an anticorporate movement. "This living, aggressive art was a perfect fit with the same antiestablishment attitudes that ruled at punk landmarks like CBGB," writes Nelson George in *Hip Hop America*. "If punk was rebel music, this was just as truly rebel art."

And graffiti, like punk, is riddled with contradictions because it is a product of two opposing forces, freely lending itself to both. For some it is just a way to be heard, the voice of the invisible that allowed a generation of city kids to brand themselves and become famous, that morphed into guerrilla marketing at its most potent. For others it is the establishment's archnemesis, the scribbling democracy, a tool for bombing the system. This conflict within graffiti is mirrored by another that exists around graffiti: Is it good or bad? Some art critics see it as the most important art form of the twentieth century, and the increasing amount of space it now takes up in art galleries stands as testament to that. But other people regard it as a scourge on the landscape that should be wiped out entirely.

Either way, it was certainly important enough to start a war, and as any economic historian—or Halliburton executive—will tell you, wars are good business. Graffiti is no different. It spawns creativity and new ways of reclaiming public domain, both of which are co-opted into tagged products and cool corporate entities such as the Ecko empire. And like many wars, it has also strengthened civic-

---

*Ecko wasn't the first person to think of this. Back in the 1960s one of the earliest writers, CORNBREAD, tagged the Jackson 5's 747 when the pop group made a stop in Philadelphia.

minded people's desire for freedom and equality, and consistently generated artists who produce exciting, socially relevant work, giving us all pause to think that little bit harder. Perhaps most important, graffiti produced something else that emerges rapidly in times of war: innovation.

Like Dogs Need Lampposts

Humans have been writing graffiti since time began. "I am amazed, o wall, that you have not collapsed and fallen," reads an ancient wall in Pompeii, "since you must bear the tedious stupidities of so many scrawlers." The Mayans were into it, the Vikings were at it, and the ancient Romans even tagged over Egyptian graffiti on the pyramids. Carved inscriptions from nearly eight thousand years ago are still visible on a boulder known as the "Writing Rock" in Fort Ransom, North Dakota. The phrase "Kilroy was here" was scribbled on thousands of walls, bombs, and fighter planes around the world during World War II. From cave paintings to crop circles, leaving our mark in public is an urge that people from all walks of life have been unable to resist.* We need graffiti like dogs need lampposts.

For all that, the graffiti that emerged in the 1970s and 1980s in New York was different. These artists were on a mission, risking life and limb to forge their identities and define a generation with spray paint. By creating new ways to organize and operate that society has only recently begun to recognize, they transformed a conventional tool of self-expression into a relentless, creative global movement.

Writers put themselves under more pressure than a well-shaken can of paint to experiment and diversify daily. In the struggle to get up higher than anyone else, stay a step ahead of the police, and develop

---

*Even mayors of New York, archnemeses of the subway artists, have a long history of graffiti in their own home. Parts of Gracie Mansion, the mayor's official residence, have been secretly covered with the tags of the privileged few. Mayor Giuliani's daughter, Caroline, scratched her name on a windowpane in the library in 2001, as did Mayor Lindsay's daughter, Margie, in 1965 and Millie, granddaughter of Noah Wheaton (not a mayor but who lived there before it became the mayor's official residence) in 1893. There is also rumored to be a wall in the basement where the mayors *themselves* have been leaving their own tags for centuries.

ever more elaborate new styles, writers have ensured that graffiti remains one of the most dynamic art disciplines of our time—and the discipline behind the art gives us a formula we can use to make anything extraordinary.

All-City Diversity

Diversity can be an empty corporate buzzword, a strategy pursued because it is politically correct or mandated by law. But smart CEOs and business leaders are waking up to the fact that diversity actually encourages people to be much more creative and productive than when they work in nondiverse groups. Way to go, CEOs. Teenage graffiti artists worked this out forty years ago.

The way graffiti writers organized was a harbinger for the way many successful groups operate today. An overwhelming amount of business research points to the fact that diversity helps us broaden our networks, open up to fresh ideas and perspectives, gain a competitive advantage, crack new markets, and increase organizational effectiveness. Globalization shortened geographic distances; diversity is shortening cultural ones. Diversity has become a multibillion-dollar industry, and the most successful boardrooms, more often than not, recruit like graffiti crews did.* With cities and nations becoming exponentially more diverse, as migration and urbanization quicken, this openness to new ideas, influences, and people is more important than ever.

After TAKI, graffiti writers began forming crews who painted in numbers, giving them the strength, security, and freedom to move through dangerous, gang-dominated locales. But crews differed from gangs in that they had a radical new HR strategy. Where gangs were fiercely territorial and localized, crews actively recruited from outside their immediate neighborhoods. They were deliberately multiethnic and multigender, attracting youths from all neighborhoods and walks

---

*According to a survey by international recruitment firm Korn/Ferry, the most successful companies in America report a greater concentration of female and minority directors on their boards.

of life in a bid to collectively go all-city. "The gangs kept neighbor-hoods apart . . ." writer LEE Quinones told Ivor L. Miller in his book *Aerosol Kingdom*. "This movement brought people together: blacks, Puerto Ricans, whites, Orientals, Polish, from the richest to the poor-est, we were equals. We took the same energy that was there to stand by your block with bats or guns and flying colors all night long and used it to go painting, to create."

The wide range of backgrounds, perspectives, and ideas that crew members brought to the table rapidly infused graffiti's palette with a broad range of styles and influences. "Being able to do a vari-ety of things gave me an edge. Not just being a one trick pony," says Sandra "LADY PINK" Fabara, one of the New York scene's original and most accomplished artists. "I think the diversity in graffiti was something that the cops looked out for; they looked for groups of teens that were mixed-race 'cos they were probably graffiti writers. I think bringing everyone together was a big factor. . . . All those races and rivalries made for better, stronger work, but there wasn't always cohesion."

Graffiti looked like an illegible confusion of tongues to outsiders, but to those in the know it was a language of an uneasy unity, the intensely creative product of crosscultural contamination powered by fierce competition.

The influences and perspectives that fed into graffiti included the civil rights movement, antiwar protests, the Black Panthers, feminism, flower power, and countless strains of youth culture, fused with a slew of traditional influences as diverse as New York's immigrant popula-tion itself. "[That] was the first time in the '60s that young people found a voice," says LADY PINK, who started writing in 1980 at age fifteen. "I think we just tried to keep that alive somehow."

Say It Loud

The voices got louder, and as the subways became buried under the clutter of tags, the only way to cut through was to go bigger. Tags burst out from the stomachs of subway cars and began covering their exteriors as well. Graffiti soon became an arms race as writers battled to become "kings"* of the train lines, armoring their supersized letters, inventing imaginative new fonts, filling them in with color, and adding drop shadows, characters, and backgrounds. By 1973 pioneering artists such as PHASE 2, RIFF 170, TRACY 168, and BLADE had evolved tags into "masterpieces."

Pieces were huge, detailed works, colorful splashes of the stew of diverse ideas bubbling up from the New York melting pot that could cover the entire side of a subway car, sometimes two, three, or even more, windows included. They trundled through the city like mobile art galleries, broadcasting the new language of an invisible generation. "Letters were being battled with," pioneering hip-hop MC and graffiti artist RΔMM:ΣLL:ZΣΣ† told me. "New York is the biggest melting pot on the planet and we had the baddest gallery known in the world: the transit system, the city's blood system. We hit the blood system first. We were the so-called cancer."

This was the ultimate high for PINK and many others, "seeing your first train roll by. Your reaction, your friend's reaction. Seeing the doors open, people coming out, then it rolls away roaring all dirty and loud. It was pretty amazing."

"The transit system was like a wind tunnel where new designs were developed," remembers RΔMM:ΣLL:ZΣΣ. Space on the trains was finite, but the imagination and ambition of the artists were not. Pieces reinvigorated the alphabet into something fresh, splitting, distorting, and restitching letters into new forms known as "wild style." Soon mind-bendingly futuristic hieroglyphics were rolling through the city, charged with more energy than the third rail that carried them along.

---

*Becoming a "king" meant you owned an entire subway line, or you were the originator of a certain style of writing. The lowest rank in graffiti is to be considered a "toy," a term for someone who was inexperienced or incompetent that, oddly enough, was first used in this way by Francis Bacon in 1597.

†RΔMM:ΣLL:ZΣΣ (pronounced ram-el-zee) is one of the most far-out forces in hip-hop culture. His tag is a mathematical formula, and he was one of the pioneers of rap music. RΔMM:ΣLL:ZΣΣ has developed his deep understanding of quantum physics and fifteenth-century calligraphy into an entire philosophy, loosely based around graffiti, known as "gothic futurism." He also has twenty-one different personalities, which he expresses by rapping dressed as one of twenty-one different giant robots made of trash, known as the "garbage gods." He is huge in Japan.

Bite Me

The kings and crews who ruled the New York subways were a social experiment in diversity, but the way they operated also tells us something about how intellectual property rights can work without legislation, something becoming increasingly important in a world where the Pirate's Dilemma is all-powerful.

Graffiti writers aren't the only people creating new systems around intellectual property. Oddly enough, the way style emerged and evolved in graffiti among the elite kings and crew members is very similar to the world of elite French chefs.

In a 2006 paper, Emmanuelle Fauchart and Eric von Hippel of MIT looked at how informal "norms-based" intellectual property systems work, studying the way France's culinary establishment is organized. What they found bears a striking resemblance to the system used by graffiti artists. In an absence of intellectual property law, the paper makes the case that informal systems act as important substitutes or complements. Both graffiti and French cooking involve highly complex styles that are not usually covered by copyright law, patents, or trademarks. In both instances, "biting," or stealing someone else's idea, can have serious consequences. Whether you're making a sumptuous béchamel in a Parisian restaurant or spray-painting a sweet burner onto the side of a train, there is an informal system in place that both communities adhere to and which ensures that both remain innovative.

In an informal system, policed by its community members, such as graffiti crews and high-class chefs, breaking the rules will result in a loss of reputation, which in both communities is an extremely important form of capital. Worse still, such violations could get you thrown out of the inner circle, which in both cases would be disastrous. The paper argues that there are three ways by which French chefs protect their work:

1. "A chef must not copy another chef's innovation exactly." In graffiti, this is called biting; being accused of biting can be a fatal blow to an artist's status.

2. "A chef who asks for and is given a secret recipe by a colleague will not pass that information on to others without permission." Graffiti artists share information about how to perfect new styles in the same way—it is not uncommon to see the copyright © symbol sprayed next to a piece.

3. "Colleagues must credit the original innovator as the author of the recipe they had created." Graffiti artists sometimes write the names of their influencers alongside their work, and there are even tribute pieces to grandmasters such as DONDI on walls and trains around the world.

In both cases these informal, implicit property rights protect innovators but encourage future innovations. Chefs and graffiti writers often learn by apprenticeship with those who are more accomplished, and you are more likely to be invited into the higher echelons if you are deemed trustworthy enough to abide by these rules. Both groups run in packs: chefs have their kitchens, graffiti artists their crews. Within these communities intellectual property is traded between peers, and artists work together, bringing out their own unique styles and flavors. Only the best get to work with the best chefs. Similarly, initiation into a world-class graffiti crew is granted only to those worthy enough. RΔMM:ΣLL:ZΣΣ, for example, once shared a studio with Keith Haring and Jean-Michel Basquiat.

In both cases, the mass market might occasionally rip off your work (French chefs might find their work copied by chain restaurants, graffiti artists could see their ripped-off designs on T-shirts), but this will help your status rather than hurt it. In both instances, it is reputation that drives innovation and lays down rules, not the law.

Drowned Out

Diversity and an informal copyright system forced styles to develop on the subways at light speed, but space on the trains was running out, and the city was stepping up its campaign against graffiti under pressure from the many residents of New York who were sick of it. "They hated us," remembers LADY PINK. "We were the dirt beneath the dirt. They always imagined we were evil villains, 'cos the subways were visually dirty-looking, it all reeked of fear. The authorities had no control and we were the visual proof. It was mayhem and chaos out there, South Bronx looked like Hiroshima, but most people didn't see that. But the trains came out of there and crept through the squeaky-clean neighborhoods, it scared the hell out of 'em."

This fear became the backbone of the resistance that would eventually eradicate graffiti from the subways. Security was stepped up at the train yards, making it more difficult for artists to get in and paint the trains, and the ones that were painted were cleaned before they had even left the yards, depriving writers of the fame they craved. "We saw the subways were being stainless-steeled and there was nothing you could do about it," says accomplished writer SMITH, husband of LADY PINK. "In 1985 they cleaned the number 4 line. I mean they *cleaned* it. We were just like in shock. Then they went to the 7, then the 1, then the F, R, every line." It took millions of dollars to stop the artists from risking liberty and limb to bomb the trains with their noms de plume, but stop them they did. In 1989 Mayor Koch declared that the last graffiti-covered train had been removed from service.

Many artists faced fines and prison; others, including LADY PINK, RΔMM:ΣLL:ZΣΣ, and SAMO (better known by his real name, Jean-Michel Basquiat) found fame elsewhere, transferring their attentions to the downtown galleries now enamored with this new art form. Thanks to pioneering works such as the film *Wild Style* and the book *Subway Art*, graffiti culture escaped from New York and went all-globe. But in New York, graffiti-proof trains replaced the cars covered with paint and pen, and many trains were decommissioned and dumped in the sea.* Works by legendary artists that should rightfully be in museums are instead at the bottom of the ocean, as corals form their own elaborate masterpieces on their rusting sides of faded paint.

---

*Although, according to SMITH, it is rumored that one entire ten-car graffiti-covered train somehow made it to Disneyland, where it resides today.

Space Invader Strategy

The city declared victory, and the authorities patted themselves on the back for doing a heckuva job. But while graffiti had been all but stamped out in the subways, a new legion of space invaders had already developed a strategy that would take graffiti, quite literally, to new heights.

As the 1990s set in, the movement took a new turn in response to the less tolerant urban environment. A new generation reacted to harsher laws with a more considered approach, focusing on location as much as anything else. "My tag was simplistic, readable, it was a total placement thing," says SMITH, who once placed a huge piece on the Brooklyn Bridge. "It wasn't like totally mindless, 'I'll tag wherever,' it was 'I'll tag that.' We transferred that as high as we could. It was so it became something to see. You had to place it correctly and as big as possible."

By moving away from the competition and subway authorities into new spaces, graffiti survived and remained relevant and exciting. It's a strategy that can work in many other situations.

Like pirates, graffiti artists know the value of finding spaces outside the market. One of the best ways for writers to compete is to make their rivals irrelevant, by moving away from the spaces where everyone else is competing—in this case, the subways—and into new, uncontested territory that the competition hasn't yet figured out how to reach. When graffiti artists emerged bleary-eyed from the dark subways into the city streets, they saw new territory everywhere they looked.

The steel shutters of shop fronts, freight trains that went "all-nation," and highway walls became new targets. Artists found new spaces known as "permaspots," locations so far out of reach that other writers couldn't touch them, new markets where their work could be consumed exclusively. Writers such as COST and REVS began hanging over the rooftops and bridges, defying not just the laws of the city but also seemingly the laws of gravity, to write their names in block letters with paint rollers, to create huge, simplistic pieces that defied all the conventions of wild style. "COST and REVS did the craziest, hugest rollers, they *destroyed* Manhattan" remembers Ad, one half of street art duo Skewville, "not just with graffiti, but with posters. So we were like 'Holy shit, what's happening?'"

What was happening was the movement's evolution. The authorities raised the stakes once again with harsher vandalism laws and sentences, so artists, now operating across the world, worked faster and smarter, using techniques borrowed from the advertising industry and the high art galleries that had adopted graffiti. The stakes had been raised; artists had to take up more space in less time.

Speed was everything. Stickers, stamps, wheat-paste posters, stencils, and installations that could be applied quicker than spray paint found new favor with street artists. Inspired by COST and REVS, artists such as Skewville took the idea of finding uncontested spaces to new heights. "No one is ever going to go bigger than that," says Skewville's Ad, "so our mentality was just to do something totally different. . . . We really felt like we had to go beyond everyone's reach."

Skewville is twin brothers Ad and Droo, who, inspired by the graffiti they grew up around in New York, embarked on their own street art campaign, with the intention of creating "a new medium, 'cos we felt everything else was kind of played out." They first got noticed when they began manufacturing fake footwear, silk-screen printing sneaker designs onto boot-shaped wood carvings. Moving invisibly like modern-day shoemaker's elves, they've thrown counterfeit kicks tied at the laces over power cables in locations as far and wide as London, Amsterdam, Mexico, and South Africa. Hundreds of pairs still hang from the wires in the sky.

Ad and Droo are also known for subverting street furniture, leaning wooden pallets that have hidden messages carved into their frames against buildings. Upon further inspection, a ventilator grate bolted inside a doorway in SoHo, New York, is a false front, its grill bent to form the word FAKE. They once erected a full-sized construction fence outside a public park; the fence was actually a huge 3-D piece carved in wood and spelling the word SKEW. "The hugest things we have done are the easiest to put up on the street as far as the heartbeat factor goes," Droo told me. "With that SKEW thing, we just pulled up, we looked like construction workers, and walked out with it." "We always bomb at the crack of dawn," continued Ad. "When you do shit in the dark, you always look like you're doing something illegal. When you're two fat thirty-year-old dudes driving around in a van, a lot of kids walking around think *we're* the cops."

Growing into new locations like painted poison ivy, context has become critical as graffiti artists hijack spaces like pirates but blend into public spaces unobtrusively.

© *Skewville*

Covert Creativity

Instead of just invading space, artists such as Skewville subtly subvert existing structures. By blending in with the scenery, graffiti has once again evolved. Mark Jenkins, the artist who turned parking meters into the lollipops in the introduction, constructs sculptures from Scotch tape, which he then places in public; most of which can be easily removed. By floating homemade tape ducks in ponds, leaving life-sized tape men sleeping in public, and dangling Scotch tape babies from street signs, Jenkins has become something of a minor celebrity (albeit an invisible one) in his hometown of Washington, D.C. "What I'm doing isn't as risky as using spray paint," he told me. "There aren't laws specifically designed against what I do. The most I could get charged with usually is littering or trespassing."

In the past, writers wanted their work to stay up on the trains for as long as possible. This is less of a concern for modern artists, because the fame game has changed in more ways than one. Writers now snap pictures and videos of their work, which they throw onto photo-sharing sites such as Flickr.com or designated graffiti websites such as WoosterCollective.com. The latest strains of geeked-out graffiti use advanced technologies to beam pieces made by projecting light onto surfaces, leaving no trace at all other than in their afterlife in cyberspace. British artist Paul Curtis puts his art onto dirty urban surfaces the same way people write "clean me" on dirty cars, using industrial cleaning fluids in a process known as "reverse graffiti," which breaks no laws at all. "It's refacing, not defacing," he said to *The New York Times*, "just restoring a surface to its original state. It's very temporary. It glows and it twinkles, and then it fades away." Skewville even remove their work themselves after they think it has been up long enough. The new way to achieve status is virally, via the information supersubway, so street art can afford to be more temporary than ever.

These cautious bombing techniques and easy-to-remove efforts have kept artists such as Mark Jenkins and Skewville out of serious trouble, but something else is going on here. Because so much street art is deliberately less intrusive and often in tune with its surrounding environment, it has yet to meet the huge opposition graffiti came up against in New York in the 1980s, and is in fact winning fans fast. Instead of shouting at passersby, street art quietly engages the public, but only the people who choose to notice.

In 2005 *Time* magazine described street art as "ingenious." Banksy, an artist from Bristol, England, who began working with stencils in his hometown in the 1990s, is now one of the world's most famous street artists. He was labeled "the next Andy Warhol" by *Esquire* in 2005, and his work can be seen from Los Angeles to Palestine to Harajuku. He has become so well known in the United Kingdom that his 2006 stencil-based piece on the side of a city building in Bristol (of a naked man dangling from a window, through which his female lover and her angry husband are peering out) has been made a permanent fixture after 97 percent of the residents polled voted to have it left there.

Banksy has also hung his own works unsolicited at the Museum of Modern Art and the Metropolitan Museum of Art in New York. When he hung a fake cave painting of a Neanderthal pushing a shopping cart in the British Museum, they made it part of the permanent collection. "Graffiti has more chance of meaning something or changing stuff than anything hanging indoors," argues Banksy in his book *Banging Your Head Against a Brick Wall.* "Graffiti has been used to start revolutions, stop wars, and generally is the voice of people who aren't listened to. Graffiti is one of those few tools you have if you have almost nothing. And even if you don't come up with a picture to cure world poverty, you can make somebody smile while they're having a piss."

The first graffiti artists lost the battle for the subways, but a new, retooled generation is winning the hearts and minds of the people. By harmonizing with its surroundings, it has become digestible to a wider market that sympathizes and identifies with it. But there is another reason why there is more public support for graffiti, and it has to do with the rise of another powerful visual phenomenon that is just as intrusive and that shares graffiti's history and natural habitat: advertising.

Corporate Vandals Not Welcome

Graffiti and advertising have been intertwined in a love/hate relationship since prostitutes in ancient Pompeii used to graffiti heart shapes on walls to advertise their services. Graffiti and advertising are, when you locate their roots, one and the same thing, only ads are tolerated, graffiti is not. The kings in the advertising world live and die by the mantra "If you're not everywhere, you're nowhere." The New York graffiti explosion was the blowback caused by this attitude, and it deliberately mimicked it. "We were influenced so much by advertising," explains PINK. "The sheer act of writing our names is based on advertising, logos, and the mass media intruding into our everyday lives. Coca-Cola, Newport, Pepsi, TAKI 183, it's the same thing. You see my logo a million times, I will be famous."

Since the New York epidemic, advertising has followed trends set by graffiti, appropriating its style for commercial purposes. Graffiti artists (PINK included) make a living doing work for ad agencies. Many artists have remixed sneakers for Nike and Adidas. Some such as KAWS, have created limited-edition T-shirts for brands such as A Bathing Ape and Ice Cream, or started their own streetwear lines. Others are commissioned to tag everything from Xboxes to skateboards.

Some corporations have even stopped flirting with the art form and taken to doing the graffiti themselves. IBM, for example, bombed the streets of San Francisco in 2001 with logos stenciled on sidewalks, facing the wrath of city officials. "It's an urban visual blight issue," snapped the director of the Department of Public Works to CNN afterward, talking about graffiti and advertising as one and the same thing. Sony proved his point in 2006 when it hired street artists to draw pictures of kids playing their PSP games consoles on walls across the United States. Many of the covert ads were quickly written over with messages such as: "Stop hawking corporate products and big business on our neighborhood walls" and "Corporate vandals not welcome."

In January 2007 Cartoon Network launched a guerrilla marketing campaign in ten major cities across the United States. Several square black placards, each the size of a place mat and dotted with electronic LEDs, were covertly installed using magnets onto street signs, walls, and bridges all over the country. Displayed in lights on the placards were two pink and green pixilated alien life forms giving passersby the finger. The aliens were characters from the Cartoon Network's new *Aqua Teen Hunger Force* movie. The placards were covert ads for the film. But to a transit worker in Boston, who noticed one of the devices on the morning of January 31 near the Sullivan Square train station, they looked more like bombs.

An alarm was raised, and panic quickly swept through Boston as more than a dozen highways, subway stations, and bridges were shut down. Emergency vehicles and TV news helicopters circled the city, frantically following as the police and the bomb squad uncovered more of the devices. Some were destroyed in controlled explosions. The coast guard was alerted.

A handful of bloggers uncovered the bomb scare as guerrilla marketing gone wrong a few hours later. Finally, at 4:30 P.M., Turner Broadcasting System, the Cartoon Network's parent company, issued a statement taking responsibility. After the incident, which became known as "Aquagate," Turner settled with the Police Department and Homeland Security, paying $1 million to each to cover the costs incurred. The two guerrilla marketers who installed the signs in Boston were arrested. Police in other cities began removing signs, too, often beaten to the crime scene by members of the public (after Aquagate, the signs were changing hands on eBay for up to $5,000 each, and bootleggers did a brisk trade selling a range of unofficial T-shirts and stickers created to commemorate the event). As a result of the incident, Jim Samples, the head of the Cartoon Network for thirteen years, was forced to step down. Boston mayor Thomas M. Menino said Turner had committed "an outrageous act to gain publicity for their product."

Graffiti might be art, but on many occasions it also can be a public nuisance. It costs taxpayers millions to remove and is often an eyesore, denying a view from a train window, damaging property, and interrupting us when we'd rather be left in peace.

New York became a safer, cleaner city after the cleansing of the subways. Modern laws in many cities are incredibly harsh on artists, and artists have responded with new tactics. But even some graffiti artists agree it's not a bad thing that it is regulated.* All this begs an important question about that other hidden public persuader: advertising. If all those tags are so bad for our state of mind, what are all these ads doing to us?

Taking a leaf from the street artists' playbook, advertisers now turn everything into ads. A steaming sewer grate becomes a fake cup of coffee. In the Netherlands, a herd of sheep wear billboard coats that advertise a website.† It seems there is no final frontier for corporate graffiti.

---

*Although most share LADY PINK's view that "the punishment does not fit the crime."

†These advertising sheep were following Banksy, who once tagged a herd of cows in England with the words "Turf War." Banksy borrowed the strategy from CORNBREAD, who was mistakenly reported shot dead in 1971 by local papers in Philadelphia. To prove he wasn't, he broke into the Philadelphia Zoo and tagged both sides of an elephant's behind with the words "CORNBREAD LIVES."

Pizza Hut tags Russian space rockets with its logo. And in the Nevada Desert, KFC placed an eighty-seven-thousand-square-foot Colonel Sanders, which can be seen from orbit should any low flying astronauts need a bucket of chicken. Ad agencies and brands around the world are currently plotting to create cosmic permaspots, launching into space glowing logos that would appear to be about the size of the moon, seen by everyone on Earth, permanently disfiguring the night sky.

Product placement has been with us for years, but today product placements are sneaked into movies, news broadcasts, TV shows, and even children's schoolbooks. Graffiti in the subways became an "urban visual blight issue," and advertising has evolved in the same way. Being "everywhere" used to mean within the confines of TV, radio, billboards, and press ads. But now it means being *everywhere*, arresting our attention to the point where entire cities grind to a halt for cartoon aliens.

Commercial Breakdown

One reason ads are getting in our faces more is because we no longer pay attention to them. "Bad advertising is no longer working," says Duncan Marshall, the man behind the Ecko campaign from Droga5, "because you now have a choice as to whether you engage with traditional advertising. People are now able to filter out the crap. It doesn't matter how big you make your logo or your price point, we can filter it out, our brains will just ignore it, and we will choose to engage with the little thing sprayed on the sidewalk because that's more interesting. I think anything invasive is a bad thing." Chicago ad agency BBDO Energy came to the same conclusion in a study done in 2005. "Consumers are no longer buying what everyone else is selling," they announced. "What happened? For starters, being 'different' is no longer a difference for a brand. And being disruptive no longer gets consumers' attention. After years of being told what to buy, consumers have changed their minds. They view brands as less relevant in their lives. And even in their most familiar brand relationships, they say they feel disconnected and unimportant—bystanders rather than participants." We get shouted at by so many ads, one on its own is about as relevant as a single scribbled tag in a train car full of them. We tune them out like white noise.

While we don't pay attention to ads as much as we used to, a lot of research suggests that some of the advertising we do engage with is having very negative effects on us. The United States and New Zealand are the only two countries in the world where it is legal to advertise prescription drugs. The United States accounts for almost 50 percent of all monies spent on prescription drugs worldwide. But according to a 2006 report by the *Journal of the American Medical Association*, U.S. residents are nearly twice as sickly as their English counterparts, despite the fact that the former spend almost twice as much on health care per person.* A study commissioned by Unilever in 2005 found that 67 percent of all women aged between fifteen and sixty-four withdraw from life-engaging activities due to feeling badly about their looks, a phenomenon they concluded was linked to advertising. In 2004, research by the American Psychological Association concluded that children under age eight accept advertiser messages as truthful, accurate, and unbiased, which is thought to be a strong cause for unhealthy eating habits and the current youth obesity epidemic.

When graffiti irritated subway commuters, the authorities ripped out an entire train fleet and threw it in the sea. But the negative side effects of advertising are being largely ignored.

Ads are messing with our heads. "The underlying message is that culture is something that happens to you," says Naomi Klein in *No Logo*. "You buy it at the Virgin Megastore or Toys 'R' Us and rent it at Blockbuster Video. It is not something in which you participate, or to which you have the right to respond." But for advertising's evil twin, graffiti, responding is a specialty.

The Bubble Bursts

We've become inundated by a daily onslaught of ads, and street artists are taking notice. "The government, more and more, is whoring the public domain to big business," Mark Jenkins tells me. "Street artists

---

*It's worth remembering that the two systems of health care are very different. The United Kingdom has free health care; the United States has forty million people with no health insurance.

are countering all of this visually by reclaiming public space, and in return mayors are targeting them and putting them in jail for increasingly minor offenses. My putting works up aren't motivated by any sort of political agenda, but gradually I've been getting drawn into thinking about these things." A lot of artists share Mark's sentiments, but no one in the world is as annoyed about all this as a former advertising guy from Estonia named Kalle Lasn.

Lasn is the founder of Adbusters, a nonprofit organization and magazine set up to counter advertising and zombielike consumer culture (*Adbusters* magazine is itself consumed by 120,000 people in sixty countries). A marketing industry dropout, Lasn has a pretty extreme position on advertising. He always resented the control he felt ads had over people. One day, in a grocery store parking lot, he encountered a shopping cart that demanded he pay a quarter to use it. Lasn lost it, jamming a quarter into the cart so hard, it could no longer demand money from shoppers. This incident brought to life a phenomenon that eventually became known as "culture jamming."

Culture jamming is the act of subverting any kind of corporate control, especially advertising. A loosely connected global network of culture jammers remix billboards with graffiti, changing the meaning of their messages in the spirit of the Situationists, while preserving their brand identities to make them seem as authentic as the real thing. Adbusters also make TV "uncommercials," encouraging us to spend less (which, nine times out of ten, the major networks refuse to air) and to organize events such as "Buy Nothing Day." Culture jamming is branding's blowback, a way to strike up a conversation with the advertising industry by heckling it.

Over the years the wrath of the culture jammers has been felt by fast food chains, sneaker companies, and fashion giants, leveling their multimillion-dollar corporate identities by using them to answer back in an effort to free captive audiences. "People now use culture from the bottom up," Lasn told me. "There has been a reaction to having culture spoon-fed to us from the top down. . . . We are in an era of rising mood disorders and cynicism. Mental disease is up by three hundred percent since World War II. The World Health Organization thinks it will soon be the number two killer in the world." Lasn's position is that ads are "mind-fucking" the people and should be banned outright. "If we don't have clarity of mind," he says, "we can't tackle these problems. With a cynical population hypnotized by mass media, we have wars started under false pretenses and so on. We need a tax on advertising similar to fining graffiti artists. We need to take seriously our relationship to television, because it's getting much more serious. We have six companies controlling half of all the communications on the planet. Media diversity is as important as biodiversity."

His resentment is shared by many. Since culture jamming first took hold in the 1990s, its practitioners have clearly had an influence. We might be responding to ads less, but corporations are responding when we criticize those ads. McDonald's is selling salads. Unilever's Dove brand uses "real" women in its ad campaigns and is on a mission to rebuild their self-esteem. Some companies are learning to shout at us less and engage us a little more, the same way graffiti does. "Advertisers are having to find different ways to get their message across," says Duncan Marshall. "What they are finding is, it has to be mutually beneficial. I don't have to watch advertising, so if I am going to interact with brands, I want it to be doing something for me. I want to get something out of it. Brands realize that unless they are the most entertaining, people are just going to choose not to see them." "Consumer culture is throwing shit at us at an incredible rate," Kalle Lasn complains. "These bubbles burst in your face all the time. But people are waking up to this now."

Another adman disenchanted with the industry is fighting these bubbles with bubbles of his own. Korea-born Ji Lee was always influenced by graffiti, first in São Paulo, Brazil, where he grew up, and then in New York, where he studied design and fine art. He was hired by ad agency Saatchi & Saatchi after designing a 3-D alphabet, but after a successful four years in the business, he was becoming agitated. "I was frustrated by these boring and often offensive to our intelligence ads all over the street," he explains. "I felt I needed to do something to change this back somehow." Lee printed twenty thousand blank speech bubble stickers, sticking them up on advertisements everywhere he went. A few days later, he would go back and photograph the results.

Passersby had quickly replaced targeted corporate messages with a bevy of political, social, and personal commentaries, humorous or otherwise. Through the speech bubble, a hipster's silhouette in an iPod ad now informs you "I steal music, and I'm not going away!" An impossibly smiley loving couple on a private health-care ad ask themselves, "Why doesn't the government insure our health?" "What country would Jesus bomb?" asks a cartoon villain from a *Grand Theft Auto* poster.

Lee,* now an art director at the Droga5 agency, is influenced by culture jamming, but feels that "bashing advertising is not really positive. With the bubbles, there are no sides. I enjoy the neutrality of the bubbles; they are just a platform for people to express themselves. So even if it's gay-bashing or a Republican NRA message, it's all valid. What counts is freedom of expression. What I learned from this is people have a lot of things they want to express. People have started their own bubble websites, one in Italy, one in Argentina, one in Romania. I love the inclusive aspect of it."

Lee's project has become wildly popular. It spawned a book, *Talk Back*, and an international army of bubbleheads reclaiming ads across the planet. Consumers are already creating even more powerful bubbles, posting their own anti-ads on sites such as YouTube, leveling criticism at brands that have angered them or treated them unfairly. Talking back has never been easier. But behind the visual sound bites was Lee's belief that advertising should be regulated in public spaces. "I have a problem with the proliferation of advertising on the street and the frequency of which we encounter this advertising," he told me. "When we are watching advertising on television, there is a kind of unwritten agreement that we are watching this ad for the price we pay for watching the programs, but I find it very different when we are faced with advertising on the street, because we never really agreed to it. That's when the bubble project comes in; it instantly transforms a million-dollar corporate monologue into a free public dialogue without censorship."

---

*Ji Lee also designed the Pirate's Dilemma logo for this book. Visit www.thepiratesdilemma .com, where you can steal it and create your own version.

Graffiti used to be like the glass skyscrapers that crush old neighborhoods in the development of modern cities, unique masterpieces that dominate the environment and alienate those around them. But graffiti has moved on, and many advertisers and those in control of public spaces are following suit. Today Banksy's stencils, Skewville's fences, Mark Jenkin's tape sculptures, and Ji Lee's bubbles work within the urban environment, not against it.

As the remix turned intellectual property into shared rights, so graffiti is turning statements on the street into conversations. "Graffiti is a strange thing," says Kalle Lasn. "It doesn't say anything conclusive about issues of the time, there is no content, but it reminds me there is a resistance to the status quo. It reminds me it is still possible to change the world."

Space: The Final Frontier

Graffiti started an argument in public with advertising, shouting at it from the pavement. As the argument escalated, the flaws in both disciplines became exposed. "I seen no difference," RΔMM:ΣLL:ZΣΣ observes. "One's tragic, and one is tragic. There are civic-minded people in both of them. One's commercial and one is commercial. It all depends on how you inform the public." Both disciplines are starting to think on a deeper level about their social responsibilities, and so the argument is evolving into, as Ji Lee puts it, "more of a dialogue and an exchange." In the battle between advertising and graffiti, we can see the public domain of the future taking shape.

This ongoing debate about public space is something that will become even more important to us in the coming decades, because public space is set to become something else entirely. Ubiquitous advertising and the role of graffiti will become even more of an issue with the advent of ubiquitous computing.

Ubiquitous computing is a term used to describe a world driven by nanotechnology that is fast approaching. A nanometer is one billionth of a meter (the amount your fingernail grows in one second), and we already have computers that measure just thirty nanometers across. Computers have become so small and cheap to produce, they can be both invisible and everywhere. "For the better part of a century," writes Howard Rheingold in *Smart Mobs*, "people have lived among invisible electric motors and thought nothing of it. The time has come to consider the consequences of computers disappearing into the background the way motors did."

The consequences are what some people are referring to as "the Internet of things." This is a world where objects are connected via tiny but widely distributed computers, such as radio-frequency identification chips (RFID), which cost less than 5 cents each and are already being used in products by Wal-Mart, Target, and Tesco to track goods. They are being used in passports, money, car keys, credit and travel cards, and are being embedded in livestock and even people. Aside from uses in the military, some nightclubs in Barcelona and Rotterdam have implanted chips into their VIP clientele, which verifies who they are and even lets them pay for drinks.

Graphical and virtual tags that attach themselves to things in the same way are also on the horizon. Visible through the screen on your phone or laptop, and even through glasses hooked to computers in your clothes, these create "augmented reality" environments. Augmented reality research projects are under way in media research labs such as the one at MIT, and have been for a number of years. A report done by the United Nation in 2005 predicts that the changes this type of ubiquitous computing will bring about will dwarf those already caused by an Internet confined inside computers.

Imagine a world where massively distributed yet impossibly small computers operate. Buildings and roads are covered in invisible tags, relaying information to passersby wearing nanocomputers that can sense and communicate with the millions of other tiny network-aware computers already around them, providing all kinds of real-time information on everything from weather and traffic conditions to where your friends are, or a sale taking place up the street. Instead of picking up a free newspaper on the corner, you download a video file of the day's top stories as you pass by. You avoid slipping on an icy patch on the next corner, and leave a virtual marker warning others, as you follow the large arrow you (and only you) can see in the sky, pointing out the directions the friend you are meeting sent you. An mpeg home movie of a lost dog is pinned to the lamppost in front of you. It seems sad, like those new gravestones hooked into memorial photo albums and posthumous MySpace pages, giving everyone an electronic after-life. Perhaps the scariest thing about this world is that all this technology is already here.

The means to display this kind of information through eyeglasses, overlaying the natural world with additional information, has been a possibility since 1989. Although these kinds of applications haven't yet been rolled out far and wide, they could one day blanket the real world in an extra layer of information. If the United Nations' predictions are right, the Internet was in fact just a 2-D blueprint for the coming re-ality. People have already been heavily annotating virtual space with tags for years. Sites such as beermaps.com overlay Google maps with information on the nearest place where you can grab a brew. But think how useful a real-world version of this would be at 3:00 A.M. on a Sat-urday morning, virtually embedded in your beer goggles?

The idea of graffiti is central to ubiquitous computing. "Tags" are already used in search engines: you get the results you want by search-ing for tags or keywords. Tags are attached to sites to give information visibility and make it accessible, and they will be even more important in the Internet of things.

When people begin virtually annotating real space, the nature of privacy, the public domain, and the role of graffiti suddenly changes. Who will and who will not have the right to tag the virtual environ-ment? How will advertising work when we can block out billboards from our vision, like human TiVos? Who will scrub out the giant pieces done by graffiti artists floating through the sky like clouds? How will we talk back?

Governments and corporations will make many of these decisions, but norms-based systems of trust, like the one used by graffiti artists and French chefs, will likely become more widespread and effective in such informal, transient environments. Our reputations may become a visible commodity, like the ratings of a vendor on eBay, floating around above our heads. Tuning out unwanted information is going to become even more important to our quality of life. Spam could become a dan-gerous eyesore. Advertising will have to become more targeted if we are to pay any attention to it; you may only see virtual billboards related to the things you are genuinely interested in, based on the list of tags and preferences you may (or may not) choose to broadcast. Some of the technology being developed could threaten our freedoms if used the wrong way, but the history of graffiti shows us there has always been a way to use information and the tools in public spaces to respond. It is calligraphy repurposed as kung fu: it lets us use the power of our opponents against them to answer back.

In the future graffiti, it turns out, may become a last bastion of free speech. Rules and regulations will be put in place, but graffiti will be an important tool, a digital scribbling democracy keeping the legislators in check. The future of the public domain is uncertain, but one thing's for sure: it's going to be a colorful story.

CHAPTER 5

Boundaries

Disco Nuns, the Death of the Record Industry, and Our Open-Source Future

Sister Alicia Donohoe moving the crowd in the party room,
Christmas 1947.

Not many nuns kick-start revolutions, and almost none have done so by DJing at children's birthday parties. But Sister Alicia Donohoe was never out to change the world—she was just trying to make sure the kids were having a good time.

Alicia grew up in 1930s Boston, in the suburb of Dorchester, the daughter of Anna and John Donohoe—a child of the Great Depression. "It was a dead town," she remembers. For the Donohoe family, a family of pianists, music would save the day during these hard times. "My parents played classical and my sister played popular music," she told me. "My parents would be playing and I'd be singing along and turning the pages, and they'd do duets. All our friends would come over, too. We were surrounded by music."

John Donohoe liked sharing music with strangers, using his piano to bring many of the unemployed people in the neighborhood together and give them something to smile about. "We had a very nice baby grand piano in the bay window," Sister Alicia told me. "When my father would sit there at the piano during the day, he'd push the draperies back and open the windows. People who liked music would be standing outside listening and my father would invite them all in. He was not an inhibited man by any means," she says with a chuckle. "We never knew who was gonna be in the house!"

Music inspired her, but by age six she had already decided she wanted to take care of children, "to see if we can make them as happy as we are at home," she remembers telling her mother. "I always wanted to be a Daughter of Charity (the order of nuns she was to join). I knew a lot of Sisters, because I had two aunts who were Sisters." And so it was that at age twenty-one, Alicia became a nun, and soon found herself at St. Joseph's Home, an interfaith home for orphans and troubled children placed into care from birth to age six. And it's there the revolution began.

The year was 1944. The world was at war. Scientists involved in the Manhattan Project were hard at work developing the most destructive force known to mankind. But at St. Joseph's in Utica, New York, Sister Alicia was getting another experiment under way—a social experiment so powerful it is still repeated all around the world every night of the week.

St. Joseph's embraced children from all cultures, religions, and backgrounds. It was a transient place: kids came and went all the time; some were there for a month or two, others for years. When Sister Alicia arrived, the young rascals at St. Joseph's were an unruly little mob—she remembers one day having to stop them beating a very overweight nun with sticks and brooms. "I had no control," she told me, "I'd be running after them, then they'd be running after me." But Sister Alicia saw they were a troubled bunch, and she just wanted to make them happy. "At first the children were all so down. I was so sad that they all had to be there. Then I decided I'd be no help if I was crying all the time." She thought back to her own childhood and the difference she knew music could make to a group of strangers, and suddenly she was inspired.

With the limited resources at her disposal, she created what the children called the "party room"—a space replete with a refrigerator and a record player, which she and the children filled with multicolored balloons and crepe paper decorations. The room also had a piano and a small stage, though the Sister in charge told Sister Alicia that the children were forbidden from using either. Sister Alicia ignored her; she could see the last thing these kids needed here was strict hierarchy. "It was a playroom and they were in there, so I said go ahead and use it." She decided that this room would be a place where the kids had options instead of rules.

She began to throw parties for the children as often as she could; she wanted them all to feel like stars. "Everybody had a birthday party. If there were three birthdays that month, we had three parties. They'd be all dressed up with party hats and I'd play the records. And the noise was something! But that didn't bother me at all. It bothered some other people, but y'know, they were having fun."

Sister Alicia manned the turntable, spinning tunes like a pro to keep the party moving. "We had many, many very nice records," she says. "We were very blessed. It was all kinds of music, children's music, party music, and then we had nice, quiet music for when they were getting ready to go to bed. I played whatever records we had. If I heard about any new records, I went to the store and bought 'em."

She would go digging in the crates at the local record store like this every week, the same way obsessed DJs all over the world still do today, and she soon learned to manipulate her dance floor with expert precision, cutting between party favorites while introducing the crowd to the latest tracks. "If I put a record on and they didn't like it, they'd let me know. If one didn't like it, I'd ask the other children. I'd say shall we play this record just once, and then play the records you like? That way everybody had a turn, so it all worked out. And they danced!"

In the party room, these children from disparate and often desperate backgrounds ate, drank, played, and danced together like they never had before, connecting through sound and sharing shiny, happy moments that would have serious effects not just on them, but, some years later, on the rest of us as well.

It was 1949 when a five-year-old named David Mancuso left St. Joseph's and was reunited with his mother. As he grew up, the memories of the party room became hazy—distant and water-colored, as the song goes. But subconsciously, a seed had been planted. David was a troubled youngster. He didn't get on well with his folks, the people around him seemed narrow-minded and racist, and even at the impressionable age of six, he was not cool with that. "I didn't believe in the things Mom believed in," he told me. "When I was told at a very young age, I don't even like to use the words, 'the spics or the niggers or the Jews or this . . . ' none of this made any sense to me. . . . Money, a lot of things didn't make sense." Time passed, but he refused to fit in. He'd forgotten the party room at St. Joseph's, but it was clear that David was singing from a different hymn sheet. After nine years, living with his mom wasn't working out, and he ended up in a reform school.

Mancuso wasn't much of a student, either. The only thing that held his interest was sound. He was consumed by it. He noticed acoustics everywhere he went, clapping when he walked into rooms. At his mom's house he sneaked friends in when she went out, and they would dance around the record player. At the reform school he would listen intently to the faraway crackle of R&B stations in his dorm room as he drifted off to sleep at night. "Music reminds us that everything is okay," he asserts. But everything was not okay. By age sixteen he'd given up trying to fit in with his dysfunctional family. He ditched school and moved into his own place. He realized he needed options instead of rules, which is why two years later he packed his things and headed for New York City.

He started out shining shoes, renting a place, and reveling in his newfound independence. Mancuso seemed to fit in here. He began hanging out in Tompkins Square Park in the East Village by the bandstand, where a group called the Grateful Dead were just getting started, as was a guy named Jimi Hendrix. The sixties were kicking in; everybody was dropping out. He begins experimenting with acid and soon met a young Timothy Leary, the legendary high priest of psychedelia, in a macrobiotic food restaurant. "The man was one of the coolest human beings ever. It wasn't like he was this high priest. . . . I mean, well, he was high, and he was kind of a priest," he explains. "And LSD was good. I mean there was some *good shit* out there. It certainly made you aware. And when you came down, you wanted to change things."

The desire to change things stayed with him. During his experiments with LSD, Mancuso experienced reality in wild new ways, soaring to great heights and hitting bottom so hard he briefly ended up in the psychiatric ward of Bellevue Hospital. No doubt the staff saw another burned-out hippie who'd been on one trip too many. But Mancuso had seen something else. A vision, a fleeting memory, a revelation—he wasn't exactly sure—but an idea was taking shape, one that seemed strangely familiar. There was something he had to do.

He flitted between jobs, disinterested in money, just trying to pay the rent. It was 1965 when Mancuso moved into a disused loft at 647 Broadway. He did so because it was cheap and large. Twenty years later, yuppies all over the world will pay fortunes for any old studio described by overimaginative Realtors as "lofts," but back then they were cold spaces in deserted and often undesirable parts of town.* Mancuso decided to warm things up with a housewarming party, which, like all good parties, went on a little longer than expected. In fact, this party is still going on today.

"I was having social things there, having all that space, I would let other people from the area come in and throw parties, too. There was a group that threw one that was all-nude . . . it was the sixties," he says with a shrug. "It wasn't until 1970 that money became tight, and then I decided to have rent parties and charge a couple of dollars. I could pay my rent and continue to live there and have parties. None of my friends objected to this."

Maybe that's because Mancuso's loft party wasn't any old shindig. His obsession with sound had grown, and over the years Mancuso had

---

*David did have a couple of neighbors. The legendary blues artist John Hammond Jr. also had taken on space in the same building, where Bob Dylan was hanging around regularly. Just across the street, another musician, named Miles Davis, had recently moved into a loft, too.

amassed so much high-end audio equipment, he had designed and installed in his loft what was reputed to be the finest sound system in New York. Mancuso was (and is) so persnickety about sound quality that the only needles good enough for his turntables are Koetsus, which retail for up to $15,000 each, designed and hand-built in Japan by a family who once made samurai swords. The original design and layout of Mancuso's sound system was so groundbreaking, many of the innovations he pioneered, such as bass reinforcement, sub-woofers, and tweeter rigs are now still used in sound systems all over the world today.

Music was just as important, and he hit the decks concocting aural journeys of R&B, jazz fusion, rock, world music, funk, anything with a groove. On top of this he served up hot food, snacks, and fruit punch. He also installed a huge mirror ball; a huger shrine to Buddha; and for some reason he couldn't put his finger on, he was moved to fill the entire room with multicolored balloons.

"It was never intended to run as a business," he explains. "I didn't want to draw attention to myself, I did not want to get involved with the Mafia—they left me alone, they knew it wasn't about money—so no liquor. I didn't want any real hierarchy; even a social club was too much for me."

Instead of membership, Mancuso sent out invitations to his many friends from all walks of life, inscribed with the words *Love Saves the Day* (you don't need to be tripping to spot the hidden acronym here). The "Loft," as it came to be known, became an institution. Soon more than two hundred people were packing out the forty-foot dance floor every week from midnight Saturday until well into Sunday, paying the $2.50 entrance fee. "It became more and more planned," Mancuso says. "The sound, the music, every full moon we had ice cream. Everything was organic. It was all home cooking. It was always about being able to be with your friends, you were definitely gonna eat—'cos maybe you didn't eat that day—who knows. That happened 'cos I had all kinds of people. Yeah, there were celebrities that came there, but the reason they came is they could be themselves. It wasn't about who's this, who's that, it was about people getting together, outcasts mixing with people who were part of the system. We were all stars."

The Loft became a legend, the original dance floor on which many elements of the emerging disco scene were formed. Word of Mancuso's parties spread, which is how a childhood friend named Eddy, also from the children's home, tracked him down. Eddy paid a visit to the Loft, and immediately felt as though he'd been there before. "My friend is really shook up by my space, the balloons and everything," Mancuso remembers. Eddy looked around the room in disbelief, and the heightened sense of déjà vu gave way to a moment of clarity. He turned to Mancuso and said, "You're not gonna believe this."

Eddy had recently reconnected with Sister Alicia, who had given him some pictures of the old party room. When he showed them to Mancuso, it all came flooding back. "In this room was a console record player with records sitting on top, these little tables with kids sitting around, and the kids had little party hats, then there was the balloons. We both just started freaking out. This picture triggered my memory. Suddenly we're in this living picture. It was so powerful, but it had been totally subconscious. The whole function of the room was socializing, playing, you look at this room and you look at the Loft and you see the same ingredients. I just wept at this picture."

Mancuso realized he had being trying to recapture these feelings from his childhood at the Loft, feelings he was transmitting through his dance floor that were now appealing to other people. Lots of them.

Disco, which emerged from the psychedelic haze of flower power infused with R&B and social progress that was being cooked up at the Loft, was the most direct descendant, but the Loft's influence spread into many other areas. Among its patrons were some of the world's most renowned DJs, who would forge their own new movements. Frankie Knuckles, the infamous resident DJ of Chicago's Warehouse Club (from where house music stems) was a regular, as was his close friend Larry Levan, the legendary DJ from New York's Paradise Garage (where "garage music" originated). Influential spinners such as Nicky Siano, David Morales, François K, and Tony Humphries were just some of Mancuso's other disciples. The history of modern dance music, rave, and club culture as we know it can be traced back to the Loft. Its legacy is difficult to overestimate.

The sentiments of Sister Alicia and Mancuso reflect an ideology bigger than music. "The Loft party was all about going through life and sharing," says Mancuso—now in his sixties and still partying.* "This whole thing about social progress through parties—the parties were a blueprint for a way for things to work or function without a hierarchy as much as possible. That sense of community was really the wind in my sails. We have to have a system, and if it doesn't work, it has to come down. Music and artists suffer a lot of the time because the system hits the wrong note."

The system has always hit bum notes, but ideas of sharing and inclusiveness are striking a chord more than ever. The Loft helped birth dance music, now a multibillion-dollar industry operating across the world, a flashback to the ideals promoted by flower power, a sonic yearning for a system without hierarchy.

Sister Alicia's social experiments with sharing and sound reverberated around the world. In recent years the music business has been torn to pieces by a new way to share. The open-source movement is revolutionizing many other industries as people collaborate, turning old hierarchies upside down, creating new business models and open resources that can improve the lives of us all.

Disco bit the dust, but ideas based on collaboration are hotter than ever. And it might not have happened in quite the same way if it were not for a nun in the 1940s, throwing children's birthday parties.

All hail Sister Alicia, the patron saint of sharing.

Talking 'bout Boundaries
(Territorial Disputes)

Each story in this book is about boundaries coming down. Punk democratized the means of production. Pirates ignored old restrictions on new ideas. We have seen how useful the remix can be, and how graffiti artists reclaim public spaces from private interests. All of these ideas are about sharing and using information in new ways.

But each story in this book has another side to it. As quickly as soci-

---

*Loft parties are still held regularly at secret locations in New York. Mancuso also throws parties in Los Angeles, Tokyo, Osaka, Sapporo, London, and Glasgow, using specially designed sound systems in each city.

ety figures out new ways to share ideas that advance the common good, private interests move in to stop this from happening, to maintain the old systems that benefit only the elite. This has happened throughout history. As Machiavelli once said, "It must be remembered that there is nothing more difficult to plan, more doubtful of success, nor more dangerous to management than the creation of a new system. For the initiator has the enmity of all who would profit by the preservation of the old institution and merely lukewarm defenders in those who gain by the new ones."

This new system being created from the ground up is a new kind of open society. As we have observed, the powers that be are resisting the Pirate's Dilemma in many cases, but the truth is that new ways of sharing can benefit the old systems, too.

More recently than Machiavelli, a tumultuous renaissance has taken place in the music business, thanks to file-sharing. The story of the record industry's response to file-sharing is relevant to every other business, because the communities and technologies that changed music could affect every area of the economy. As new economic systems underpinned by sharing begin to outcompete markets, understanding the Pirate's Dilemma will become a priority for nations, organizations, and individuals alike.

Less Fences = Better Neighbors

The open society disco dreamed about is a space with fewer fences. There will always be a need for gardens with good fences and gated communities, but boundaries can be damaging, and we live in a world where this is becoming increasingly obvious. Our nineteenth-century intellectual property laws suited the past, but they are not quite right for the future, and today they often stifle creativity rather than encouraging it. Sometimes progress happens only when pirates jump fences, going on garden runs over unreasonable licenses and patents to get us to a better place.

Good fences make good neighbors, but take the fence away and you have a bigger lawn. Get a few more neighbors involved and soon you've got a park.

The birth of dance music was based on the idea of sharing, channeled through David Mancuso, influenced by Sister Alicia and 1960s youth culture. But electronic dance music was not the only unforeseen side effect of flower power. Another was the birth of the personal computer.

The PC, as we shall now see, also was designed to be a social machine like the Loft—a way of sharing information that offered new freedoms and possibilities while posing a serious threat to some oppressive systems of old. It has since birthed what is known as the open-source movement, which started out as a way to build computer operating systems but is fast becoming a design for life.

There are two underground clubs from the 1970s that will go down in history as major influences on early twenty-first-century ideas about sharing. Both were involved in the death of the twentieth-century music business, and both were inspired by the possibilities of sharing, that we all need to comprehend. One was the Loft. The other was known as the Homebrew Computer Club.

(Disco's) Revenge of the Nerds

Youth culture built the personal computer. The ideas that shaped it came together at Stanford University's campus in Palo Alto, California, during the 1950s and 1960s. There a handful of young tech students, who were involved with both the antiwar and the hippie movements, fed their psychedelic social ideas into the development of the computer. Many scientists working on similar projects at nearby R&D facility Xerox PARC also were influenced by flower power. Some were hippies themselves. According to John Markoff, author of *What the Dormouse Said: How 60s Counterculture Shaped the Personal Computer,* "There was this very interesting parallel between the way they worked with psychedelics—which was about augmenting human potential—and the works of a man named Doug Engelbart [a pioneer of human-computer interaction, who, among other things, invented the mouse], who was attempting to build a machine that he thought would augment the human mind."

The pioneers of Palo Alto had the same D.I.Y. attitude that energized punk. Their ideas for a new social machine were a reaction to the war machine and the establishment in general. Computers weren't invented by narrow-minded number crunchers; they were the combined efforts of a group of anarchic radical left-wing activists, who had a desire to expand science, technology, and our collective consciousness, which they began to realize in the research lab. As Markoff tells it, "The great transformative technology of our lifetime was more than just a triumph of engineering and finance. It was, just as compellingly, the result of a concerted effort by a group of visionaries—fueled by progressive values, artistic sensibilities and the occasional mind altering drug—to define the idea of what a computer could be: a liberating tool to expand and enrich human potential."

Computers became social tools rather than just giant calculators as a direct result of the influence of 1960s youth culture. In 1972 *Rolling Stone* ran an article about the link between psychedelic drugs and computers returning power to the people. The piece upset Xerox so much, they shut down the Palo Alto research facility. In doing so, they lost out on their early lead developing the PC and word processing—and squandered one of the greatest business opportunities of the twentieth century.

So instead of being controlled by Xerox, the next stage in the personal computer's development was overseen by a D.I.Y. activist named Fred Moore. Moore was a radical pacifist known for protesting throughout the late fifties and sixties. He saw money as the root of all human problems* but thought computers might offer us some new solutions.

In 1975 a company called Altair released the first home computer kit, which was to whiz kids such as Moore what the turntable was to DJs. Fred Moore and fellow programmer Gordon French founded the Homebrew Computer Club in the same year, the geek equivalent of the Loft. Its membership was a left-leaning mix of hackers and activists who also grew up under flower power's influence. They met in the garage of French's home in San Mateo County, California, to

---

*In 1971 Moore unwillingly had $20,000 of seed money bestowed on him, which freaked him out so much that he buried it in his backyard.

ponder the future of computing, using new technology such as the Altair kit. Here the idea that became the personal computer was formulated.

The club's members included a college dropout who occasionally dropped acid named Steve Jobs, and his future Apple cofounder, Steve Wozniak. They remixed early programs, fixing and debugging them, publishing their findings in a regular newsletter, and recruiting more members along the way. Like disco, computer software was something of a loose-knit, collaborative effort with an open social structure. And like disco, it would change completely once it went commercial.

In 1976, a twenty-one-year-old programmer (another college dropout rumored to have dabbled with LSD) wrote the Homebrew Computer Club an angry letter, saying the club couldn't use his software anymore, a program called BASIC, without paying for it. "Who can afford to do professional work for nothing?" the letter asked the club, which had formed to do exactly that. "What hobbyist can put three man-years into programming, finding all bugs, documenting his product and distribute for free?" he asked, even though hackers, researchers, and companies such as IBM had been treating software as a public good since the 1950s. This young programmer was brilliant, but he had a different point of view to that of our sharing, inclusive Homebrew Computer Club. He was not doing this for nothing; his software was not a public good; it was intellectual property he had created to make a profit. He had a point: Why shouldn't he be paid for his time?

It was the early 1980s, and disco was approaching a similar fork in the road. Disco was becoming the kind of social hierarchy David Mancuso and the original pioneers were trying to escape, spearheaded by commercial superclubs such as the infamous Studio 54 and the rise of manufactured, formulaic disco records being churned out by the major labels. Its original ideals were getting lost in a blizzard of sequins, cocaine, and flared polyester.

At the same time, in the world of computer programming, the letter-writing geek managed to turn the tide of opinion, and software was widely considered private property by the early 1980s. He ended up scratching a good living from his software, too. The letter-writer was Bill Gates, founder of the Studio 54 of personal computing,

Microsoft. Software, which had previously been as free to use as a public park, became a gated community. Gates became the richest man in the world.

Studio 54 and Microsoft monetized the ideals of sharing and networking, but other Homebrew and Loft regulars decided to take the road less traveled. Disco's revenge was house.

As the commercialized disco scene died a slow death, its original source code was hacked by DJs such as Frankie Knuckles and Larry Levan, who forged it into the new house and garage sound, cleansing the music of crass commercialism and reinvigorating it with disco's original progressive ideals. House music drifted across the Atlantic in the mid-1980s and found favor with partygoers on the Balearic island of Ibiza, where it was combined with a new drug known as ecstasy.

Music, one of our most precious forms of information, has always wanted to be free, spreading across the globe and mutating into new forms. The music from Ibiza was transmitted to the United Kingdom, where it caught on quickly, devoured the entire country, and evolved into a new sound: acid house. Huge, illegal outdoor parties attracted tens of thousands of people, who gathered in fields and disused structures such as airplane hangars, setting up massive sound and light systems, overwhelming local police forces across Britain. Huge crowds united for the night to thumb their noses at the authorities and imagine a different world. "Rave visionaries revived the utopian hopes of the 1960s," wrote Ken Goffman in *Counterculture Through the Ages*, "believing that the vibe coupled with the communications technology and the open information channels . . . could now effortlessly effect a rapid, global, mass transformation of consciousness." Rave's giddy optimism whizzed around the planet, and has since been reimagined as many different youth cultures and strains of dance music, attracting partygoers to venues all over the world, infecting people everywhere, from Texas to Tehran.

Rave became popular because it generated community, even if it was an imaginary one contained in a disused warehouse that only lasted for twelve drug-fueled hours, fading as the sunrise blotted out the ultraviolet lights. Rave was flower power's wild grandchild; it was the perfect accompaniment to the digital counterculture that began to creep into the early 1990s. It's no accident that one of the richest veins of rave culture in America, an anything-goes culture also based on the idea of giving people options instead of rules, is in Silicon Valley.

The Homebrew Computer Club's revenge on Microsoft was the open-source movement. While many agreed with Gates and saw software as intellectual property, others didn't, and continued to develop their own free software. In 1983, a hacker/activist named Richard Stallman founded the Free Software Foundation, writing a new operating system that was as open as possible, arguing, "Free software is a matter of liberty, not price. To understand the concept, you should think of 'free' as in 'free speech,' not as in 'free beer.'"* Hackers who weren't ready to drink Gates's pricey Kool-Aid instead started chugging Stallman's free beer, and a range of new code was created, code that would revolutionize society.

The idea behind open-source software is to let others copy, share, change, and redistribute your software, as long as they agree to do the same with the new software they create in the process. This way, it can spread and progress as quickly as house music. The Internet was founded on free software such as USENET and UNIX, which is why no one can own it but everyone can use it. USENET is a public good free for the rest of us to build on. It was the early 1990s when Tim Berners-Lee, a British researcher working at the Swiss particle physics center CERN, designed the Web on top of such open-source software as a social experiment rather than a technical one. Free software was officially rebranded as open-source software in 1998 by the company Netscape (which then rebranded themselves as Mozilla, and created the hugely popular open-source Internet browser Firefox). As the Web spread its tentacles around the world, it became clear that open source was a way to maintain a wealth of new public goods, as well as a great way to promote private enterprise. In the words of Linus Torvalds,

---

*Open-source culture has since developed free beer, too. A group of students and artists in Copenhagen created VoresØl, the world's first open-source beer, to demonstrate how open source can be applied outside the digital world. Released under a Creative Commons license, anyone can use the VoresØl recipe to brew and remix their own beer, and as long as they publish their recipe under the same license, they're free to make money from it and use VoresØl's open-source design and branding.

founder of open-source software Linux, "the future is open-source everything."

Open for Business

Just as house produced new sounds such as acid house, drum 'n' bass, and U.K. garage, which became industries in their own right, the open-source movement has created new business models. Open source isn't just a case of letting others use your work; it's also about allowing your work to be transformative, so both you and others can benefit. Some businesses use the open-source model as it was intended by the hackers who created it; others just play with the basic idea of options as opposed to rules, enabling a community to build on their brands (but without giving up any copyright to those brands).

The open-source model is also known as a "wiki," which is defined by Wikipedia as "practices in production and development that promote access to the end product's source materials—typically, their source code. Some consider it as a philosophy, and others consider it as a pragmatic methodology."

Wikipedia is a great example of an open-source model. It is an online encyclopedia, the largest encyclopedia in the world, which can be added to, updated, and edited by anyone who wants to. Before Wikipedia, encyclopedias were painstakingly constructed by scholars. Wikipedia is built entirely by amateurs. Instead of authority, Wikipedia embraces a new, decentralized way of working. At the time of going to press, Wikipedia had seventy-five thousand contributors, 5.3 million articles, and was available in more than one hundred languages. Every day thousands of new entries are added, and thousands more are edited and improved on.

Wikipedia's open-source nature does leave it open to tampering and inaccuracy. In the United States, TV comedian Stephen Colbert has encouraged viewers to change Wikipedia entries during his show on more than one occasion, which they did as he spoke. In the United Kingdom, two BBC Radio 1 DJs defaced each other's pages live on air. In 2007 both the U.S. government and Microsoft were caught by Wikipedia editors tampering with their own entries (editing your own page is a practice frowned on by Wikipedia users). A 2005 study by the science journal *Nature* compared forty-two science entries in Wikipedia and the *Encyclopaedia Britannica*. They found an average of four errors per entry in Wikipedia, three errors per entry in *Britannica*. But as Chris Anderson noted in *The Long Tail*, "shortly after the report came out, the Wikipedia entries were corrected, while *Britannica* will have to wait for its next reprinting."

Wikipedia is usually pretty reliable, and covers much more ground than a traditional encyclopedia ever has. It may not be perfect, but if you want detailed information on the history of the Jedi, the Pamela Anderson sex tape, or the Homebrew Computer Club, Wikipedia rules *Britannica* every time. But the site itself makes no guarantees about accuracy. So instead I asked Jimmy Wales,* the founder of Wikipedia, to define the wiki/open-source business model personally. "A wiki is a website that anyone can edit," he says. "It's a place where people can edit and share information. It has tools where people can monitor the quality and revert to older versions if anyone has done something bad."

Jimmy Wales is to encyclopedias what David Mancuso is to DJing. Both Mancuso and Wales changed the game, because they saw new possibilities in the idea of sharing. Jimmy Wales grew up in Huntsville, Alabama, close to where NASA's team of rocket scientists were headquartered. He attended a small, private school run by his mother and grandmother. "I remember the windows shaking in my house when they were testing the rocket engines. It was a big deal to me that these people were going to the moon. That sent me off in a very scientific frame of mind. We had a really flexible environment. I had a lot of spare time, which allowed me to be very diverse in my interests, and I had a real passion for the encyclopedia. I loved following the links to other knowledge and learning different things."

Making money was not rocket science to Wales, who made a fortune in the 1990s as an options and futures trader in Chicago, and then decided to pursue his passion. "I'd seen the growth of open-

---

*I interviewed Jimmy Wales before a panel discussion at the Columbia School of Journalism in 2006. While he was talking, the dean of students purposely altered a Wikipedia entry on the screen behind him. Five minutes later, the dean rechecked the site. The mistake had already been corrected.

source software coming together online. I recognized that the free-license model gave us a new social paradigm, a way for people to share their work. People are able to use the software for commercial and noncommercial stuff. It's not about nonprofit versus profit—it's about proprietary versus closed. If I share my code, I'll share it under a license that says you can use it for anything you like, but you have to share your changes as well. And that provides a level playing field—we're all agreeing to share our knowledge. It struck me that this kind of social structure and social agreement could be used much broader than just software. One of the things that came to mind was an encyclopedia."

Like Linux founder Linus Torvalds, Wales recognized that our future could be open-source everything. "Some of the general principles apply almost anywhere. In many cases, businesses are losing out on opportunities because of their information-hoarding mind-set. They don't realize that their customers know more than they do."

Wildly successful Net-based businesses such as eBay, Amazon, and MySpace are based on the strength of their communities and the content their users contribute for free. The technology these businesses are based on—the code that powers the Net—is also free. If there was a huge cost involved with adding pages to the Internet, or using it, none of these businesses would be able to function in the same way.

Many businesses that give content away for free are making money and growing fast. The open-source Linux software set up by Linus Torvalds as a hobby in 1991 is today used by Google, in Motorola cell phones, TiVos, and BMWs. Many companies, including Intel and IBM, have programmers working full-time developing new free software for Linux, as they obey the laws of Linux and put back some of what they take out. By distributing their core software for free, Linux now powers forty-three million personal computers worldwide. By selling customized software that runs on top of the free open-source software, it's predicted the market for Linux products will be worth $35 billion by 2008. To paraphrase Stewart Brand, author and founder of the *Whole Earth Catalog,* information wants to be free, but customized information wants to be really expensive.

The value of openness is something most of us are only just getting to grips with. Harvard Business School published a report in 2006 that surveyed a range of businesses and concluded that introducing problems to outsiders was the best way to find effective solutions. A European Union report released in 2007 specifically endorsed open-source software, claiming that in "almost all" cases, long-term costs could be reduced by switching from proprietary software to open-source systems such as Linux. The study also claimed that the number of existing open-source programs already available would have cost firms 12 billion Euros (£8 billion) to build, and estimated that the programs available represent the equivalent of 131,000 programmer years, or "at least 800 million Euros [£525 million] in voluntary contributions from programmers alone each year."

Systems based on sharing expand the way information is used, and in doing so expand the market for that information. As this dawns on more of us, the question will not be "How do we stop this happening," but "How do we facilitate it?" The challenge of successful social networks in the twenty-first century will be figuring out how to create a dedicated dance floor like the one at the Loft, and how to keep people contributing to open-source projects and social networks, devoting their time and expertise the way they did at the Homebrew Computer Club. To better understand how this might work, let us look at an example of an industry that decided to fight a new system based on sharing, when it should have been adapting to it.

From Loft Space to MySpace

Today, major record companies claim that they are facing a threat from file-sharing unlike any they have ever known. But this is a case of history repeating itself. The majors have been confronted by the threat of new distribution methods before—in the 1980s the British Phonograpic Industry believed that the cassette tape and home recording would kill music, and campaigned against it. The industry also was confronted by what they saw as a threat from new ways to share music back in the 1970s at the Loft. But just as it was with cassette tapes, in the end, they realized that this threat was an opportunity.

Then the disco DJs were figuring out new ways to share vinyl. Now people are figuring out new ways to share MP3s. As it turns out, David Mancuso is not just the godfather of dance music, he is also the grand-daddy of file-sharing.

Back then, the influence of Mancuso and the handful of twenty or thirty club DJs in New York City was so powerful that the obscure independent records they sought out and spun in the clubs could become so well known, they could break into the top forty charts without any support from radio stations. At the Loft and the other discos springing up around the city, records that were hits on the dance floor became so popular that the majors began swooping in, signing and releasing them commercially. Many hit the pop charts, making a lot of money for the major labels in the process.

But according to Mancuso, the record companies didn't understand these new club DJs. They had no idea who was who, or which of them were breaking these records, so the labels responded by making it very difficult for the disco DJs to get ahold of promotional copies of new records, refusing to share their new records before they were released. They discriminated against disco DJs in favor of radio DJs. Even when they would give records to the disco DJs, "labels would only let DJs go get records between 2:00 P.M. and 4:00 P.M.," remembers Mancuso. "The record industry was exclusive, it was racist. . . . I would just go buy my records." It was becoming harder and harder for the disco DJs to get new music from the labels, even though they were promoting their records better than the radio stations, even though, as Mancuso says, "in those days you didn't make any money playing records. You were lucky if you got paid."

Mancuso and the other DJs found the situation incredibly frustrating—so frustrating that, as Mancuso tells it, he stayed up for *three days* in 1975, taking speed and thinking intensely about the issue until he came up with a solution. Mancuso and fellow DJ Steve D'Acquisto called all New York's disco DJs to a meeting at the Loft. "DJs and DJs only met to figure this stuff out. And we did," he told me. "I said why don't we do something like a car pool, something where we can all get together and pool our energies?"

The club DJs wrote a declaration of intent at the Loft, setting out the blueprint for what would become known as the "record pool." The disco DJs who were breaking and promoting records presented themselves to the labels and convinced them that what they were doing was legit. "The record companies would give us test presses,* there were no favors, no this, no that. It was eliminating payola—that was the beauty of it. The way to get your record distributed was to give us enough copies; that was *it*. If they sent us twice as many as we needed, I would send them back. I kept it really clean. Many people felt threatened by it, but we just wanted our records, in exchange for feedback, and that's what it came down to. It was a great concept, it worked, there was no executive director—we were all DJs."

The record pool would legitimize the club DJs. For DJs to belong to the pool, they had to pay a small subscription fee to cover postage and costs, and supply a letter on headed paper from the clubs they played at, stating how many nights they worked. In exchange for this supply of free records, the DJs had to supply written feedback to the labels about each new track, letting them know what worked and what didn't. The DJs got access to new music, the labels got a new kind of R&D department they could use to road test their products. It was brilliant—so brilliant that the record pool system is still used by labels and DJs all over the world today.

"Some people found everything I was doing very intimidating," Mancuso remembers. "It took a lot of work to form this pool. We used the word 'discotheque' and called ourselves 'disco' DJs. I only started to realize how significant all this was later."

This story has never been more significant than it is today, because in the past ten years, this story of the majors responding the wrong way to a Pirate's Dilemma has manifested again, only this time on a global scale. Just like with the record pool, the majors are being forced to work out a better way to share music, so that the system benefits both them and the people promoting their records and making them money. Only this time it is not disco DJs promoting their records, it is every single one of us.

---

*A test press is a prototype vinyl record, typically with no label, also known as a white label, pressed in small quantities to test the sound quality of a record before the larger batch is pressed up.

Farther down the bloodline of geek royalty from Steve Jobs and Bill Gates, is Shawn Fanning, the seventeen-year-old college dropout and convert of rave culture who created Napster, the file-sharing community that turned the music industry on its head. In 1999, Fanning figured out a new way to share music just like the disco DJs did. Napster was born, allowing users to share and exchange vast quantities of music online—illegally. Together with MP3 players, which allowed consumers to carry around the vast amounts of music they had downloaded onto their computers, Napster changed music history. At its height, the Napster file-sharing network had some seventy million users trading 2.7bn files (most of which were music files) every month. Fanning was the consummate pirate, creating a new space and upsetting the status quo. The industry responded with a bloody legal battle, bankrupting Napster by 2002 (it has since relaunched as a legal online music store). The majors continue to rage against download sites and those who use them. But Napster was like the record pool on steroids, and downloading would change the balance of power in the music business for good.

Artists not getting paid for their work is a problem. But the fact remains that file-sharing sites such as Napster make an abundance of music available that we otherwise would not have access to. Most of the recorded music ever made is no longer available for sale on CD (only about a fifth of all recorded music is ever actually on sale; the rest is deleted and no longer in circulation). It is clear that file-sharing can offer us something more than record stores, the same way disco DJs could offer new music in a way radio couldn't and wouldn't.

Getting a major label advance has traditionally been the holy grail for aspiring musicians. But many are shelved or dropped before they've been given a chance to develop. Those who do sign their rights away and are then subsequently shelved find their careers held up indefinitely. As musician Courtney Love said in a speech in May 2000, "Somewhere along the way, record companies figured out that it's a lot more profitable to control the distribution system than it is to nurture artists. And since the companies didn't have any real competition, artists had no other place to go. Record companies controlled the promotion and marketing; only they had the ability to get lots of radio play, and get records into all the big chain stores. That power put them above both the artists and the audience. They own the plantation."

The same way the record pool made things fairer and better for both the disco DJs and the record labels, file-sharing also could make the business of music much more efficient and equitable for consumers, artists, and labels alike. Artists are learning to make it without the majors, the same way disco DJs made hits without radio. File-sharing and online social networks are giving rise to a new type of infrastructure that allows artists to become self-sufficient and that gives music fans more choice.

Having the backing of a major label with the marketing muscle to put you on every record store shelf and TV channel used to be the only way to the top, but who needs the majors in a world where people watch music videos online and record store chains are going out of business? File-sharing has created a new middle class in music. The musicians in this middle class might not go platinum, but they are making a living.

DJ Jazzy Jeff—who made a name for himself as Will Smith's DJ and producer (back when Smith was the Fresh Prince), is one such artist who left the majors to do his own thing and who is still making a living as a successful producer and DJ. He explained to me why he decided to go the independent route in 2004:

"The business of music is more influential than the music itself. It sucks, and that's why now I'm very supportive of downloading. The Internet has given music back to the people; right now the industry has to be doom and gloom to wash out all of the bad. Artists fight over how they split up the dollar they get per record, but nobody is talking to the guy who gets nine.

"One day I really sat down and did the numbers. You get a dollar per record, and after the recording and promotion of the record, it might be $800,000 spent, which comes out of your cut. You sell 500,000 records, which means you wind up owing the record company $300,000. You've blown the record up, toured all around the world, how in the hell do you owe them $300,000? If they sold half a million records and got $9 per unit, they made nearly $5 million! And you still owe them!!!

"We have to change the structure. You know what made me realize? I did a mixtape about four or five years ago. I went to a couple of the stores and they were like 'we sell mixtapes for $10, and we'll give you $5.' And I was like 'Shit! That's 50 percent! That's more than the record company gave me! And when you get to the big time, you get 10 percent? If your tape blows up, you might sell 10,000 tapes. And you made $50,000. You can't make that when you sell 1 million records. That's why the industry is dead. I know a lot of artists that made records without record companies, but I don't know any record companies that made records without artists."

Many artists welcomed the changes file-sharing brought because they felt the same way as Jeff. A study by the Pew Internet & American Life Project asked three thousand musicians and songwriters their views on file-sharing in April 2004. A total of 35 percent of those polled said that file-sharing was not necessarily bad, because it helped market and distribute their work; 35 percent said file-sharing had actually boosted their reputations. Only 23 percent of those asked agreed that file-sharing was harmful; 83 percent said they had deliberately put free samples of their music online.

Until recently, the record industry had made no real attempt to legitimize file-sharing. The majors responded the same way they did to the disco DJs, treating the prospect of a legitimate file-sharing business as a second-class way of doing things. Instead of responding to this Pirate's Dilemma by competing, the industry fought against file-sharing, imposing unworkable restrictions of digital rights management* on paid-for MP3 files, criminalizing legitimate music fans.

In 2005 Sony-BMG covertly added "rootkit" software in their products, a type of spyware that secretly installed itself on to the computers of their customers, allowing them to make only three copies of their CD and relaying private information about how their customers were using their computers back to Sony-BMG. This was done without customer permission or knowledge, and trying to uninstall the soft-

---

*Digital rights management (DRM) is a flawed protection system used on some legal music download sites that prevents you from copying your music the way you would a CD or a tape. It has not stopped piracy at all, but it treats fans as criminals, preventing them from backing up music legally.

ware from your computer could potentially melt down your entire system. Millions of computers worldwide were affected by this corporate-sponsored virus, which did nothing to combat piracy but outraged many customers who had chosen to legitimately purchase their music rather than download it illegally.

As founder of O'Reilly Media, Tim O'Reilly once noted, the thing to fear is not piracy, but obscurity. Instead of figuring out how to embrace digital formats, when the labels decided to turn their customers into the bad guys, many customers turned their backs on them. Ten years ago there were six major labels. Now there are three. Soon there will probably be two. Suing consumers trying to figure out a new distribution system makes about as much sense as only allowing the DJs who promote your records to collect them between 2:00 P.M. and 4:00 P.M.

The hip-hop group Public Enemy was one of the first to understand this new business model, and Chuck D of the group was one of the first to grasp what was happening. When he was invited to address the U.S. Congress Committee on Small Businesses hearing on downloadable music in May 2000, he told them the music business "had to be eradicated for everybody to participate and start from scratch. . . . A business model will come out of this new century," he said. "It won't destroy the old companies, but it will reconfigure their ways."

Chuck's prophecy is coming true.

Downloading is blamed for all the majors' woes, but the reality isn't so straightforward. It was the majors' *response* to downloading that was the real problem. A 2004 Harvard study that matched the hard data on downloading against the actual market performance of the songs and albums being downloaded found that any negative effect downloading has on CD sales was "statistically indistinguishable from zero." The study concluded that file-sharing was actually *boosting* CD sales for the top 25 percent of albums that had more than six hundred thousand sales. According to the study, for every 150 songs downloaded, sales jumped by one CD, because the people downloading these songs and albums were not people who would have bought these albums or singles in the first place.

File-sharing created a new market and is attracting a new type of music fan. The problem is the same as the problem with the disco DJs. The music industry hasn't yet worked out how to legitimize this new way of sharing. When an industry responds to a Pirate's Dilemma by fighting rather than competing, it runs the risk of missing out on new opportunities.

The Recording Industry Association of America (RIAA) blames file-sharing for the industry's decline, ignoring many other factors. Radio ratings have plummeted in recent years, as more people tune into MP3 players or talk on their cell phones rather than listening to the top forty on their drive home from work. The RIAA has refused to recognize the potential of file-sharing as a new format. According to their statistics, in the first half of 2005, U.S. music retail sales fell by $266.1 million. But as a paper on the effects of file-sharing by MIT published in late 2005 noted, this figure "does not take into account digital music sales (such as iTunes) which have increased by $124.5 million (169.9 percent) compared to the same period last year. However, when this is taken into account, the loss is almost halved."

The paper concluded that "allowing the recording industry to proceed with their lawsuits is not the solution. Despite these suits, online piracy is still rampant. The recording industry somehow needs to work with these software companies and come up with a system that is mutually agreeable and effective." A study commissioned by the Australian attorney general's office in 2006 similarly argued that the music and software industries were attributing sales losses to piracy, with no solid evidence to back up their allegations.

The truth is that the CD market went into decline because it became an obsolete format, peddled by an out-of-touch industry too stubborn to change. The only reason why the majors had it so good for so long was they could keep selling people back their entire record collection on tape, then CD. Once the majors became multinationals, complacency set in and output suffered. Add to this the consolidation of radio stations into similar conglomerates, and suddenly you have a business with a range of products as diverse as a McDonald's menu. The death of the record industry was the best thing that could have happened to the business of making music.

It took a company that truly understood sharing to make the first steps to legitimize downloading on a grand scale. It was no coincidence that this company was Apple, a product of the Homebrew Computer Club. iTunes proved that music no longer needed a physical system of distribution to be a legitimate, profitable business. Selling music online independently has been made easy, allowing bands to grow fan bases independently. Suddenly radio playlists, MTV, and A&R guys aren't the all-powerful gatekeepers anymore. At long last the music industry is becoming a democracy.

This new democracy looks a lot like the model used by the music business in China. A total of 95 percent of all CDs sold there are pirate copies. This is because there are such tight restrictions on the legitimate sale of foreign media, and also because in Chinese society, the idea of paying for downloading music is, by and large, considered ridiculous. Recorded music is effectively a public good, free at the point of consumption. Yet a large middle class of artists make a living there, primarily from live performances. As columnist Kevin Maney wrote for *USA Today*, "Chinese rock stars aren't getting as wealthy as, say, Michael Jackson, but . . . why should they? Only a relatively few American rockers ever sell enough CDs to get fabulously rich. Should society care if rockers can't afford to build their own backyard amusement parks?"

Celebrity magazines might not have as much to write about, but as far as the business of music is concerned, file-sharing has meant that every aspect of the business (apart from selling the little plastic disks part) appears to be doing better. Since 2005, the legal download market has begun to flourish, with sales worldwide tripling that year, to $1.1 billion. Demand for live music, from barroom acts all the way to stadium-filling rock stars, has grown exponentially since the advent of downloading, as local bands use online social networks such as MySpace to promote themselves beyond their hometowns to worldwide audiences.

Live music has grown because music has become more important to us as it has become more accessible. As MP3 players converge with other products, music is becoming a feature of everything we do. Apple sold thirty-five million iPods in 2005, but Nokia sold forty-five million cell phones that could play music, two years before the iPhone came along. Meanwhile Oakley plumbed an MP3 player into its range of sunglasses and Swiss Army installed one in its latest penknife. The year 2006 saw the first single go to number one on downloads alone. "Crazy" by the group Gnarls Barkley (aka singer Cee-Lo Green and our friend from chapter 3 DJ Danger Mouse) hit the number-one spot in the United Kingdom. "You really think you're in control?" sang Cee-Lo, maybe not intentionally to the record industry. "Well, I think you're crazy." And just to prove it, Koopa became the first unsigned band in history to enter the U.K. top forty, in January 2007, with their aptly named single "Blag, Steal, and Borrow."

Recently the major labels have begun to see the benefits of this new reality, learning to work with file-sharing the way they learned to work with disco DJs. "Digital is no longer a disruption but the bright future of our industry," announced Alain Levy, CEO of EMI, in October 2006. "Over 10 percent of music revenue worldwide is now in the digital format and we predict digital will account for around 25 percent of EMI's revenue by 2010. That's a hell of a change in a very short time. We are living in a world of beta products/services waiting for consumer traffic . . . we have to be increasingly flexible and open to the outside world. Closed media companies will quite simply die."

In the summer of 2006, Peter Jenner, former manager of the Clash and Pink Floyd and now a professor at the London School of Economics, became a modern-day Mancuso, proposing a new way for the artists and the labels to pool their resources and earn money from music shared online. "If there were, for instance, a charge of $10 a month for all the music you can use," he said, "and there were 300 million subscribers worldwide, the recorded-music industry would have the same retail turnover that it has now. If we also consider that over 800 million mobile phones are sold every year, which will all be able to receive music, and study the growth of new technologies and their application in the last century, the industry should be confident." The jury is still out on Jenner's solution, but EMI and Universal became the first major labels to begin selling MP3s without DRM encryption in 2007. That February, Apple's Steve Jobs made a plea to all the record companies to abolish DRM completely, saying it was "clearly the best alternative for consumers, and Apple would embrace it in a heartbeat." John Kennedy, the CEO of the IFPI (the International Federation of Phonograph Industries), summed up the music industry's new position on the Pirate's Dilemma it faced: "At long last the threat has become the opportunity."

The sad truth is that it was an opportunity all along. By the end of 2007, some of the world's most successful musicians, including Madonna, Radiohead, and Oasis, had all stopped working with major record companies.

The music industry's response to the Pirate's Dilemma is a lesson all others need to learn from. Movies, video games, magazines, and newspapers have all suffered losses as they make the transition to business models based on electronic distribution. The music industry found out the hard way that resistance is futile. The best way to stop piracy, as Steve Jobs said, is to compete with it.

Instead of fighting change, his computer company saw a way to "embrace it in a heartbeat," legitimize it, and became one of the most powerful players in the music business in a few short years. Apple beat the majors for the same reason the Homebrew Computer Club beat Xerox back in the 1970s: they were the first to treat the threat as an opportunity. The trick is not to fight, but to be the first to market.

When I say that the Pirate's Dilemma is something all other industries need to consider, I mean literally *all* other industries. There are many already using new ways to share electronic information to change things, but sharing isn't just making waves online. A world full of 3-D printers, where downloading sneakers becomes as easy as downloading music, could be just as scary a place for those in the business of selling physical goods. But a world full of open-source 3-D printers could be terrifying.

3-D.I.Y. Part 2: The New Batch

As we saw in chapter 1, the big machine that punk raged against is being broken into smaller, faster, more efficient ones, albeit ones that can print machines of their own.

Even so, Adrian Bowyer, the 3-D printer developer we met previously, sees even more profound possibilities in the 3-D printer's future.

Bowyer and his team are developing an open-source 3-D printer that can print a 3-D printer called the "Replicating Rapid Prototyper," or RepRap for short.

"I realized that it ought to be possible to design a 3-D printing machine that could make almost all its own parts," Bowyer explains. "You'd have to put the machine together yourself. But it would effectively be reproducing, albeit with help from a person. . . . The best definition of biology is that it's the study of things that reproduce. My proposed machine would reproduce, and so a lot of biological laws would automatically apply to it, the most obvious one being Darwin's law of evolution." Not only will the RepRap reproduce faster than a wet gremlin eating chicken after midnight, it will be able to improve itself and evolve.

"It has the potential to create wealth like nothing that has gone before," he envisions of the RepRap. "But immediately this leads to a paradox: the RepRap machine itself, and the idea of it, are both worthless. The reason is that nobody can sell a machine that copies itself, because one is all they would ever sell. The machine's cost has got to drop to the price of its raw materials plus the labor cost of assembling it—it kills the whole idea of added value."

Bowyer and his team are on a mission to subvert the status quo. Using open-source licenses that do not allow anyone to patent the technology, the RepRap's design will be free to download, kicking down the last barrier to the world stage once and for all. "We all know that, if it were not for trade restrictions imposed by the rich, the poor would be growing all the world's food," he says. "They would thereby cease to be so poor. My primary aim is that RepRap will turn manufacturing into agriculture, and that the poor—who will have the most competitive labor cost of assembly—will thereby be able to use it to elevate themselves.

"3-D printing will completely replace vast swathes of manufacturing industry. Our initial RepRap machine will be quite modest. . . . But then Darwin will take over. Anyone with a RepRap machine can redesign it to improve it, then use their machine to make their redesign. Those improvements will be posted back on the Web, and so I think it will evolve very rapidly in a number of directions. We will also see something akin to speciation as the types of machines diverge. But, of course, any change that makes a machine unable to copy itself becomes a dead end, just as with living organisms."

Perfect Information

Open-source culture has the potential to turn the 3-D printer, or any other object or idea, into a living organism. And this radical idea based on sharing and D.I.Y. is making some profound changes in the way we live.

A concept exists in economic theory known as perfect information, which describes a state of complete knowledge about the actions of others, instantaneously updated as new information comes to light. It is a purely theoretical, impossible construct, but in a world where Wikipedia is growing exponentially, the Gawker Stalker map gives you George Clooney's exact coordinates in real time, and you can spend hours Googling the crap out of that girl you met last Thursday, we may be edging a little bit closer to it.

Schools and colleges have always shared the hackers' sentiment that information wants to be free, and many are freeing theirs. Educational resources are being made available to the public all over the world. Free, open-source educational tools and podcast lectures from some of the world's finest institutions, such as MIT's OpenCourseWare, are now available to people who would previously have been denied access to academia. Free education for billions of people would have a profound, positive effect on the planet. Mark Twain once said that he never let schooling interfere with his education; now getting into a school doesn't have to be a barrier to entry for anyone who wants to learn.

Sharing information in new ways is affecting who is educated, but also *how* they are educated. Blogging assignments, educational podcasts, and class wikis are becoming increasingly popular as school 2.0 becomes a reality. Education has never been as exciting as other content on offer to kids, such as video games, but it would appear that that is changing. "Never in twenty-five years of teaching have I seen a more powerful motivator for writing than blogs," teacher Mark Ahlness told the *Seattle Times*, "and that's because of the audience. Writing is not just taped on the refrigerator and then put in the recycle bin. It's out there for the world to see. Kids realize other people are reading what they write."

Many open-source collaborations are educating even the smartest of us. The Human Genome Project is a great example of this. The project was the result of some of the best and brightest scientists from academia and several huge pharmaceutical companies getting together to collaborate and create a public good: a map of our DNA—the human operating system, a living Linux.

Because so much information is being shared so widely, knowledge and power are being distributed farther than ever before in history. The stock of human knowledge is doubling every five years. "The walls dividing institutions will crumble," predict Anthony D. Williams and Don Tapscott in their book *Wikinomics*, "and open scientific networks will emerge in their place. . . . All of the world's scientific data and research will at last be available to every single researcher—gratis—without prejudice or burden."

The open society forming around us is utilizing resources to achieve greater efficiencies than markets alone can. It's also creating some new killer applications, tackling some of our biggest questions.

A great example of this is community computing. Community computing is a way to create vast amounts of decentralized computer power by connecting home computers together like Voltron, using their spare disk space to do massive calculations and process vast swathes of data that no single supercomputer could handle. By signing up online to services such as SETI@home, which processes radio frequencies from outer space (SETI stands for the search for extra terrestrial intelligence), instead of just going on standby, your laptop joins more than five million other PCs linked together to search for flying saucers whenever you're not using it.*

Community computing uses distributed networks of PCs, Macs, and

---

*Maybe SETI should look in the museum at Fort Eustis, Virginia, or the Smithsonian Air and Space Museum in Maryland, where there still exist two prototype flying saucers that were built by the U.S. Army and U.S. Air Force between 1958 and 1959. The saucers, known as "Avrocars," were originally developed by a Canadian company in 1954 and bought by the U.S. military. The project was abandoned after more than $10 million had been sunk into the secretive operation and the highly unstable craft could only make it three feet off the ground. It's clear that the flying saucer business should have gone open source a long time ago.

laptops to work on potential cures and medicines for cancer and AIDS, render digital animation for movies, predict the weather, and crunch huge numbers so we can better understand global warming. By sharing disk space like it was Loft space, distributed computer networks are faster than our most powerful supercomputers with enough PCs in the chain. Stanford University had signed up fifteen thousand PlayStation 3 users by April 2007, who donated their console's spare processing power to biological research. This distributed computing network of PlayStation 3s is faster than the fastest supercomputer in the world.

People are figuring out new ways to share knowledge that have serious implications for many industries, most of them positive. Lawunderground.org is attempting to democratize the legal process, using law students and volunteer lawyers to pool their knowledge and provide free access to legal information in the form of a wiki, which generates legal advice based on the questions you ask it. Doctors are using a Google search of more than three billion medical articles to help them diagnose patients (a study carried out in 2006 showed that 58 percent of the time, Google made the right diagnosis). Several projects, such as the Science Commons, are making scientific knowledge and findings more accessible to the general public. Systems creating free substitutes for all kinds of basic processes and services that used to be based on sharing are things you had to pay for, as advice from doctors, lawyers, and teachers becomes as downloadable as music. The customized information that lawyers, doctors, and teachers give will still be expensive; this isn't about undermining their ability to earn money. What's actually being undermined is the very idea of why we work.

When Work Stops Working

The success of open-source initiatives proves that money isn't the only thing making the world go 'round. As Pekka Himanen observes in *The Hacker Ethic*, capitalism is based on the notion that it is our duty to work. The nature of the work doesn't matter; it's just about doing it. This notion, first suggested by St. Benedict, an abbot in the sixth century, evolved into the Western work ethic (where we do work that doesn't always matter most to us, but it's for money rather than the monastery). This work ethic has never been perfect (even for Benedict—some of his monks tried to poison him), but is increasingly coming unstuck.

We live in a world that has been governed by competition for several millennia, but increasingly competition has to compete with cooperation.

Work-centeredness was long ago replaced with self-centeredness, but this drive to express ourselves is also forging a new community spirit. As Linus Torvalds writes in *The Hacker Ethic*, "The reason that Linux hackers do something is that they find it to be very interesting and they like to share this interesting thing with others. Suddenly you both get entertainment from the fact you are doing something interesting, and you get the social part." Our work ethic is more of a play ethic.

We've always harbored desires to create and share, long before the Loft and the Homebrew Computer Club came about. Building community is part of human nature. This previously unseen economy has long been ignored by mainstream economists, but it is now encroaching on the monetary system itself. But rather than eating into the foundations of the free market, it's bolstering them.

Historically, societies have always been more successful when they boast a wealth of public goods on which free enterprise can be founded. Open-source social networks and other systems based on sharing are about a still unimaginable wealth of new public goods on which even more unimaginable new business ideas will be established. It's about new industries creating new value. The Internet was built on UNIX; free code, a public good. On top of that, millions of new community-based private enterprises have been built, from the new media giants such as Google and Yahoo to millions of niche and special-interest businesses even weirder than the "weird" section on PornoTube. The music industry is being replaced by a new middle class, but this isn't just a class of musicians, it's also a new democracy that offers businesses and citizens more opportunities, which is redefining our economic system.

Based on a $9 million research project into open-source culture, authors Don Tapscott and Anthony D. Williams published their 2007 book *Wikinomics*, which concluded that "smart firms can harness collective capability and genius to spur innovation, growth, and success," but to fully realize the potential of an open-source future world require "deep changes in the structure and modus operandi of the corporation and our economy."

The changes that need to be made are largely in our perception. Many think that open-source models are about giving everything away and not making any money. While this is true of some, it's a choice. They are about sharing information, but it is possible to manage what you share so it's a win-win situation for you and others.

How to Build an Open-Source Platform: The Four Pillars of Community

We know how to go about creating a great remix, but how do you encourage others to remix your ideas in an open-source system or social network in ways that will benefit you both? Open-source systems work like the youth cultures that dreamed them up, open environments that can infect people with the passion of those who built them and become self-perpetuating, growing sustainably and often substantially.

Pulling a crowd into an open-source project is a lot like pulling a crowd into a nightclub. To build a great open-source platform that people will want to go to, you need to be a great party promoter. Handing out flyers is not enough. What can you offer the potential users who will turn your idea into the hottest ticket in town? There are four ways to motivate people to participate. To create a great platform people will flock to, you need to build it with one or more of the four pillars of community.

Pillar 1: Altruism
Inspire Your Audience to Help You Start Something

Successful clubs and open-source projects are driven by the passions of their audiences. Clubs inspire partygoers with new sounds. Open-source projects inspire people with new ideas. The Loft gained support because there was nothing else like it. It was worth being a part of. The same is true for Wikipedia, the cause of amassing all our knowledge in one place, for free, is a worthy one. The lawyers who contribute to open-source pro-

jects such as Lawunderground.org do so for the same reasons
disco DJs promoted obscure records in the 1970s for very little
pay: they believe in carving out a different way of doing things.

Pillar 2: Reputation
Let Your Audience Create New Identities and Distinguish Themselves

Altruism inspires people, but so does self-interest. A form of
self-interest that powers both youth cultures and open-source
culture is the desire to create identity. Ravers might wear
brightly colored outfits as a form of conspicuous consumption
designed to communicate something about themselves to
others. Open-source systems flourish when they encourage conspicuous collaboration. Many open-source networks have an
inner core of extremely dedicated users. To encourage this, you
must empower your most dedicated contributors. Reward
users' efforts by making their hard work visible to others. Users
of Internet forums are often graded under a points system,
depending on the number of posts they have made on the
forum. The most dedicated Webmasters on forums are often
volunteers who are motivated by their position of status in the
community and the power they have to control the discussion
and ban unruly members. Reputation drives many of the hard-
core users who make Wikipedia the largest encyclopedia in the
world. It has many contributors, but only about 10 percent of
them contribute ten or more entries. They are competing with
one another. It's a social activity, a form of conspicuous creation
that ups the reputation of users among their peers. Open source
is about decentralization, but in many cases an upper echelon
of core users, working hard just to get a rep, is vital.

Pillar 3: Experience
Give Your Audience a New Experience and the Chance to Improve Their Skills

Flower power, disco, and house all offered their audiences
incredible new experiences on the dance floor. The payoff for

being a collaborator in these movements was walking away with a new experience and being part of something that mattered to you. Old hippies talk about being at Woodstock with reverence for the rest of their lives. Old ravers love telling younger generations that they "weren't there in '88." Open-source models also offer users experiences they might not otherwise get the chance to have.

Collaborators are attracted to great open-source projects so they can say they are a part of it, but many are also looking for experience in a more practical sense: they want to hone their skills and gain hands-on experience. Free blogging software gives users the chance to learn to be journalists. Programmers all over the world support Linux not just because they share Linus Torvald's passion for free software, but also because they want to learn the finer points of the system to boost their own careers. For those interested in getting into the video game industry, creating open-source mods of games is a great way in. The cost of contributing to open-source projects is usually just time. To convince collaborators to spend time on your project, you must make sure their return on this investment is high.

Pillar 4: Pay Them!

At the Loft, David Mancuso paid his partygoers back for coming with homecooked food and fruit punch. Increasingly, paying users back will be an answer for many companies that are attempting to make a profit from open-source and social-networking ventures. If contributors are to share expertise, revenue-sharing models will become more commonplace as more organizations jockey for our spare time, helping to grow a sustainable open-source economy. Already people make full-time jobs out of selling goods on eBay. Online editors will increasingly be paid, too, adding further to the growing number of self-employed people.

Open-source collaborations have to be a win-win situation for the system and its users. Everybody needs to benefit in some way or the model is not sustainable. Creating a great open-source model is about striking a balance between encouraging users to innovate and create without giving away so much that you cannot sustain the model. This might mean you don't give away all your information, but in other cases giving away all of it may be the best solution.

Weaker Boundaries = Stronger Foundations

Some critics argue that open source will completely destroy free enterprise, but what it is actually threatening to do is facilitate free enterprise on a truly democratic basis. The huge disparities of income that exist in the world could be significantly eroded by the free distribution of all kinds of knowledge and information, and if the 3-D printer succeeds, the free distribution of physical goods, too. Open source isn't going to end free enterprise on a global scale, it's going to make it fair.

"I think that we are in for some really radical changes in a lot of social structures, because of the ability to flatten things out and have really open sharing of information," says Wikipedia founder Jimmy Wales. "How it's going to play out in a lot of fields I have no idea. But there are huge opportunities for people who come to things with a new perspective."

Resources are being made available that could decentralize power in unimaginable ways. Giving resources away, exploiting others less, and relinquishing control are defining the most progressive and innovative businesses, movements, and ideas, and have been since the 1970s. The mass market isn't going out of business, but it's learning to do business in a new way.

The new democracy in the music industry gave us more choice, but for the old industry machine it means less dominance for marketing-led manufactured music and more opportunity for organically grown niche acts. We find ourselves with a unique opportunity to share anything that can be transmitted electronically the same way we share music, and all industries could face the same changes. The future depends on whether we fight these changes, or see them for the opportunities they are.

We still need boundaries. But our boundaries now need to be porous. In many areas, ideas of collaboration and collective intelligence are met with fear and contempt. But others are proving that if you let your users add their two cents' worth, soon you have a pile of money.

Some think that open source is digital communism, but it's exactly the opposite. We are laying the public foundations for new ecosystems of private enterprise that will reinvigorate competition and break inefficient monopolies.

The antiauthoritarian ideals of youth culture are becoming something nobody saw coming: a new more extreme, invigorated, and equitable strain of the free market—the decentralized future of capitalism.

As organizations and systems become more open and transparent, as the balance of power between consumers and producers is leveled as we become more connected, another important idea is gaining traction. As we shall now see, it's not enough for new systems to just be connected to their audience; the dialogue between systems and their users needs to be genuine above all else. Our new connections need to be authentic.

CHAPTER 6

Real Talk

How Hip-Hop Makes Billions
and Could Bring About World Peace

Secretary-General Kofi Annan (center), flanked by Christina
Norman (right), president of MTV, and Shawn "Jay-Z" Carter (left),
president and CEO of Def Jam Records, addressing a press
conference to launch the United Nations–MTV global campaign
on water, at U.N. Headquarters in New York.
August 2006 © U.N. Photo/Paulo Filgueiras

One-man corporate behemoth Sean Combs/Puff Daddy/Diddy/What-
ever-his-name-will-be-by-the-time-you-read-this flounces in to Burger
King with his camera crew in tow. Bedecked in oversized Jackie-O
stunna shades, a black and gold Biggie T-shirt, and a leather jacket,
he's shooting a promotion with the multinational fast-food chain that

is almost as famous as he is, to air online on TV site YouTube. "If y'all don't know, I'm here to announce to y'all that Burger King has named me the king of music and fashion," he crows in the grainy video clip.

The sight of a Burger King uniform alone should be enough evidence that this company isn't really in a position to be dishing out such sartorial endorsements. But the real problem here is where Burger King and Diddy were at. The comfort zone for this type of collaboration is the one-way, mainstream media where the broadcaster controls the message and celebrities can get away with the cheesiest of cheesy promotions. But this isn't how you roll on interactive two-way streets such as YouTube. Here, hip-hop legend or not, if the crowd catches you slipping, you better be ready for some real beef.

The video shows Diddy making for the counter and ordering a Whopper before turning to the camera to explain how Burger King had bought a channel just for him and his celebrity friends. A few seconds after ordering, he starts throwing a hissy fit at the poor kid behind the register for fixing his burger too slowly, then muttering begrudgingly when actually asked to pay for it.

The spot was a bad look for Diddy, normally a master at manipulating the media. It drew widespread disdain from the blogosphere, a 2 out of 5 rating on YouTube, and more than seventeen hundred mostly negative viewer comments within a few hours. It served as a depressing reminder of the stagnant state of mainstream hip-hop and how far removed it had become from the ideals that birthed it. On YouTube this kind of posturing was, as MTV News later put it, "about as welcome as a Whopper at a PETA convention."

Diddy failed to keep it real. He didn't show any respect to his audience, delivering a viral video devoid of value, stumbling on to YouTube waving money around, showing no understanding of the medium (you don't need to wave any money around on YouTube—you can post up as many videos as you like and create your own channels free of charge). This was why it wasn't long before the self-proclaimed king of music and fashion was taken down by one of YouTube's democratically elected court jesters: amateur filmmaker Lisa Nova.

Lisa stepped up to battle Diddy with her own viral counterpunch, a video of herself walking to her local fruit stand, with no makeup on, hair scraped back, ensconced in an old hoodie. Matching Diddy's swagger with an equal measure of sarcasm, she said, "I'm here to announce that me and the fruit stand have gotten together, and the fruit stand has decided to name me the queen of music and fashion." Ordering her fruit with everything on it (salt, pepper, mayonnaise, chili . . .), Lisa explains, "Me and the fruit stand have gotten together to buy our own channel on YouTube, even though they're free . . . just 'cos we're *that* smart," before giving the fruit vendor grief for not getting her stuff fast enough, muttering when asked to pay for it, etc.

It was an instant hit, scoring 5 out of 5, much online worship, and sparking even more Diddy TV parodies. Nova was crowned queen of YouTube for the next five minutes (which is the maximum amount of time you can be the king/queen of YouTube before the next online viral video sensation comes along), while Diddy's people quietly removed his original clip. Nova has no hip-hop credentials whatsoever, but she still managed to bring it to one of the movement's most famous icons because she kept it real.

The importance of authenticity is one of the most misunderstood factors in hip-hop—even Diddy gets it wrong sometimes. Hip-hop has dominated youth culture for decades, and has bred brilliant entrepreneurs who are now among the richest people in America. It is also increasingly informing thinkers, politicians, and decision makers as the hip-hop generation come of age.

Keeping it real and striking a chord with a huge audience is how hip-hop took over, but keeping it real is a trend bigger than hip-hop, now used to speak to consumers, voters, and entire nations. As we saw in chapter 4, we are becoming more immune to marketing—consumers are as brand-savvy as ad agencies, and we only respond to advertising with a genuine value for us. It doesn't matter if you are a student sending out a résumé, a CEO repositioning a brand, or a rapper promoting a mixtape. Your audience is real, and as Jay-Z once put it, "real recognize real," so you have to be, too, or they won't listen.

Technology has connected us in new ways—we have the opportunity to speak to more people than at any time previously in history. Now we need a way to communicate effectively. In youth culture, the dominant language is hip-hop. In the grand scheme of things, the root of this language is real talk—the art of making authentic connections.

Reality Used to Be a Friend of Mine

Today consumers crave reality. Previous generations grew up on TV shows such as *I Love Lucy*, wanting to believe in an ideal dream world. Now magazines snap celebrities warts, nip slips, and all, and "reality" TV thrives on half-truths stranger than fiction. We take comfort in how weird everybody else is.

In the past thirty-years, the hip-hop generation* has discarded the concept of cultural authority. In a world where product placements are broadcast by trusted networks as news pieces and we are approached by make-believe MySpace friends made of spam, it's getting harder to believe what we see and hear.

As a result, we thirst for authenticity like never before. With mass personalization has come the need for everything to feel more personal. The only way to move the crowd and rally a community is with genuine connections. But the need to forge a real bond with a mistrusting audience is not new.

As Saul Alinsky, the godfather of activism and rallying communities, wrote in *Rules for Radicals*, "In the beginning the incoming organizer must establish his identity or, putting it another way, get his license to operate. He must have a reason for being there, a reason acceptable to the people." The way hip-hop initially took shape as a grassroots movement and evolved into a global language of authenticity could have come right out of the radical activists' textbook.

In the beginning, hip-hop got its license to operate in the South Bronx because it was an escape, a way for people to stop fighting and to channel that energy into breaking, rapping, DJing, and graffiti. It got

---

*The term "hip-hop generation" loosely refers to those who grew up or are growing up after the boomers. Just as every boomer isn't a rock 'n' roll fanatic, I'm not suggesting that everyone who grew up after them is a hip-hop nerd who has memorized every KRS-ONE lyric ever recorded. But as KRS-ONE once said, "Rap is something you do, hip-hop is something you live." In the same way that rock colored the mind-set of a generation, all of us, boomers included, now find ourselves living in a hip-hop world.

acceptance outside of the Bronx by borrowing and remixing elements from other scenes, such as punk, funk, and disco, and whole new audiences found themselves identifying with it. Anyone can be part of hip-hop, anyone can borrow it, but nobody can own it. It is defined by participation and collaboration.

Hip-hop is not a sound, culture, or movement at all. It is an open-source system, which is why it has become such a great business model. Sociological shifts usually rob youth cultures of their value. Teddy boys, new romantics, and greasers no longer seem relevant or threatening to most people, but hip-hop is still right there because it evolves constantly. Many youth cultures stop evolving at some point, develop too many rigid structures and pretensions, stagnate, and die. Others are devoured by the mainstream until nothing is left. But hip-hop refuses to go out like that, instead using the remix to devour everything in its path.

Globalization has only worked to hip-hop's advantage. But it is not a colonial powerhouse with lesser regional outposts; it is a decentralized network that has self-sufficient hubs on every continent. It is a model of how globalization should work. Around the world it has been appropriated into many localized versions, which together form a loose-knit, open-source network through which people can communicate, collaborate, and empower themselves.

The world music on sale in the front of Starbucks won't unite the planet in this way, but hip-hop is truly universal. It uses cultural differences as instruments to celebrate our similarities, as part of a global drum pattern beating out a desire for change. Hip-hop doesn't recognize or respect tradition in the traditional sense. It grew from a community who'd had their history stolen, and while many cultures have long been defined and confined by their histories, hip-hop took over because it didn't have to stick to just one, and as a result it is now capable of speaking to us all.

Hip-hop had a license to operate in the Bronx, but by relying on authentic connections, it now has a license to operate everywhere. Burger King and Diddy didn't make this kind of connection, but the story of one of the first hip-hop entrepreneurs to turn the scene into a brand, outside the world of music, is a story of authentic connection that begins in another chain restaurant.

Escape from the Red Lobster

Many good stories are told in three acts. But Daymond John's is a story better told with three hats. Hat one, scene one, opens in Hollis, Queens, in the early 1990s, where John is working at the Red Lobster restaurant. Under the waiter's hat is a frustrated entrepreneur obsessed with hip-hop culture. "It was always huge to me," he reminisces. "When I was eleven, twelve years old and it was just the mixtapes, it was huge, it was as big as the world is."

Maybe there was something in the water in Hollis, because more than a few visionaries who grew up there could clearly see there was something in hip-hop. In his immediate circle of friends was Irv Gotti, who would go on to found the multimillion-dollar record label Murder, Inc., and Hype Williams, who would become rap music's most legendary video director. Russell Simmons, founder of Def Jam Records and one of America's most prolific entrepreneurs, also hails from there.

Daymond John started in hip-hop as a break-dancer, calling himself "Kid Express." He caught a lucky break in the 1980s when yet another prolific teen from Queens, named James Todd Smith III, better known as LL Cool J, went on tour. John got the chance to tag along, and was fast-tracked into the scene's inner circle. "At that tour I met everybody else and ended up going to a lot of tours," he remembers. Here his role in the hip-hop world began to take shape.

Enamored with hip-hop fashion, John became something of a style scientist, rocking classic hip-hop brands such as Ellesse, Le Coq Sportif, and Fila, and pulling old skool power moves such as lacing his kicks chessboard style, pin-tucking his pants into his socks, and perfect-creasing his Levi's. Daymond John's fashion game was mighty healthy, and it led him to a revelation. "Kids would wanna buy the clothes off my back! I realized that this was a culture and that people were dying to get ahold of it. This was a movement that could rival the civil rights time, the Harlem Renaissance, it was a movement where everybody was on the same page, it was more than just the songs."

But John's idealistic vision became clouded when some of the brands he worshiped seemingly betrayed him. "Right around 1990, 1991, I heard that an executive over at Timberland had made a comment, something like 'we don't sell our boots to drug dealers,'" he recalls. "What that is basically saying is that the African Americans that were buying his boots were drug dealers. If you add that to the other rumors that I heard about Tommy Hilfiger saying he doesn't make clothes for us, and Calvin Klein . . . whether they were true or not, now being in the business I know that 90 percent of the rumors you hear are bullshit. But at that point, it was all coming back to the community. I was frustrated because I knew how religiously I bought a lot of those products."

The tours ended, and Kid Express's fast track slowed to a halt. By the time he found himself sidelined at the Red Lobster, John's enthusiasm for hip-hop was clashing with his resentment of the brands he had idolized and their seemingly negative attitude toward the culture.

John came across the second hat to shape his destiny while out shopping in Manhattan one afternoon. Shocked at the $20 price tag of a knitted cap, he thought, *For $20, I could make twenty of these a day.* And suddenly it all clicked. His entrepreneurial spirit, belief in the power of hip-hop, and passion for fashion came together, and so begins the story of Team FUBU.

John recruited three friends and formed For Us, By Us—FUBU for short—a name that stood for the team's genuine commitment to the hip-hop community. They began stitching together their own D.I.Y. hats, and after making $800 in one day selling them outside a mall in Queens, they realized they were on to something. Soon they were turning out T-shirts, baseball caps, and polo shirts, too. The money began to roll in. John quit Red Lobster in 1992, and Team FUBU turned pro.

John set up FUBU's headquarters and factory floor in the basement of his house, which he remortgaged to finance the business. Through friends such as Hype Williams, he persuaded many major artists such as ODB, Mariah Carey, Busta Rhymes, and Run-D.M.C. to wear FUBU clothing in their videos. "They wore them for different reasons," Daymond explains. "They wore them to support us, and secondly we were genuinely fans when we came there, we were honored just to be in their presence. When the artists' stylists would go to Gucci and them guys, they would say, 'Get the fuck outta here, we don't like rappers.' And if a company did come down, they would barely even know the rappers' names and have no respect, it was like, 'Here, wear this, you're lucky we're even here.' And at this point these rappers are millionaires. They don't need the stuff like that, y'know? So it was a movement that was happening that nobody else realized. It was us starting to empower ourselves."

The story of hip-hop is one of a new generation empowering itself by taking down the mainstream from the inside, and the next turn Team FUBU would take was classic hip-hop. By the midnineties FUBU was doing well but found itself stuck under a glass ceiling, unable to get distribution in many mainstream stores. This ceiling was cracked by hat number three, worn by John's old friend and unofficial ambassador for FUBU: LL Cool J.

FUBU was one of the first clothing lines to spring from the font of hip-hop culture, but by the midnineties many brands had caught on to the movement's power as a marketing tool. So it was no surprise when in 1997 the Gap hired LL Cool J to do a TV spot, kitted out in Gap clothing. When LL told John the news, the FUBU CEO made an audacious request.

"LL didn't want to do it at all at first," he told me. "I understand why, he had several endorsement deals on the table. But believe it or not, in the end LL said to me, 'You know what? I'm gonna do this, and it's really not something that's good for my career.'"

On the day of the shoot, LL walked onto the set wearing Gap jeans and a Gap shirt, as per the advertising agency brief. But he was also sporting a powder-blue baseball cap. As John tells it, LL said to Gap's people 'I got this little company that I have, can I wear the hat inside the commercial?' And the Gap says 'No problem.' In their mind it's like, 'Who gives a fuck?'"

With cameras rolling and music booming, LL launched into his thirty-second freestyle as required, dropping watertight rhymes. None of the ad execs saw anything out of the ordinary when he turned and looked directly into the camera, the FUBU logo on his hat clearly visible, finishing his verse with this line:

For Us, By Us, on the down low.

The ad shattered FUBU's glass ceiling, not to mention a few ad execs' careers. "What he was saying to every hip kid in America was this is a FUBU commercial, and I'm slipping it in here and they don't even know," says John. "It was like the Freemasons' sign. It took Gap about a month to find out. When they did, they pulled the commercial, fired the agency and a lot of people at the Gap because of it. A year later, they come to find out that sales at Gap to African Americans had gone up by some astronomical number, because people were going to the Gap because that's where they thought our goods were! They reran the commercials after that, and it aired for a long period of time."

Team FUBU is now a multimillion-dollar brand playing in the big leagues. It grossed an estimated $370 million in 2006, and it operates in more than five thousand stores in some twenty-six countries. The glass ceiling is a distant memory, but FUBU has continued to grow by operating on the down low—stenciling FUBU graffiti onto storefront shutters, transmitting more Trojan horse–like commercials inside other companies' ad campaigns,* and even recording and releasing FUBU-branded albums with the artists who helped them build the label.

FUBU is a classic hip-hop success story. Like hip-hop, FUBU is a grassroots D.I.Y. outfit that came up from the streets, remixing existing media into its own pirate material and forging a strong authentic connection with a massive audience. The start-up from Queens now reigns supreme.

Daymond John and the FUBU brand told the story of a movement that lacked power but that was in a position to seize it. He told it so well that he was able to convince stars to endorse his product for free, pulling off stunts that could have wrecked their careers, but instead converted more fans. The hip-hop community made an authentic connection to John's brand, and FUBU turned that connection into a multimillion-dollar business. If a story doesn't speak to an audience, they will tune it out. And this is not just a truth in hip-hop: there is a long history of brands losing millions because they failed to do so, while others make billions because they did.

---

*In 2005 rapper Mike Jones also "pulled an LL," wearing a FUBU T-shirt in an ad for Reebok.

Blowin' Up Without Going Pop

Let's look at authenticity through the bottom of a beverage glass. Douglas B. Holt observes in his book *How Brands Become Icons*, how PepsiCo's Mountain Dew soda successfully made a name for itself by championing extreme sports and slacker culture, but over a decade it tried three times to co-opt hip-hop, and three times it wiped out and fell flat on its face.

Instead of communicating genuinely with hip-hop, PepsiCo acted like a cultural tourist who didn't speak the language, looking in from the outside and creating a parody of the culture it observed. First, in 1985, Mountain Dew launched a commercial centered around break dancing and BMXing titled "Bikedance." It was so far off the mark, it actually caused sales to decline for the next *two years*. Then in 1993, the drink spawned a hip-hop–inspired but poorly executed cartoon character called "Super Dewd," a hip-hopping, skateboarding, basketball-dunking buffoon who went down so badly that PepsiCo pulled the entire campaign, limping back to their extreme sport comfort zone.

Finally, in 1998, a fleet of reps in Mountain Dew–branded Hummers fanned out across the country, hanging out in urban areas blasting loud music and offering free samples to teenagers outside schools and malls—a strategy borrowed straight from hip-hop labels who promote records in this way. The hip-hop labels had in turn borrowed this strategy from drug pushers, but unlike drug pushers, Mountain Dew hadn't established its license to operate.* Dew then shot an ad featuring rapper Busta Rhymes, which placed him, as Holt tells it, "incongruously, in Dew's world. The spot showed the rapper ice-picking his way up a mountain, dreadlocks and all. . . . The ad seemed to make fun of Dew's existing cultural home while failing to do justice to the hip-hop nation, an unfortunate and unintended effect."

Because they didn't make an authentic connection with the culture, Mountain Dew didn't connect with hip-hop's audience, and the mar-

---

*Uncomfortable as it is, there would seem to be some logic behind promoting a highly caffeinated beverage to kids the same way drug dealers try to sell them dope.

keting moves alienated their core slacker audience, too. Instead of coming off cool, hip, and down with the kids, Mountain Dew ended up looking like your dad dancing to "Baby Got Back" at a wedding.

Contrast that failure with the way designer water company Glacéau worked with Curtis "50 Cent" Jackson in 2005. Glacéau produces Vitamin Water, a line of colorful drinks enhanced with electrolytes and vitamins. It's marketed as an upscale, less sugary alternative to soda, popular with gym bunnies, metrosexuals, and the stroller set. Twenty-six-year-old 50 Cent was hip-hop's favorite cartoon villain, telling street-tough tales of life growing up as a crack dealer. The two brands couldn't be more different. So how did they work together to create a soft drink that became the choice of a new generation?

The partnership between 50 Cent and Glacéau was forged on authentic connections. It started with a story similar to LL Cool J and FUBU, when Glacéau executives spotted 50 Cent drinking Vitamin Water in a commercial he did for Reebok. They decided to reach out to him, and were surprised to discover how much they had in common.

Again, both hailed from Queens, and a healthy lifestyle was something 50 Cent took seriously; he'd already turned down several offers from companies selling sugary soda and alcoholic drinks. "Being as healthy as I am—I don't drink alcohol—Vitamin Water helps me live a healthier lifestyle and control what goes into my body," he explained in a carefully crafted PR statement.

Even though they were both from Queens, there are clearly many differences between a bottled water turned flavor of the month and a crack dealer turned rapper. So to work together, they focused on, to paraphrase MC Rakim, not where they were from, but where they were at.

Both brands were at a similar point in their careers. Despite Diddy's YouTube claim, 50 Cent was the newly crowned king of commercial hip-hop in 2005. He came up by shifting fifty thousand mixtapes on the streets of New York by himself, to become a one-man brand on a par with Donald Trump or Oprah, and getting shot nine times along the way. The year before, he'd made $50 million without releasing a single record. He had a clothing line; a line of Reebok sneakers (that in 2005 was outselling all of Reebok's shoes endorsed by sports personalities); and his book, video game, and movie were all hits that year, too. When he released his second album, *The Massacre*, he told me, "I actually had number one, two, and three in the *Billboard* charts the week the album came out. I was the first artist ever to do that and I think that says it all."

Vitamin Water was also a hot young upstart. As consumers shifted away from traditional carbonated sodas to energy drinks and flavored waters, it was climbing a hockey-stick sales curve, growing 250 percent since 2000. "We both grew in a similar sort of way," said Rohan Oza, senior vice president of marketing for Glacéau, to the *New York Daily News*. "He is the hottest music star, and we're the hottest beverage company in the country, so it's a natural fit."

By 2005 both 50 Cent and Vitamin Water had both accumulated some serious swagger. This is where Glacéau found a real connection to the hip-hop star, so they decided to capitalize on it. They did so with a sophistication that has eluded most big brands that try to buy their way into youth culture.

Instead of throwing 50 Cent some money and slapping his face all over their products, they negotiated a deal, and 50 Cent bought a small stake in Glacéau. They then asked him to collaborate with them creatively and design a new flavor of Vitamin Water.

The bright pink grape-flavored drink they created, Formula 50, was branded in the same understated way as the rest of the Vitamin Water line. Packaged simply and clinically in one of their trademark oversized medicinal bottles, there is hardly a mention anywhere on the purple label of an affiliation with 50 Cent. This might seem absurd; why align yourself with a celebrity and not shout about it?

If Vitamin Water had branded Formula 50 with images of a gun-toting, bulletproof-vest–wearing 50 Cent that looked similar to his album covers, they ran the risk of alienating Vitamin Waters' core consumers. It also could have alienated hip-hop fans increasingly turned off by corporations trying to sell them products irrelevant to hip-hop culture, using crass hip-hop stereotypes. It made sense for neither audience; it wouldn't have been real to either of them.

Instead 50 Cent pushed the beverage on his fans covertly, drinking it at shows and subtly slipping it into his 2005 video game *Bulletproof*, in which a virtual Formula 50 bottle makes a cameo as a health power-up, replenishing the pixilated 50 Cent's energy level. Back in the real world, a special-release bottle featuring a platinum and purple label dropped in certain stores (which still only mentioned 50 Cent once, in fine print, and had no other logos or photos), released on the hush-hush like a limited-edition sneaker, to celebrate the release of 50 Cent's *The Massacre*. It was packaged and promoted to 50 Cent's fans so they knew it was his drink, but a soccer mom could buy it and have no idea; 50 Cent hid himself in Vitamin Water in plain sight, like a FUBU hat in a Gap commercial.

Vitamin Water then launched print and TV ads for the drink, once again veering away from 50 Cent's tough-guy image.* Instead they portrayed the drink as a genuine part of the rapper's daily superstar routine. "Fiddy" was pictured drinking it in his private gym before going into his studio, and sipping some with breakfast as he perused *The Wall Street Journal* at his Connecticut mansion. Vitamin Water put 50 Cent in the same upscale limelight as the beverage, where together they shone side-by-side as beacons of a health-conscious lifestyle. And 50 Cent was presented as an inspirational figure to both their core audience and his, without compromising either brand's integrity.

Vitamin Water put together a genuine collaboration that made sense for 50 Cent, Glacéau, hip-hop, and gym bunnies, too. The flavored-water market grew 57 percent in 2005. Vitamin Water grew 200 percent. Coca-Cola bought Glacéau in May 2007 for $4.1 billion in cash.

The Best of Both 'Hoods

In previous chapters I've talked about the ideas behind a youth culture, and then looked at how these ideas impacted the rest of society. But with hip-hop it's impossible to separate the underground youth culture from the mainstream. Hip-hop is still an underground scene, but it also

---

*In contrast, Reebok made a commercial that stuck so closely to this image in 2005, it was banned in the United Kingdom for glorifying gun culture.

exists in every part of mainstream culture. This has long baffled cultural critics, the same way light baffles scientists by existing as waves and particles at the same time. Hip-hop seems to contradict itself at every turn. Youth cultures usually offer people realism or escapism, but hip-hop sells both.

Hip-hop is filled with gritty, unfiltered stories of poverty, tragedy, rage, and violence, but it's also a romanticized vision of the free market, bling, and big pimpin'. It maintains a country house, a fleet of luxury rides, and a private jet, but it will never leave the street, and it remains stationed on the corner, hugging the block. You'll also find it in every middle-class suburb in between, partying in the club, disturbing the peace, or getting cerebral at the coffee shop, while its many cousins can be found in favelas, shanty cities, and slums across the southern hemisphere. It is omnipresent.

Rock can do escapism and realism, too, but hip-hop did something rock never could—it managed to blow up without going pop. It sells a way out of poverty rather than just selling out, painting elaborate pictures of wealth and success, but also by criticizing the system through blunt stories of real-life suffering and violence. In the 1990s, gangsta rap shocked the middle class the same way punk did, but it was effective in getting its message across. Before graphic depictions of inner-city life began to emerge from the West Coast in the late 1980s, many had no idea how desperate life in certain parts of America was (and still is). It was, in the words of Chuck D, "the black CNN." Since then, as acclaimed hip-hop writer Jeff Chang observed, thanks to hip-hop, "old boundaries between activism and arts blurred."

Does it glorify violence gratuitously? Without a doubt, and concerned parents, talk radio hosts, and most of all, other hip-hop artists will continue to dress it down for doing so. Hip-hop has no fiercer critic than hip-hop (it also just happens to be its own biggest fan). How is this movement going to be replaced when the antithesis of hip-hop is . . . hip-hop?

It remains true to itself as an underground movement and a multinational, multibillion-dollar industry in the same instant. In the United States, hip-hop stars rap about buying jewelry and going platinum, while MCs in South Africa talk of exploited workers toiling in platinum mines. Newsstands contain shelves of mass market glossy magazines that document excessive dreams of the lifestyle, while across the street a guy is selling subversive hip-hop literature from a makeshift table. Its contributions to fashion stretch from haute couture to hoochie mama, and it evolved into a scholarly pursuit as easily as it became violent video games and branded bathrobes. How can it constantly contradict itself without tearing itself apart?

Credit Where Credit Is Due

Once again, the answer lies in authenticity. Hip-hop has managed to make connections with several audiences in several different regional and national markets. It works with every scene, sound, and culture it can.

By appropriating everything and authentically connecting to other scenes, hip-hop has gained so much cultural credit, it is now accepted just about everywhere. Nobody in the scene personifies this universal acceptance better than the man who created hip-hop's first major label and later hip-hop's first major credit card: Russell Simmons.

As Simmons tells it, he started out hustling drugs and running with a gang in Queens, but he made his fortune selling a lifestyle. "Hip-hop has many different voices, although [it has] a common kind of social, political, and environmental backdrop," he told me. "There's so many billions of dollars and there is space available that young people can occupy." He's right—but that space is there only because Simmons helped create it. There has been no greater contributor to hip-hop's worldwide acceptance than Simmons, and he managed it because he believed in hip-hop as a cultural force from day one, and because he aligned himself with great people just as hip-hop aligns itself with great sounds.

Simmons started his career by managing Kurtis Blow, who in 1979 became the first rapper ever to be signed to a major label. Then in 1984, Simmons founded Def Jam Records with a middle-class Jewish kid from Long Island named Rick Rubin. Rubin was a punk and metal fan who liked the energy in hip-hop clubs and saw it as the "black punk." Rubin was a great producer, Simmons knew how to hustle, and together they signed some incredible talents such as Run-D.M.C. (a group that included Simmons's brother Joseph, better known as Reverend Run), Public Enemy, LL Cool J, and the Beastie Boys.

Although all these artists fall under the umbrella of hip-hop, this was a diverse lineup, to say the least. Under Simmons and Rubin's guidance, each act was encouraged to play to their strengths and to incorporate diverse sounds and ideas while always staying focused on the core hip-hop market. Run-D.M.C. collaborated with rock band Aerosmith and sold three million copies of "Walk This Way." LL Cool J (short for "Ladies Love Cool James") was hip-hop's original ladies' man. Public Enemy did political and the Beastie Boys were rapping *and* being white at the same time, ten years before Vanilla Ice officially invented it. All of these Def Jam artists are still popular today.

Simmons had always seen hip-hop as more than music, and went on to sell it in many other areas. Today Simmons has a hand in the movie business, fashion, television, energy drinks, online, jewelry, hip-hop/yoga workout DVDs, financial services, and more, all underpinned by hip-hop culture. He's managed to keep an authentic connection to his core hip-hop audience while keeping an eye on the mainstream, in order to stretch his brands like limos and broaden his markets without losing fans along the way.

Swaggernomics

Simmons inspired a generation of hip-hop entrepreneurs; then again, hip-hop was always an outspoken advocate for entrepreneurship. No other subculture has ever been as celebratory or savvy when it comes to the free-market system. Rappers don't just *talk* about getting money, they've become some of the most versatile businesspeople in America. When producers such as Dr. Dre, Timbaland, and Lil Jon work on tracks for other artists, they don't just produce the records they make, they also *brand* them, appearing in the videos and singing hooks, often cross-promoting their own product lines at the same time. For commercial hip-hop stars, having several side hustles is as important as having several clean pairs of kicks.

Hip-hop is a game of braggadocio, and conspicuous consumption is no longer enough to impress. The more you can successfully build and extend your brand and still manage to keep it real, the more you can exaggerate your swagger. Diddy didn't invent the remix, as he claimed on his 2002 album *We Invented the Remix*. But he *became* a remix, permanently rebranding himself and extending his Bad Boy label into one acting career, two restaurants, three apparel lines, several lucrative licensing deals, and fourteen different types of "luxury sneaker."

Meanwhile, rapper Snoop Dogg's endorsement endeavors make most logo-covered professional athletes look like anticorporate prudes. Aside from the requisite clothing line, sneaker deal, and Hollywood career most rappers now feel naked without, "Bigg Boss Dogg" has his own brand of pornographic DVDs, malt liquor, foot-long hot doggs, a skateboard company, a youth American football league (the Snooperbowl), and a line of action figures, not to mention endorsing everything from mobile phones to scooters to "Chronic Candy."* A more diverse line of side hustles is hard to imagine, but Snoop pulls it off by endorsing products that reflect his personality. Hip-hop artists create business empires as a form of self-expression the way the rest of us build MySpace pages.

Hip-hop instills passion in its fans and then demands participation, making entrepreneurs out of even the most reluctant. When artist and producer Pharrell Williams was growing up in Virginia, hard work just wasn't his thing; he was fired from three separate McDonald's restaurants. "I didn't give a fuck, just as long as I didn't have to work," he told me in 2004, lounging in London's exclusive St. Martin's Lane Hotel. But the hip-hop bug bit him, and Williams worked so tirelessly to refine his craft that by 2003, 43 percent of the records played on U.S. radio that year were his handiwork. Since then the Grammy Award–winning producer turned one-man band has been inspired to launch a sneaker line, two clothing labels, and purchase a handful of Fatburger fast-food restaurant franchises. "When you love something so much," he says, "and are that passionate about it, it won't feel like work. Lazy people just gotta find their passion, man, that's all."

Hip-hop is not just about doing it yourself, but also about working

---

*A Swiss line of confectionary that tastes like weed and is banned in some parts of the United States.

damn hard for yourself. Hip-hop breeds its success stories in-house, influencing its fans to follow their example. It is an extension of the punk mind-set that retains rebellion and hedonism but constantly reminds its listeners of the importance of staying on their grind and working hard. Many artists and fans don't like the fact that money has changed hip-hop. But hip-hop also has changed how many artists, fans, and corporations think about making money.

The business acumen behind hip-hop and the fact that it made entrepreneurship cool is one of its strongest attributes. Georgia-based MC Young Jeezy constantly reminds fans he is about the business of music rather than music itself, asserting, "I'm not a rapper, I'm a motivational speaker." Part of hip-hop's appeal is that it is viewed by many as a way out—a path to success that bypasses conventional routes to the top, routes that remain closed to many. Hip-hop offers sound advice on marketing, distribution, PR, promotion, and more. No other music scene in the history of the music business has been quite so obsessed with the business of music. Ninety-nine percent of aspiring MCs won't become the next 50 Cent, but they will learn something about building a brand, and they'll gain practical experience that isn't available in any classroom. These days the first thing an aspiring MC may write is a business plan.*

Successful rappers have become multinational corporations. In 2005 Jay-Z, whose current business interests include, among other things, Roc-A-Fella records, Roc-A-Wear clothing, a line of luxury watches, S. Carter sneakers, the 40/40 Club, and a stake in the New Jersey Nets basketball team, hit this particular nail on the head. He dropped a line on the remix of "Diamonds from Sierra Leone" by Kanye West, saying, "I'm not a businessman/I'm a *business*, man/So let me handle my business, damn!"

He was also referring to the fact that he had recently been made president and CEO of the record label he had been signed to for years: Def Jam Records. The move looked like a publicity stunt at first, and

---

*According to a 2006 survey by the Junior Achievement Worldwide organization, more than 70 percent of teenagers are interested in starting their own businesses, and 83 percent think self-employment will provide greater job satisfaction.

this was not lost on Jay-Z. "I know people think that this is a vanity job or that I'm the guy that just brings in talent and I'm out of the office three months a year and I only come in once in a while, you know, like the real president," he joked to *The New York Times*. "But yes, I'm really there." It may have seemed crazy, but it makes perfect sense. If rappers are experts at extending brands, as Jay-Z certainly is, why not hire a rapper as CEO? And why stop at record companies? Could Russell Simmons head up GlaxoSmithKline? Should 50 Cent take over Blackwater?

But these are not the most pressing questions we need to ask about hip-hop's destiny. Hip-hop has forged such a strong connection with so many, it can create change like no music scene before it. "I don't think there is any place it doesn't exist," says Daymond John of the movement he grew up with. "Hip-hop artists are addressing the U.N. It could actually overthrow governments. This is the communication of the poor. Music is one of the most powerful ways people communicate with each other. There is no limit to this." Hip-hop has proved to be a great way to generate money, but it's now in a position to generate some serious social change, too.

Don't Believe the Hype

Yes, hip-hop is a commercial juggernaut. It is a high-gloss, well-oiled, intelligent commercial machine able to transform to stay on top like Optimus Prime. But in addition to conquering the commercial sphere, it has simultaneously become the common voice of people around the world. It's a way to express ourselves in common terms, something we've been trying to do since the Tower of Babel fell.

Commercial hip-hop is often perceived as nothing but an empty, misogynistic, violent culture obsessed with hos, bling, and little else. In contrast, the baby boom generation remembers themselves using rock 'n' roll to shake things up in the sixties and end the Vietnam War, as we are now reminded in TV ads for retirement plans. The criticism leveled at commercial hip-hop is justified. Rock 'n' roll certainly changed the world. But the dirty secret is that generation hip-hop is doing it even better.

Many baby boomers consider this generation apathetic compared to themselves. But before the war in Iraq even started, the hip-hop generation had organized the largest protests in history against the decision to go to war. Between January 3 and April 12, 2003, a total of thirty-six million people across the globe took part in almost three thousand protests.

According to hip-hop writer Jeff Chang, evidence for the hip-hop generation's growing political and social clout also can be found in 2004 U.S. election data. He wrote in 2006, "4.3 million more voters between 18 and 29 came to the polls than in 2000, a surge unseen in decades. In other words, the 2004 election marked a historic moment, the electoral emergence of the hip-hop generation." Chang also cites studies such as the UCLA freshman survey that points out that "the hip-hop generation's rate of participation in voluntarism, in political protest and in activism on a wide range of issues is much higher than that of the baby boomer generation during their youth. . . . The myth of an apathetic generation—one even upheld by some of our youngest public intellectuals—is one of the most baseless and insidious lies of our era."

It's Not About a Salary, It's All About Reality

Hip-hop has been right on the money when it comes to building businesses, however, the corporate hustle hip-hop loves so much isn't always about keeping it real. But many hip-hop entrepreneurs are Punk Capitalists; they are social entrepreneurs. In the spirit of keeping it real, hip-hop entrepreneurs use their celebrity status to benefit the communities that put them in the limelight in the first place.

Russell Simmons has long looked at hip-hop's influence in this way. Among his more recent projects, he launched the Rush Card—a Visa debit card aimed at the forty-five million Americans whose credit situations mean they can't qualify for a credit card, as well as a range of conflict-free diamonds.* "The African American community chooses

---

*Conflict diamonds are defined by the United Nations as diamonds that originate from areas controlled by forces or factions opposed to legitimate and internationally recognized governments, and are used to fund military action in opposition to those governments, or in contravention of the decisions of the Security Council.

what cool jewelry happens in the world," he said to me in 2004 before the launch, "but none of us are in the bling bling business. If we gonna buy bling bling, then we gotta bling all the way. I don't know if that industry is gonna like us highlighting the conflicts going on there, but I don't do shit for money."

Another great example is sportswear and sneaker brand Starbury, owned by basketball star and hip-hop fan Stephon Marbury of the New York Knicks. Hip-hop has long harbored an unhealthy fetish for sneakers, from Run-D.M.C. recording "My Adidas," to kids getting shot for their Reebok Pumps in the 1980s, to people camping outside sneaker boutiques all night to cop a limited-edition pair of Nike Dunks.* The more sneakers are hyped before their release, the higher the prices have climbed.

Marbury grew up obsessed with basketball, under hip-hop's shadow in the housing projects of Coney Island, Brooklyn. But top-of-the-line basketball shoes, manufactured cheaply and targeted at kids from low-income families like his, were way out of his league, at $100 to $200 a pair. When Marbury became an NBA star he was, like many NBA stars, offered multimillion-dollar endorsement deals from these same companies. But Marbury saw an opportunity to do something different, a chance to take keeping it real to a whole new level.

Teaming up with low-cost retail outlet Steve & Barry's, Marbury developed his Starbury brand of sneakers and apparel, which retail at rock-bottom prices. The basketball shoes on sale at Steve & Barry's for $14.98 are actually the shoes Marbury wears on the court. "Now parents can afford to go to a store and buy five kids something . . . and the kids can feel good about it, and not feel like 'I've got something on that's wack,'" he says in a promo video on Starbury.com. "We're just flippin' it and turnin' it around."

Starbury proved to be a slam dunk. At Steve & Barry's stores,

---

*A riot broke out at a sneaker store in New York in February 2005, at the launch of Nike's limited-edition "Pigeon" Dunk—a gray and orange shoe with a pigeon embroidered onto the heel. Some people camped out for two nights straight to obtain one of the twenty pairs being released in New York. (One hundred fifty were released worldwide.) The police were called in to break up the melee and escort the lucky few who managed to purchase the sneakers to safety. Knives and baseball bats were reportedly among the utensils found in the streets once the crowd had been dispersed.

demand is so high there are signs up restricting each customer to just ten pairs of sneakers from the Starbury range *per day*. With no big-name sports brand behind him, Stephon Marbury managed to create the realest sneaker ever to emerge from hip-hop culture.

Paying Forward

Hip-hop mastered the art of the sustainable sellout through the notion of keeping it real. It instilled a focus on giving back to the community in people such as Stephon Marbury and Russell Simmons, because giving back has been an integral part of hip-hop since its birth in the Bronx.

Hip-hop is once again becoming a powerful form of collective action, as it was at its birth in the 1970s, only this time it's on a much larger scale. "It's always about what we are giving back," says Russell Simmons. "It's important that we acknowledge that." Rolando Brown, executive director of the Hip Hop Association,* agrees, asserting that it's now time to start spending hip-hop's cultural capital. "We realize there is an opportunity to be change agents," he explained to me over lunch in Harlem. "What we are seeing right now is a lot of people who are tired of the same old song, but will soon have a real opportunity to do that thing." "It done got bigger than us," Diddy told allhiphop.com in 2006, clearly in a more reflective mood after digesting his burger. "It got way bigger than just us. We gotta be laying down the foundation for everybody to come after us."

Diddy's right. When mainstream brands interact with hip-hop—or any other youth culture, for that matter—it works only when the brand is seen to put something back into the culture. Because of its incredible commercial success, increasingly hip-hop is coming under pressure to participate in the world the way it wants the world to participate in hip-hop. It is hip-hop's time to give something back.

This is happening in a number of ways. Hip-hop megastars are starting charities and nonprofits just like other multimillionaires. Diddy runs Daddy's House, a foundation providing funding and edu-

---

*The Hip Hop Association is a nonprofit founded in 2002 to utilize hip-hop to facilitate critical thinking and to foster social change and unity.

cation for underprivileged youths, while 50 Cent has shifted his focus from pieces to weight, launching a child obesity initiative. Russell Simmons now devotes most of his time to philanthropy, as founder of the Hip Hop Summit Action Network and the Rush Philanthropic Arts Foundation. While this in itself doesn't set hip-hoppers apart from other celebrity philanthropists and corporate giving programs, it is a sign of a sleeping giant stirring. Hip-hop is slowly waking up to the fact that it is powerful enough to start revolutions.

Hip-hop has always been a radical disrupter, incredible entrepreneur, and social organizer, but as it increasingly uses these three skills together for social purposes, we may see changes as radical and as exciting as hip-hop's commercial success stories. Hip-hop power brokers have started to jump on the world stage. Russell Simmons was inducted as a goodwill ambassador in a U.N. campaign against global hunger in 2006, while Jay-Z forged a partnership with MTV and the United Nations to draw attention to the millions around the world who do not have access to clean drinking water. "When Jay-Z talks," noted MTV News, "his words reverberate all around the world."

It seems that hip-hop has been chosen to lead. As S. Craig Watkins notes in *Hip Hop Matters*, "The hip-hop generation may soon be the most powerful constituency since the religious right in America." Whoever the first hip-hop president may be, the real power in the movement is not the few at the top leading, but the billions underneath.

Planet Hip-Hop

Former U.N. secretary-general Kofi Annan once described hip-hop as a language. Recognizing its power as a social force, the United Nations included hip-hop in its Millennium Development Goals as a tool to reach and uplift millions of young people around the world, organizing the Global Hip-Hop Summit and enlisting the help of artists such as Snoop Dogg, Gangstarr, and others on several U.N. projects. This is but a glimpse of the movement's potential.

Hip-hop is a common language and a political motivator creating cross-cultural understandings that have never before existed. Hip-hop around the world is influenced by American culture, but many local varieties exist because hip-hop allows itself to be customized in local markets to better suit local tastes.

Within America there are dozens of variations from state to state, from the East Coast to West Coast sounds of yore to southern subgenres such as crunk or chopped and screwed, hyphy in the Bay Area, and Miami bass in Florida. Meanwhile, outside of the United States, Miami bass's cousin baile funk rocks the favelas of Rio. In the Dominican Republic, hip-hop fused with merengue to create meren-rap. It collided with Jamaican dance hall and landed in Latin America as reggaeton. In Europe, France has the second-largest hip-hop market in the world. German hip-hop regularly hits the top ten, while the United Kingdom has grime, and bespoke European scenes stretch across the Continent all the way to Russia. Local adaptations flourish from Shanghai to Seoul to Tokyo. You can hear hip-hop colliding with the bhangra music of northern India and Pakistan when you listen to the hybrid known as desi beats. Scenes are spreading through Australia, intertwining with Maori cultures in the Pacific Islands and moving across to the Middle East, where some Israeli and Palestinian MCs are working together. Regional variations such as Ghana's hip-life scene have weaved themselves into African music as hip-hop negotiates Africa's complex tribal matrix of indigenous cultures, rounding the cape and fusing with house music to become a sound known as kwaito. "Within the context of hip-hop culture, there are so many places people can meet," says Rolando Brown of the Hip-Hop Association. "Hip-hop gives us an opportunity to connect with people that we did not have twenty years ago. It's undervalued, because it's become a clichéd concept, 'Oh, hip-hop is unifying people, so what?' No. It *is*. That's what *it is*. That's amazing and we have to recognize that."

Hip-hop pioneers in the United States such as Afrika Bambaataa always had a global vision for the movement, and it has developed by incorporating local insight into that vision. Hip-hop superstars have managed to connect authentically to people on every continent, even in countries they have never visited. Rozan Ahmed, a U.N. public information officer currently stationed in the Sudan and who was previously my deputy editor at urban music magazine *RWD* in London, sees a strong link between the hip-hop world she was immersed in there and the sentiments of young people she now works with in Africa. "It's uncanny how people living in the bush out here can relate to hip-hop," she tells me. "They relate because they familiarize, they see their dream of escape. It brings hope without even trying to."

For the first time ever, it would seem the world has a youth movement everyone can relate to. "It is one of the only subcultures that still represent rebellion and a sense of self," continues Rozan. But is hip-hop really big enough to make a difference? "If certain artists in places of real power lay off the hip-hop hos and platinum watches and really utilize their influence on so many millions of frustrated kids, then yes— perhaps. I've seen 50 Cent signs in the middle of nowhere, deep in nothing but jungle. I don't even know how those people managed to hear 50 Cent. Can you imagine the impact 50 could make if he took part in, say, the U.N. International Peace Day? Do you know how many more of the people who *need* to be peaceful would pay attention?"

Darfur, Sudan, 2006
© Jamie-James Medina

"Hip-Hop Better Wake Up"

Missy Elliott opened the track "Wake Up" with this statement in 2003. She was not talking about hip-hop as a language that can unite the downtrodden, but the dire state of commercial, mainstream hip-hop. The wake-up call came in 2006. Hip-hop sales in the United States fell dramatically, down 21 percent from 2005. For the first time in twelve years, there wasn't a single rap album in the top ten bestselling albums of the year. In a poll of African Americans by the Associated Press and AOL–Black Voices conducted that year, 50 percent of respondents said hip-hop was a negative force in American society. According to a 2007 study by the Black Youth Project, the majority of young people in America think rap has too many violent images. Hip-hop artist Nas released an album titled *Hip-Hop Is Dead*.

After three decades at the top of the cultural heap, it seems that hip-hop is starting to lose its footing. It is the sound track to our current economic paradigm, but the relevance of both is waning. In its relentless pursuit of the finer material things in life, hip-hop was the perfect accompaniment to late-twentieth-century capitalism. But the economic model behind hip-hop is changing.

The outlook of both our economic model and commercial hip-hop became blinkered. The way many artists evangelize drug dealing, violence, and the pursuit of money, no matter what the cost, is a message critics perceive to be damaging. Critics of our economic model feel the same about the way neoclassical economists paint abstract pictures of the world. Neoclassical economics is based on an irrational belief that unlimited growth can solve everything, without taking into account the long-term effects or social costs of such growth. This business model doesn't work in a world of finite environmental resources, only in some imaginary utopia. This business model is about as sustainable in the real world as the party at a hired mansion full of hired girls in bikinis depicted in your average rap video.

Like commercial hip-hop, neoclassical economics is increasingly coming under fire from the inside. In 2006 hip-hop fans rebelled with their wallets. Real has begun to recognize real in the ivory towers of academia, too. The Post-Autistic Economics (PAE) movement was conceived in 2000, based on the work of a Sorbonne economist named Bernard Guerrien. Today some of the most talented minds in economics around the world are challenging the disconnect between mainstream neoclassical economics and reality. It began with a group of students in France who branded the reigning neoclassical dogma "autistic." As it is with sufferers of autism, they argued, neoclassical economics is intelligent but obsessive and narrowly focused, disengaged from the real world. It advances its cause by making us believe in a set of imaginary conditions, like a rapper who pretends he's a crack dealer just so he can sell more records.

"We believe that understanding real-world economic phenomena is enormously important to the future well-being of humankind," PAE representative Emmanuelle Benicourt told *Adbusters* in 2006, "but that the current narrow, antiquated and naive approaches to economics and economics teaching make this understanding impossible. We therefore hold it to be extremely important, both ethically and economically, that reforms like the ones we have proposed are, in the years to come, carried through."

The PAE movement spread from the Sorbonne to Cambridge to Harvard to every major Ivy League school in the United States and academic institutions around the world. It now has nearly ten thousand members in 150 countries. The movement regularly makes headlines internationally, arguing that, as the great economist Milton Friedman once said, "Economics has become increasingly an arcane branch of mathematics rather than dealing with real economic problems." Dumping toxic waste in poor countries, sweatshop labor, war—all these things make perfect sense economically. They don't make much sense for the people they affect. Glorifying drug dealing, threatening people with gun violence, demoting women to garden tools—all these things make perfect sense on your average commercial hip-hop record. They don't make as much sense to the hip-hop fans switching off in increasing numbers.

It is this unencumbered pursuit of growth that has polluted hip-hop so much. The influence of risk-averse major labels and radio consolidation helped homogenize the culture. Major hip-hop releases have played it safe by sticking to a chart-friendly formula of misguided masculinity and misogyny. As longtime hip-hop fan Dart Adams wrote on his blog Poisonous Paragraphs in 2007, "I used to learn from the hip-hop I grew up on. It was filled with uplifting messages for the youth and had more than enough variety and artistic merit that you couldn't possibly generalize or pigeonhole it into being one monolithic thing. Ever since it became big business and got away from the basics, it has gotten progressively worse. How can these outsiders complain about the current state of rap music when they're part of the reason it's in the state it is now? Why can't they recognize their own double standards and hypocrisy in regards to narrowcasting hip-hop culture?"

Hip-hop can bring attention to many of the problems the world has, but first it needs to address the problems within itself. This youth culture obsessed with authentic connections needs to get real again. The same goes for our economic system. If hip-hop is to remain a rebel, and if neo-classical economics is to continue to govern, both need to wake up.

The End?

Despite its recent commercial woes, hip-hop still has global appeal, and more potential political power (albeit untapped) than any White House administration. Hip-hop has earned a license to operate on every continent by making authentic connections to people and markets the same way it did back in the Bronx. By appropriating everything in its path, it can and has built new brands, sounds, and scenes, which are all able to coexist under its inclusive umbrella. It encourages its audience to put back into the communities they take from. Tracing back hip-hop's path to world domination reveals a way to make a pile of money, or a big difference, or both.

The movement wrote a new chapter in American history, but could be the history of the world's next act. Just like the rest of society, hip-hop is being forced to make a transition because of the forces of Punk Capitalism. Hip-hop's future is uncertain, but one thing is for sure: hip-hop has expanded so far and wide that it is clear it has more than one destiny.

I predict it will have no fewer than three.

The Good Ending

The utopian vision of Afrika Bambaataa and the ancient prophets of hip-hop will be realized, and social harmony will be achieved through two turntables and a microphone. The sales blip will be overcome, and it will continue commercially into the stratosphere, until Snoop has his own airline that guarantees you stay high, and Diddy and Burger King together colonize the moon.

Rap museums and hip-hop golden-era nostalgia radio stations are already here, yet nothing has dethroned it. It will remain a voice of the downtrodden, a sound track that crosses cultural and national boundaries. It will mature from its difficult adolescence into a broad-minded thirtysomething, and it will grow tired of degrading women and bragging about violence, instead focusing on the bigger issues it faces. It is more than thirty-five years old, fully grown and ready to assume responsibility. It is the world leader waiting in the wings ready to empower the planet, all of us united under a groove.

Word to your mother.

The Bad Ending

Hip-hop took over from the inside, like a wolf in sheep's clothing. But now it's just a herd of sheep dressed in adorable little limited-edition wolf outfits with dorky matching sneakers and fitted hats. The politics, rage, and rebellion of groups such as Public Enemy have been replaced by a generation more concerned with Public Enemy member Flavor Flav's VH1 reality show *Flavor of Love*, confirming hip-hop's worst fear: a wack planet.

DJ Premier and graffiti artist HAZE summed it up best on their 1997 underground mixtape *New York Reality Check 101:* "It is the underground that put you on, and it is the underground that will take you off." Hip-hop forgot where it came from. It's about time it got whacked.

Commercial hip-hop no longer feels like it's on the side of the downtrodden. It was once a spanner in the works; now it's just another part of the machine, increasingly self-absorbed and ignorant of the world around it.

Commercial hip-hop went from angry young activist to comfortable, obedient citizen, to bloated, corrupted corporate carcass. Hip-hop sold its soul and is dying slowly, begging to be put out of its misery by a fitter, leaner, younger movement. Let's face it: at nearly forty, it's embarrassing to see it out there in the clubs still pretending it's a kid.

It has become a ridiculous pantomime so far removed from the culture that created it that all meaning has disappeared. Its basic premise that selling out is okay has left it with nothing more to sell. Soon hiphop will be so watered down, the most threatening man in the game will be Turtle from *Entourage*.

Stop kicking it. It's already dead.

The Scooby-Doo Ending

Not so fast! Hip-hop has always played at being the cartoon villain, but under its crass, commercial mask is a movement that's making a difference. Hip-hop has many masks left to shed, and it will never quit changing its identity. It will still be here in a decade, but it may be unrecognizable to its audience today.

Disco shed its skin and became house. Under the crusty chassis of classic rock lurked punk. Change is the only option for the chameleon that is hip-hop because that's how it has always responded to its changing environment. The voices of change are already getting louder. Bling will become passé, rappers will retire, but the real forces that drive hip-hop—telling authentic stories of hope, suffering, hedonism, alienation, and a desire to create change—will not.

The notion of hip-hop as a way out and as a change agent will continue to appeal to people around the globe. What it evolves into may no longer call itself hip-hop, but that's fine. Hip-hop has always acknowledged that the ideas behind it are bigger than hip-hop itself. Hip-hop's new disguises will be many and varied, operating in such a way, as we shall now see, that you may not notice their existence at all.

CHAPTER 7

Ethernomics

Pillow Fights, Happy Slaps, and Other Memes That Leave a Mark

PillowFight Club, February 14, 2006.
© *Scott Beale/Laughing Squid*

"Bohemias. Alternative Subcultures. They were a crucial aspect of industrial civilization in the two previous centuries. They were where industrial civilization went to dream. A sort of unconscious R&D, exploring alternate social strategies. Each one would have a dress code, characteristic forms of artistic expression, a substance or substances of choice, and a set of sexual values at odds with those of the culture at large. And they did, frequently, have locales with which they became associated. But they became extinct."

"Extinct?"

"We started picking them before they could ripen."

—WILLIAM GIBSON,
All Tomorrow's Parties, 1999

Is youth culture now just a relic of a past era, which marketing men and cool hunters have overfished to the point of extinction?

Rock festivals happen only with the say-so of corporate sponsors. Rap stars meet with brand managers to work out how to promote fast food and SUVs in their next record. The latest fashion sensation causing a stir with schoolgirls in Harajuku is dreamed up by marketing consultants in Europe, and then assembled by kids in sweatshops in China. In this fast-moving, hypermaterialistic, technology-saturated age, the idea of youth culture meaning anything anymore seems like a joke.

But this is just how it looks on the surface.

On the surface, commuters cross the palm-lined intersection at Justin Herman Plaza, San Francisco, making their way under the imposing shadow of the Ferry Building's clock tower, backs bowed by the weight of pocketbooks, shopping bags, and impending deadlines. A similar scene plays out in front of the Zhongyou Department Store in Xidan, Beijing, where the fluorescent tubes overhead are diluted by the morning light into a melancholy hue that makes everything feel more sequestered. The scene is no different at London's Liverpool Street train station. A crowd waits on the main concourse, standing motionless like a company of drones as others shuffle past to an accompaniment of cell phones, distant sirens, and the high-pitched hisses of other people's MP3 players. Music is just part of the white noise.

The idea that youth culture might change things seems naive and quaint in an age where new trends are sold back to us before we even knew they were happening. People who still take such things seriously are living in a dream world. The only rebels we take seriously are terrorists.

As if to prove it, a 330-pound car bomb suddenly explodes in the third-floor garage of the exclusive Nogal nightclub in Bogotá, Colombia, punching a hole through the packed leisure complex. A total of thirty-six people are killed; 160 others are injured. Paramedics pull survivors from the rubble and glass as the fiery skeleton of the Nogal sags defeated behind them. The images of the tragedy confirm the world's paranoia as they are instantly beamed back to the crowds in San Francisco, Beijing, and London. Desensitized viewers are delivered their daily dose of fear; the horrific stats scroll across the bottom of our flickering screens. There is no time for context as the network cuts to commercials.

Technology was supposed to make us feel more connected. A "global village," they said. Yet the crowd feels lonelier than ever.

But this is just how it looks on the surface.

Back in Bogotá, a ragtag battalion is moving quickly toward the burning shell of the Nogal, brandishing rifles and AK-47s. They have never known peace; their resolve is ironclad. After this horrific attack, they sound like the last thing this tragedy needs. But this is just how it looks on the surface.

This is a militia of musicians. The guns are known as *escopetarras* (gun guitars). They have been converted into instruments, strings stretched across their barrels. The militia calls itself the Battalion of Immediate Artistic Reaction. They are a loose-knit network that communicates online and that formed immediately after the 2003 car bomb blast. "We arrived there with our guitars and our music, and we realized that the victims, many of whom were crying, were able, through the music, to exorcise their feelings of impotence and pain," organizer Cesar Lopez later told the BBC. They respond instantly to any event that hurts the community, a community torn apart by forty years of fighting between right-wing paramilitaries and the left-wing guerrillas. "Since I was born," says Lopez, "I have seen guns, death, and war. . . . When we hear on the news of an incident, we move immediately with guitars and tambourines to the spot, to accompany those who are the victims."

This battalion is a "flash mob"—a group that mobilizes seemingly instantaneously, with the help of digital communication networks, to do something unusual in public before dispersing just as quickly. They are popping up all over the place, reconnecting the crowds and briefly subverting the loneliness.

As the clock tower in San Francisco strikes 6:00 P.M. on Valentine's Day 2006, more than a thousand of the people in the crowd suddenly pull pillows from their bags and briefcases and begin pulverizing each other with shrieks of laughter. This is PillowFight Club. The only rules are you *do* tell everyone about PillowFight Club. If someone doesn't have a pillow, you cannot hit him or her. If this is your first night at PillowFight Club, you must get feathered.

Feathers burst into the air, cameras flash, and the flash mob battles for a solid half hour before quickly disappearing back into the anonymity of the city. "It's just a meme," pillow fighter Amacker Bull-winkle said to the *San Francisco Chronicle* afterward. "A meme is when a thought goes out and becomes part of consciousness. . . . No injuries, no cops and lots of smiles."

It's 11:00 A.M. on Saturday outside the Zhongyou Department Store in Beijing that September when twelve people, three of them women, suddenly go down on bended knee. Each produces a single red rose and begins begging a girl, also in on the joke, for her hand in marriage. They shout her name, pleading with her as a bewildered audience forms. The group had been organized just minutes earlier by text message. A few minutes later, they disappear. "This is not the first time a flash mob has appeared in China," reported news site Crienglish.com from the scene. "Experts attribute this to the decline in heartfelt communication between people, in contrast to the highly developed communication tools of this age. On the surface, flash mobs seem to try to distinguish themselves from the average Joes; but in a deeper sense, what they are really looking for is the feeling of belonging."

At precisely 7.24 P.M. one Wednesday the following month, the crowd of commuters back at Liverpool Street spontaneously erupts into a party. They roar, laugh, and cheer in unison, each plugged into his or her own MP3 player. Everyone dances to their own tune, but the crowd has become one. They party together for more than an hour, turning one of London's busiest commuter hubs into a bizarre rave that would have been illegal, but its silence broke no laws. Instead, balloons fill the air, and tourists, railway staff, and onlookers watch in amusement. "Perhaps most bizarrely of all," reported *thelondonpaper*, "a whole station of people went home smiling."

The truth is under the surface.

Youth culture isn't dead; it evolved into a moving target and became harder to kill. New ideas are transmitted virally. New movements are ephemeral; most are never more than a blip on the mainstream radar.

Flash mobs and youth culture have been working together for some time—Situationists in London raided Selfridge's department store dressed as a squad of Santas in 1968, handing out stolen toys to children. Thousands in the United Kingdom partied at illegal raves in the 1980s, organized using pirate radio and cell phones the size of ghetto blasters. Radio listeners were told to meet at a certain petrol station, where convoys of cars would congregate and be led out to fields in the middle of nowhere to rave all night. New York's "club kids" in the early 1990s took over doughnut stores and subway cars and partied until the cops came. Temporary scenes are not new, but as old mass movements lose meaning, their temporary replacements are growing in popularity.

Today's flash mobs are the digital Situationists, increasing the peace, subverting the norm, and making us laugh. Each one is different and unique; the only thing they have in common is their transience. But flash mobs are just one new phenomenon; many things are becoming just as temporary. Nanocultures rise and fall in months. Goods are ever more disposable. Owning something is becoming less important than the right to access it. Gibson was right: things that used to be meaningful no longer carry the same weight. Youth cultures and fads have become marketing tools, but deeper underground, something else is happening.

Instead of the subversive words of youth cultures such as punk and hip-hop, the actions of a new breed of nanomovements and subversive systems are sweating the smaller stuff, tearing old models to shreds, and finding new ways to construct meaning and movements. The nanos still add up to something. It seems depth is a thing of the past, but again, this is just how it looks on the surface.

Welcome to youth culture's great disappearing act.

Traveling Without Moving

The alleged disappearance of youth movements has confused cultural commentators for some time, but times have changed.

The advent of the information age brought with it cultures, communities, and companies that are instant, informal, and fleeting. We no longer have to be physically connected to our networks to value them. We don't even care if our friends are physically tangible.* Ideas aren't held back by the constraints of space or time. Evolutionary biologist Richard Dawkins was the first to brand ideas that travel virally "memes"— defining them as units of cultural information transferable from one mind to another. As marketing guru Seth Godin points out in *Unleashing the Ideavirus*, "It took 40 years for radio to have 10 million users . . . 15 years for TV to have 10 million users. It only took 3 years for Netscape to get to 10 million, and it took Hotmail and Napster less than a year. . . . The time it takes for an idea to circulate is approaching zero."

Whether it's an idea, MP3 file, or 3-D printer design, anything can pass through the network, infect us, and take on a life of its own. "I think computer viruses should count as life," argues Stephen Hawking, citing their ability to reproduce and travel. "I think it says something about human nature that the only form of life we have created so far is purely destructive. We've created life in our own image." But not all viruses are destructive. Some man-made viruses, such as youth cultures, are fine examples of friendly bacteria.

Youth culture has been traveling virally for decades, breaking into smaller and smaller pieces along the way. The fragmenting of old systems has been in the works for a while, reaching up like a death crack from the streets all the way to the lofty spires of academic institutions and corporate skyscrapers. Activists, artists, entrepreneurs, and economists are championing an alternative worldview based on sustainable, democratic, decentralized networks. Multinational corporations now have to move as quickly as underground music scenes.

---

*A 2006 survey by the Center for the Digital Future found that 43 percent of online networkers from the United States felt "as strongly" about their Web community as they did about their real-world friends.

This is confusing. Youth cultures move so quickly that companies that used to be able to borrow meaning from them for their ad campaigns are being forced to manufacture meaning themselves. Marketers became obsessed with co-opting temporary trends, training their crosshairs on new youth cultures as soon as they emerged. Youth cultures responded by becoming moving targets, evolving constantly and seeking out new territory to stay relevant. Stay still and they shoot you.

Youth cultures today are small and loose-knit, floating on the electronic ether, making authentic connections with fans worldwide. Fans do not court them exclusively; they maintain open relationships with a number of other niche cultures at the same time. The days when punks had a uniform and were easy to identify are gone; marketers can't tell who we are just by looking at us anymore. Old demographics are becoming obsolete, and old generation gaps are beginning to disappear.

To understand how a nanoculture can take over, let us zoom in on one of the first to rise and fall this way; London's grime scene. This is a story that begins with a classic Pirate's Dilemma, which, oddly enough, was a record called "Dilemma" by a gang of South London radio pirates known as the So Solid Crew.

Original Pirate Material

Imagine for a moment that you are one of the few hundred or so pirate radio DJs who introduced this record to the world.

You're on the fourteenth floor of an East London tower block, standing in a sweltering-hot kitchen that is currently serving as a makeshift studio for the pirate radio station you are a DJ on. The room is hardly big enough for the turntables set up on the counter in front of you, let alone for the three MCs spitting into the microphone. The air is heavy with stale marijuana smoke, and there is condensation dripping from the ceiling—almost as much as there is trash strewn across the floor. You spent the last of this month's paycheck on the new handful of record promos, test presses, and dub plates shoved in the front of your sports bag. (The station manager won't let DJs bring their tunes up to the studio in a *real* record bag, in case the authorities or the neighbors figure out that's where you're transmitting from.) It's just past 2:00 A.M., so now you can't even get the tube home.

But none of this matters, 'cos you've got that feeling. You have a hunch that this record you and the rest of London's pirates will champion is about to change everything.

It's May 2000; the track you are lining up in the headphones is the instrumental version of "Dilemma" by the So Solid Crew that you picked up earlier that week. You've seen weird records flip scenes upside down before. But what you and the other pirate DJs who will spin this record don't know is that by doing so, you will catapult the forty-odd members of the So Solid Crew who produced it to national stardom, bring about the downfall of one music scene, and pave the way for another. This record will ignite a media frenzy, close a string of club nights, open a TV station, a new magazine, inspire artists worldwide, and change the very definition of British street culture.

All you know is that this record is different. It's nuts. It's too simple and it shouldn't work, but that's exactly why it does. You are a U.K. garage DJ; you spin melodic, vocal-led yet bass-heavy club anthems designed to pull girls onto dance floors faster than the tractor beam on the starship *Enterprise*.

However, this record doesn't have that sound. It doesn't adhere to any of U.K. garage's guidelines. "Dilemma" is a Pirate's Dilemma—this instrumental creates a new space, made of nothing but bass, empowering U.K. garage MCs to spontaneously create complex rhymes over the top. Instead of relegating them to the sidelines between vocal tunes, "Dilemma" works like Duke Reid's original instrumentals that changed the reggae scene in the 1960s and birthed the remix.

Through the rain lashing at the window, the city lights seem to blink in step with the lights emanating from the turntables before you. It feels like the whole town might be listening. You reach for the crossfader, cut the track into the mix right on the drop, and kill the vocal garage tune on deck two.

Everything changes.

A sixteen-bar, single, relentless bass note erupts from the system, underpinned by a paper-thin kick drum and a pair of tinny, clipped hand-claps that are almost lost completely to the overpowering low frequencies. The MCs respond instantly, transformed from sideshow hosts into snarling fighters stepping into the arena. This is the main event. The MCs' energetic lyrics ride the bassline effortlessly. This energy is converted into the radio signal traveling up to the link box tacked precariously onto the roof, transmitting to the antennae atop another block some two miles away, and from there, it falls down onto the city with the rain.

The station's cell phone erupts with calls and text messages: "DIS 1 IS NANG! PULL IT UP!!!" "UR 2 MUCH! TUNES HEAVY! RELOAD!" you read as the cell continues to blow, caller after caller begging you to rewind the track. The MCs reach fever pitch, feeding off one another in a frenzy of creativity until it becomes too much. "My DJ! I beg you take this one back!" they shout.

You hit the stop button and drag the record slowly backward across the needle; it makes a sound like a robot dying. The dead air is revived only by the relentless ringing of the phone and the breathless MCs' remarks of self-gratification. You start the track from the beginning. And that's it. That's all it takes. The right record, the right place, and the right time. A new strain of youth culture has just been born.

Dizzee New Heights

Grime traveled through London like a virus. Barring So Solid's chart success, it remained off the mainstream radar as a scene. Because it was so amorphous, for the first few years of its life nobody even knew what to call it.

That was to change on a hot summer's day in Bow, East London, in July 2002. Sitting on a wall on the outside corner of the council estate where he lives is a seventeen-year-old named Dylan Mills. In the distance is the Docklands skyline, one of its three tall towers still under construction, shimmering in the summer haze as cars and commuters hustle out of the city heat for the weekend. No one gives the black teenager in the bright yellow tracksuit and baby blue Nikes a second look as he slouches on the wall on the corner, taking it easy, watching life go by. Dylan is a pirate radio MC. He has arranged to meet me on the corner to give his first ever interview. As it turns out, for Dylan this interview will be the first of thousands.

Like the tower in the distance, Dylan is a British institution under construction. He is an MC, better known as Dizzee Rascal. What you can't see here is the bidding war going on over his first single, "I Luv U," currently the biggest tune on London's pirates even though it hasn't been released anywhere, even though the type of music he makes still doesn't have a name yet.

At the turn of the millennium, Britain's urban music scene became dominated by this angry, angular sound inspired by So Solid's "Dilemma," which was later branded "grime." Fusing together elements from house, U.K. garage, dance hall, and hip-hop, grime survived solely on hype and bravado—images and ideas. It was always more of a meme than a scene.

Emerging from the tower blocks of the capital, it had little physical capital itself. Many grime records were never released, existing only on pirate radio frequencies, recorded on simple, pirated music software programs on home computers. Some records were even made on PlayStations. It has no spiritual home in clubland; there were few clubs; many venues banned the sound; and the police continually closed down organized nights for fear of violence.

It stayed unbranded and underground, part of hip-hop's global underbelly, the ignored voice of a disillusioned section of society dealing with problems the country would rather pretend it didn't have. As music journalist Chris Campion later observed of grime artists in the *Observer Music Monthly,* "These are the bastard sons of Blair's Britain." Grime was the sound of a generation of teenagers criminalized just for wearing hoodies,* facing the myriad problems of the United Kingdom's urban centers such as soaring gun crime, streets flooded with drugs, and opportunities enjoyed by previous generations

---

*There are more than four million security cameras in the United Kingdom, one for every fourteen people. Often petty thieves wear hooded sweats to conceal their identities, and British society has started to become suspicious of anyone wearing one, which is unfortunate because they are worn by millions of people. Some British shopping centers and pubs have now banned them outright—in February 2006 a fifty-eight year-old-teacher was asked to remove her hooded top by security guards as she tried to enter a grocery store.

being washed away. "The street is my inspiration innit—everything that's going on," Dizzee Rascal told me from his spot on the wall in 2002. "It's quiet today; usually it's a bit more wild. It's safer like this, though. There has been bare change round here, it's about adapting. Like the cameras [he points up at a hidden CCTV camera], sly little cameras everywhere, more police, drugs, crime. . . . Everything is changing."

Grime emerged from the remnants of U.K. garage, a very different scene popular in the late 1990s, bristling with bright, bubbly melodies and sugarcoated vocals, underpinned by bouncy bass lines borrowed from the drum 'n' bass scene. U.K. garage was the sound of premillennial optimism in Britain. But it was rendered obsolete by the new world disorder of fear, which required a new, darker sound track.

"It's like people don't even know we exist," Dizzee told me in May 2003 at the Dairy recording studios in Brixton, South London, working on his first album, *Boy in Da Corner.* "But we're underneath. Below this whole thing and we're about to blow up and rise to show there is something."

Sure enough, thanks to a handful of vigilant DJs, journalists, and bloggers, the mainstream discovered Dizzee a few months after his single blew up, and the sound was branded grime. Its harsh portrait of reality shocked Britain's chattering classes, the same way gangsta rap shocked America in the 1990s. But for the style press it was love at first sight. Some saw the United Kingdom's first credible response to hip-hop, others a new wave of black British punk.

Dizzee stayed true to his word, winning the Mercury Music Prize and selling more than 250,000 copies of his first album. For a hot minute, grime was flavor of the month and the majors started waving their checkbooks fervently. The rest of the world began to notice as it spread. "The music has reached New York not through concerts and rare vinyl singles, but through the Internet," wrote *The New York Times* in March 2005. "In London, grime may seem inseparable from the rowdy clubs and fly-by-night pirate radio stations that nurture it. But in New York, grime is computer music—that is, music you listen to on your computer." Grime had finished downloading and successfully installed itself in the wider world. It looked like the next big thing was finally here.

But it wasn't to be. A few MCs from the scene crossed over to mainstream success, but you can count them on one hand—Dizzee was by far the most successful. The media attention was too much, too soon. Grime was pigeonholed as antisocial and violent. The harsh picture of street life painted by MCs quickly painted the entire scene into a corner. It lived fast and died young like punk, but stayed intangible as a commercial entity. Record companies couldn't work out how to sell it, and commercial radio didn't want to play it; it was "too urban," they said. U.S. R&B divas and manufactured bands put together by reality TV shows were much safer bets. Some artists had reasonable album sales, but reasonable was no longer cutting it at the majors.

By late 2005, interest in grime was dwindling in the mainstream press; even Dizzee was distancing himself as he became a bigger artist, and it became increasingly clear he might outlive the scene that birthed him. "People couldn't make up their minds anyway, from 'I Luv U,' saying, 'Wass this? Wass dat?'" he said to me in defense that year. "People are scared of adjusting. That's why I don't like to attach myself to one scene no more, 'cos people can't make up their minds." The next time I saw him was at a party thrown for him by Nike, celebrating the release of his own limited-edition brand of Dizzee Rascal/Nike sneakers. Dizzee was now a millionaire and a household name. He decided to move on.

The mainstream media was thoroughly bored of grime by 2006, and had moved on, too. On the underground it began to sound past its sell-by date and the scene began to split into even smaller ones. Many fans and pirate DJs migrated to a new strain of the funky house scene that was taking shape, or to the emerging nu-rave scene, or to grime's more cerebral cousin, a bass heavy nanoculture known as dubstep.

Grime seemed to rise and fall inside of three years. It was a flash in the pan like punk, but in a world where the media are fragmented into millions of pieces, it's hard to build consensus and a commercial afterlife around a scene the way punk did. Youth culture is now disposable. Hip-hop in the United States is championing a shiny new local interpretation of itself every month, while a hot new rock band arrives every week as last week's heads for the stage door. What has changed is the amount of choices we have. We have so much music available to us, the sample size is too large—it's impossible to observe change. Youth culture can no longer rebel against the status quo in music, because there isn't one.

Despite the backlash, grime survives, though only just. New artists continue to emerge, but remain off the mainstream grid. It is part of music's more democratic model that exists without the major institutions. Many of the scenes most respected artists have formed loose-knit networks of their own within grime, such as the Boy Better Know collective, producing their own albums and merchandise with no relationship to the majors, or the mainstream, at all. The niche market grime relies on is small, but the network at its disposal is global. Its message travels through forums and MP3 files—artists are booked to play all over the world because of Internet portals such as MySpace. It has a worldwide fan base; mainstream hip-hop artists including Jay-Z, LL Cool J, and Lil Jon have all acknowledged it.

London is just one of many cultural capitals churning out new scenes with similar business models. Inside scenes such as grime, the scene is the entire world. Outsiders see a storm in a teacup. If you weren't looking hard enough, you might not notice that the teacup had a weather system at all.

These global nanocultures are evolving. They are becoming more immune to the markets that plunder them for meaning. There isn't even time to pigeonhole new trends before they disappear. First the sections in record stores vanished, and then the record stores themselves did. Now there is just an infinite tangle of new music arriving daily, available to us all without leaving the house.

The strip-mining of youth culture has led to new movements that either blend into the mass media background instantly or die in the glare of the spotlight in seconds, so some nanocultures are staying out of the limelight altogether. Everything gets lost in the din of novelty as competing products, ideas, sounds, and sights from every corner of the globe now compete for our attention. The angry sound of grime was the sound of a frustrated generation, with no movement left to own.

But their frustration is shared by the very people who use youth movements for meaning: advertisers and brands. How can anyone make a mark when everything is eternally lost in the clutter?

Marketing Lessons from the Booo Krooo

In November 2001 I became the founding editor in chief of *RWD* magazine, then a new-music publication focused on the new sounds and cultures emerging from the London pirate radio scene. *RWD* began as U.K. garage was on its way out and grime was being born, and back then we were pretty much the only magazine that cared about either scene. We printed roughly five thousand copies a month with a staff of five, from the dingy back room of a record shop in Crystal Palace, South London. I'd quit a steady job at a big magazine company to join *RWD* on issue 3, because I thought it could be a great magazine. Outside of my day job, I was one of the pirate DJs championing records such as "Dilemma." I'd been DJing on pirate radio and in U.K. garage clubs since I was a teenager, and I saw *RWD* as a way to combine my experience in the magazine business with my love for underground music. I knew working at this start-up would be an adventure. I had no idea what was in store.

Where we were in Crystal Palace was not the nicest part of London. On a normal day in the office, fights would break out, drugs were bought and sold, and sometimes guns were waved around. When the debt collectors came looking for us, it was normal procedure to lock the doors and hide all the rented computer equipment in the garden. I was the only guy there who had ever worked at a magazine before. We had £5,000 of start-up capital. Other magazines laughed at the music we wanted to cover, and few brands wanted to be associated with it. The expert designing our website was a sixteen-year-old named Alex who designed flyers for grime crew So Solid and whose only previous employment had been as a glass collector at Crayford Dog Track (but he'd recently been fired for stealing peanuts and setting fire to a dustbin). On top of that, the music magazine market was shrinking quickly.

We didn't have a snowball's chance in hell.

What we did have was a cool niche title and a shared belief in the pirate culture we were championing. Grime was just beginning to emerge, Dizzee's success was still a few months away, but the So Solid Crew had surprised the country by topping the U.K. pop charts. At first, the majors were eager to sign the next So Solid. But not many people at the labels had a clear understanding of what this new sound was, and the wrong artists were being signed for no good reason.* RWD magazine was ahead of the curve when it came to grime. We knew the labels were watching the artists we featured; in fact we suspected people were getting deals *just because* they were in RWD.

In April 2002 we decided to test the hypothesis. We ran an April fool about a hot new act: the Booo Krooo. We shot a picture of the "Krooo" (myself and a few other members of staff hidden under hats, hoodies, and sunglasses) and ran it with a ridiculous story about them getting signed for £4 million in Japan, their single getting banned, even from pirate radio, and people vomiting on dance floors when they heard the record. We reviewed their make-believe album, giving it a 1 out of 5, and I included their manager's number in the article (which was actually my direct line). When the magazine came out, A&R people from each of the majors phoned, desperate to get a meeting with them. I had talent agencies trying to get the Booo Krooo on their books and DJs telling me they'd been playing the record since January. Stunts like that and a commitment to covering the right artists earned us a lot of credibility on the underground, but not much money to get the debt collectors and local gangsters off our backs.

By early 2002, it was clear Alex was as good at building websites as he was at setting fire to things, and we were getting ready to launch our online version of the magazine. I tried to figure out how to create an effective campaign to promote the launch, but given our nonexistent budget, this was a problem. I'd started to see some viral videos circulating the Net; most of them weren't ads, but I knew they could get an idea across.

---

*In 2002 I interviewed a crew of MCs who did a £250,000 music publishing deal, which seemed to be based on the fact that they used to go to the same school as some members of So Solid. They sold fewer than five hundred copies of their first single and were never heard from again.

We've covered many viruses already, such as the Marc Ecko/ Droga5 video. Stephen Hawking was right about viruses; effective ones have lives of their own. A good idea virus can catapult a brand into the stratosphere, but not all viruses are created equal. It's up to us to make them work.

I realized we had to create something that would be valuable to others and worth their while to forward on. Your idea is your currency; what you're buying is a few seconds of the viewer's time, in which you must gain their trust, entertain or inform them, convince them of your message, and possibly get them to act on it. But it also has to be currency for the user; it has to be funny, informative, or somehow valuable for them to pass on to someone else. In this case, we needed to direct traffic to our website. We needed to convince urban music fans that this was their ultimate destination.

RWD readers and red-faced industry people loved the Booo Krooo stunt, so our illustrator, Art Jaz, and I had kept them alive as a cartoon strip in the magazine. They had struck a chord with our audience, and when it comes to viral marketing, it's your core you need to focus on. If they like your virus, they will spread it to others.

We decided to try turning the cartoon strip into an animation to promote *RWD* online. Our target audience was fifteen-to-twenty-four-year-olds into urban music. The Booo Krooo was a unique property; there was no British equivalent of a show like *South Park*, and we already knew our audience was into the idea. We wrote a script and storyboarded it, focusing on the trials and tribulations of the crew of MCs and their hopeless quest to take over the music industry. We injected the dialogue with slang and elements of street life that would amuse the core but that would appeal to a wider audience at the same time. The magazine's drum 'n' bass editor and I recorded all the audio and music in our bedroom recording studios, and Alex put the sound track together with Art Jaz's illustrations, bringing the Krooo to life. We included the option to click through to *RWD*'s website at the end of the three-minute cartoon, and sent the video out embedded in an e-mail to our modest mailing list.

Once the Krooo hit the Net, the response was overwhelming; the cartoon quickly gained a following, and our website hits spiked. The word was out; within hours we were getting e-mails asking for more. The virus had come to life. Now we had to feed it.

The Booo Krooo virus proved to be a monster. We wrote a second episode, and when it dropped, the virus started to grow like the plant in *Little Shop of Horrors*. Web hits soared. Out of nowhere, we got a phone call from Missy Elliott's people at Atlantic Records, who wanted to know how much it would cost to put Missy in the third episode. We did a deal, and the third animation was sent all over the world and back, appealing to Missy's fans in other countries as well as to the Krooo's core audience at home. Within a few months of launching, the *RWD* site it had become one of the most popular urban music destinations in the world. The Booo Krooo had met its brief and overdelivered. All it had cost us was a little sweat equity.

But the Booo Krooo took on a life of its own. After the third episode we were offered a TV deal, and I wrote a Booo Krooo series that aired all over Europe. Thanks in part to their success, *RWD* became and remains the largest urban music magazine in the United Kingdom. A consortium of investors led by PR guru Matthew Freud and Liz Murdoch bought a stake in the company. We moved into new offices in London Bridge, employing a large team full-time and an army of freelancers.

The Booo Krooo was a great virus. It became a valuable property and revenue stream in its own right, winning our brand a host of new fans and awards. The Booo Krooo went on to release a record and their own line of New Era fitted caps. Alex is now an independent filmmaker who also runs his own design agency. The icing on the cake was when we were awarded the Prince's Trust and Royal Bank of Scotland London Business of the Year Award in 2004, and invited to tea with Prince Charles at St. James's Palace. The first thing Prince Charles said to me was:

"Who does the animations?"

How to Look After a Virus

The story of the grime scene offers us an insight into how all nanocultures can become successful viruses. Its rise and fall is the blueprint for successfully broadcasting an idea in this perpetually temporary new world—a four-step diet plan anyone can use to create and feed a successful virus.

1. **Let the audience make the rules.**

So Solid's record "Dilemma" worked because it gave MCs space to turn the instrumental into whatever they wanted, so the track became a living, breathing song that had a different MC rapping over it each time you heard it on a pirate. Every MC loved it, so all the DJs needed it in their record bag. Soon every teenager in the country had heard it, and So Solid hit the top of the charts. Because U.K. garage wouldn't give MCs that space, it was usurped by the grime scene. Grime became a virus worth spreading because it was open and evolving—it gave its users options instead of rules. The U.K. garage virus became too formulaic and predictable, so it stagnated and died. Viruses are spread by their audiences. Let them make the rules.

2. **Avoid the limelight; talk only to your audience.**

Malcolm Gladwell defines this point in his book on social epidemics *The Tipping Point,* in what he describes as "The Law of the Few." Dizzee Rascal would never have gotten a record deal if he'd just sat in his room mailing demos to records labels. Record labels can't start viruses like that—they buy into them later and take them public. They were not his audience, and he knew it. His audience was London's influential young pirate listeners, so he spoke only to them. They let the labels know who he was on his behalf, and the bidding war started.

If *RWD* had put a big ad somewhere advertising our website as the best urban music site in the United Kingdom, nobody would have believed us. The Booo Krooo pulled a crowd onto the site, giving us the chance to prove it. Even if your idea is so good that everyone will eventually get it, tell it to your core first. They'll tell everyone else afterward, and it will sound a lot better coming from them.

3. **Feed the virus according to its size.**

When the virus takes on a life of its own, you have to feed it, and you must feed it according to its size. Dizzee released his first single, "I Luv U," commercially only when the pirate listeners were going crazy for it. He and his management waited to do a publishing deal when the buzz from that single was at its height. They released the album only when they were sure the mainstream had caught the virus, too.

If we had put Missy Elliott in the first episode of the Booo Krooo, her celebrity would have clouded the cartoon's original identity. But by the third episode we knew our audience got the idea and was ready to accept an intrusion of another brand like that. Because we grew their popularity online first, when the Booo Krooo series hit TV, it pulled in the highest ratings on the digital station it was on.

4. Let it die.

All good things must come to an end. Nanocultures are temporary and won't live forever. Grime fed off the U.K. garage scene until it was strong enough to stand on its own. Dizzee detached himself from the grime virus when he saw that the association was no longer helping him or the grime scene. As grime's popularity began to wane, *RWD* decided to kill the Booo Krooo and move on. Viruses are great tools for artists and brands alike, but if you can't remain detached and recognize the right time to cull the virus, it will die anyway, and drag you down with it.

Roots Culture

These days viral videos are part of many a mainstream ad campaign. Grassroots culture isn't growing quickly enough for all the companies that want to use it, so instead many create their own synthetic grassroots buzz, as artificial as the Booo Krooo, in a process known as "astroturfing." Astroturfing is now a part of the ad industry estimated to be worth, according to *BusinessWeek*, more than $150 million in the United States alone.

Some viral videos don't always hit the spot—think Diddy and Burger King's effort on YouTube. But the Burger King "subservient chicken" website, which features a man in a chicken suit, in a room hooked up to a Webcam, who will carry out (pretty much) any instruction you send him, has been viewed four hundred million times.*

In advertising, viral marketing is one of the few efficient ways through the clutter. Even though some viral agencies charge $500,000 to produce viral spots, that's still incredible value for money if one hundred million people or more watch the video. The way videos are disseminated makes them a lot more likely to hit people actually interested in buying your product (the same cannot be said for traditional TV advertising). But competition is tough; brands are competing with thousands of videos produced by amateurs that are not ads, many of which will be funnier than anything an ad agency can dream up.

Corporate viruses are not just online anymore. They are moving through all kinds of social networks. Procter & Gamble has gone one step further than most, creating entire legions to shill its wares. It currently has more than six hundred thousand "vocalpoint moms," an army of disparate housewives with large social networks fanned out across the United States, who are given a steady supply of free samples and coupons of P&G goods to push on their friends and neighbors. This synthetic movement is bigger than the grime scene.

The vocalpoint moms give feedback to P&G as to what its customers want to see in the marketplace, and have been incredibly effective. According to *Business Week*, sales of Febreze Air Effects increased by 17 percent after the network of moms had at it. P&G also has a junior company of marketers in its ranks, the 225,000 teens who make up the "Tremor" team, who have done promotional stints for third-party music and movie companies on P&G's behalf as well. The company has received criticism for not requiring its buzz armies to disclose their relationship to Procter & Gamble, and for commercializing human interaction. P&G's Steve Knox explained their stance to *Business Week*, arguing, "We have a deeply held belief you don't tell the consumer what to say." However, the article goes on to note, "the company does provide its stealth marketers with product pitches."

---

*Like the Booo Krooo, the Burger King video is a work of fiction. The chicken man isn't live; the whole thing is done with the smoke and mirrors that are prerecorded video clips and word recognition software.

What's also interesting is that P&G defines its voluntary marketing team as consumers, whereas many protesters believed they were acting more like company-sponsored pushers. But just as D.I.Y. blurred the line between producers and consumers, customers are now replacing the R&D and marketing departments, too.

Meanwhile, "pop-up" stores are appearing in urban areas for a few weeks at a time, like commercial flash mobs. These stores, either in conventional retail spaces or temporary spaces of their own, such as converted shipping containers, populate city streets like interactive ads, which is what most "flagship" stores in prime locations aspire to be anyway. A pop-up store gives a brand a temporary shot of kudos, without the lasting hangover effect of an expensive long-term lease that premium retail spaces come with. Target, Kodak, Illy coffee company, *Wired* magazine, and Nike are just a handful of brands that have set up such temporary stores.

The advent of pop-up stores is another indicator of the trend away from physical places. Catalog sales, according to *Fast Company*, increased in the United States from $61 billion a year in 1974 to $133 billion in 2003. Online shopping has been growing 25 percent a year on average since 2001 and is now worth an estimated $65 billion by comScore networks. Browsing times in stores are falling, too. Whether it's shopping or youth culture, we just don't have the time for long-term commitments anymore.

We still need devices of mass production, but they are taking a backseat. Viruses are center stage, the only real capital we have left. We don't need marketing people to pigeonhole music or compartmentalize scenes anymore, because we do it ourselves.

We can transmit to the world a carefully managed perception of who we are, what we think is cool, what we wear and listen to. We need the network or no one will hear us, but we retain the power. Marketers can't sell us meaning; we have to find it in their products, and if we do, and we're passionate about them, we'll happily tell everyone we can. But by the same token, if a brand or an idea makes one wrong move, it can cause the entire crowd to walk away.

Companies have to fight harder for our attention, youth markets are becoming increasingly difficult for brands to penetrate, and so they are working harder than ever to jump on the next big thing. When they do, the effect is sometimes terminal.

Running on Empty

In 2001, viral videos started circulating widely of a new urban sport known as free running. Free running, also known as "parkour," is the spontaneous act of street acrobatics—vaulting, climbing, and jumping on and off street furniture, buildings, and even bridges, performing death-defying stunts. Initially championed by limber youths in the suburbs of Paris, parkour is like skateboarding without the capital requirement—a skateboard. Participants focus on moving in a fluid, uninterrupted style, running and jumping like mime artists pretending to skate. This grassroots movement jumped off in a big way in 2001, but it was branded even before it landed.

Parkour was instantly devoured by media piranhas because of its incredible visual appeal. Free runners appeared in films, advertisements, and news stories within months. BBC Television used it in three separate campaigns and programs in 2002. Toyota, Canon, Nike, and Microsoft all made free-running commercials. James Bond can be seen practicing parkour in the opening sequence of *Casino Royale*. It appeared in several video games; Madonna was soon doing it in a music video; and Adidas released a line of free running–inspired sneakers. It was a real movement, but it was turned into a corporate circus almost instantly. The founders of the sport started as one group who saw free running as a way of life, but soon split over disagreements about what parkour pioneer David Belle described as "the prostitution of the art."

Parkour barely survived the media frenzy, ducking back underground, but it was worse off for it. It's difficult for a movement to gain grassroots appeal if Madonna, James Bond, and the BBC are already into it. Increasingly, when new forms of youth culture survive, it's because they are things the media wouldn't touch with a ten-foot pole—this was very much the case with hip-hop at its inception, for example. With everything from urban legends to conversations with our neighbors about detergents becoming a carefully placed marketing message, it's only at the outer limits of acceptability in society that grassroots movements can find meaning. And pushing people to the limits of acceptability isn't always a great idea.

Hit-Driven Culture

At the same time parkour was being branded to bits in Paris, across the English Channel in London, set against a grimy score, another very different craze was taking off on the 106 bus route in Hackney.

"Happy slap TV" videos started to appear in numbers in 2004, filmed on camera phones and transmitted virally to other phones and over the Net. Happy slaps are videos of teenagers approaching unsuspecting members of the public of all ages and slapping them across the face. It was the ultimate fast track to fifteen seconds of fame. "One of my videos is quite popular and in circulation. I've slapped grown men three times my size before," a twenty-year-old woman from Northwest London boasted to me in an interview. Teenage camera crews moved through the streets and across the nation's playgrounds in packs as the happy slap meme spread. Schoolkids were ruthlessly beaten on film. Commuters who had fallen asleep on trains were rudely awakened with violent slaps. Old people taking the bus home were punched in the face for fun. One boy was stabbed for the camera; another, in North London, is said to have died after being hit over the head with a traffic cone. The homemade snuff film is still circulating on the Internet. A thirty-seven-year-old named David Morley was killed live on camera phone by four youths on London's South Bank. "We're making a documentary about happy slapping. Pose for the camera," said one of the attackers, a fourteen-year-old girl, before kicking him in his head as he bled to death.

The frightening fad became a national nightmare. Commuters worried for their safety as more and more people were slapped, punched, or kicked on the way home. In January 2005 more than ten people were charged with serious assault for happy slapping in London. Soon after, the police announced a mandatory five-year jail term for anyone caught making happy slap videos, and for now, at least, the virus seems to have been contained.

The reason happy slaps were a hit was because they were off-limits. What could be more appealing to a generation brought up on the staged, gonzo-style violence of prowrestling, ultimate fighting, and Jackass? Happy slap TV was the one thing left that kids could own without fear of a corporate takeover. Unlike free running, this was something that the mainstream couldn't go near, except to condemn it. New youth cultures can't be as safe as those of days gone by, because if they stay within socially acceptable limits, marketers pounce, and before long they are just another branded spectacle. Teenagers are going to such extremes to create space for their identities because some of the gaps between them and their parents have gone.

Parents Just Do Understand

The hip-hop generation was the first to grow up in a brand-saturated world. Before hip-hop, as Will Smith and DJ Jazzy Jeff once postulated, it was a given that parents just didn't understand. But now parents who are the age of Smith have the same albums on their iPods as their kids, and the same reissued retro sneakers on their feet. This has serious ramifications for youth culture, commerce, and everything else.

Using youth culture to sell things was once a trusty way to tap into the elusive young audience. Now a cool product, if it can remain cool long enough, can trickle all the way up, even to grandparents. What does it mean now to "grow up" in a world where thirty-year-old men collect designer vinyl toys like they collected Garbage Pail Kids when they were fifteen, where sixty-year-old women have plastic surgery in an effort to look thirty again, and where we all want a Nintendo Wii for Christmas?

The generation gap seems to have become obsolete, and the marketing men have noticed. "People who grew up in the '60s and '70s didn't have brands and the music was very different," says Carl Christopher, manager of content and sponsorship at Sony Entertainment U.K. "A lot of brands revive culture. Nike Air Force Ones just keep getting revived and resuscitated because the brand knows it can get more change out of them. If you have a good product you can aesthetically re-present it. Younger generations will always find a way of rebelling; now it's been done with media and technology rather than clothing and music. That whole shock factor isn't there. Rebellion now is about being a bit cleverer."

"I think the rebellion is that kids aren't rebelling," says Rana Reeves, creative director of PR agency Shine Communications. "They aren't rebelling against the marketers; they want to *be* marketers. That's the rebellion. Rebellion is there, but I think that MTV and culture and society have become so much more permissive, that there is a lot less to rebel against. The way people rebel is in a technological sense now. It's that power of the remote or the power of the mouse that your parents probably don't have. Also it's down to things like health and age, people live longer, so the category of youth is longer. These are angry times. Kids are angry. But I don't think they know what they are angry against."

Richard Russell, the founder of independent label XL Recordings, has long marketed some of the world's most credible music acts to young people, such as the Prodigy, the White Stripes, and Dizzee Rascal. The disappearance of the generation gap troubles him. "The way the media pounces on subculture is new," he told me. "There was no press around rave, the papers didn't write about music. The Prodigy didn't used to get press anywhere; now subculture is the press's favorite thing. Think about Dizzee Rascal. That should have been a generation gap, but the *Guardian* were like 'Dizzee's quite good.' I was quite pained by that. The generation gap has just been obliterated. A lot of aspects of that are fantastic. A lot of that teenaged rebellion was a bloody nightmare—to have your parents not understand you was a right pain in the arse really. It's much better if these people you've gotta live with do understand you. They are more understanding now because we've got some mutual interests; it's gotta help things a bit. Maybe music will suffer, but then again we have other stuff to rebel against, the world's still fucked, but you don't need your parents to be fucked, too, if you can help it."

And Like That . . . It's Gone

The way ideas and youth cultures grow and spread has changed. We've gained a lot as society has embraced the rules of youth cultures, but we lost something along the way, too: organic youth cultures such as grime and free running are covered in branded pesticide before they can develop; only social weeds such as happy slaps are left alone.

As every area of life is being mined for its cultural value, and ideas from youth cultures can spread quicker than ever, these ideas don't last long enough to mature. In the West, youth culture as a method of communication has lost some of its value. How likely is it that there will be another scene like punk? In its place are tiny scenes and great ideas—they are the mainstream. If you were in your early twenties in the 1970s and there was nothing good on TV, dyeing your hair green and forming an alternative rock band with your friends to complain about it was a good idea. Today it is just as easy for three guys in their twenties to start an alternative to TV, as the three guys behind YouTube did, sell it to Google for $1.65 billion twenty-one months later, and revolutionize the way television works. Music isn't the only way to rebel anymore. It's likely the future of youth culture will look very different.

The Next Big Thing?

Youth culture's past held the keys to our future. But the future of youth cultures belongs to those who aren't celebrated here. In the West, youth cultures will continue to grow, and we'll continue picking them before they ripen. Youth movements become successful when social change is desperately needed. They start with someone making a hot new record, throwing a party, or cutting their hair differently just for the hell of it, but gain traction if they express society's collective desire for change.

The source of future youth movements will just as likely be the rage, desperation, and hope transmitted from the medinas, favelas, and shanty cities of the southern hemisphere. According to a 2005 report commissioned by the National Research Council and the Institute of Medicine on trends affecting youth in developing countries, there are currently 1.5 billion ten- to twenty-four-year-olds on Earth, and 86 percent of them live in a developing country. In many places in Asia and Africa, this generation is the first generation of teenagers their countries have known. This is where the new youth cultures will be, because this is where the new generation gaps are.

In many places, there is no middle ground in transition from child to adult. One minute you are a child, the next you are at work. The concept of the teenager didn't come into existence in the West until after World War II, but now that similar advances are being made in the developing world in health care, education, and technology, new generations of young people are growing up. As their economic and political power grows, new sounds, movements, and ideas will grow, too.

The 1.5 billion young people across the world equal 1.5 billion potential youth movements. Almost half of all unemployment in the world is among young people. A quarter of them live on less than $1 a day. A total of five hundred thousand people under age eighteen are recruited by military and paramilitary groups, while some three hundred thousand have been involved in armed conflict in more than thirty countries. Thirteen million adolescents give birth each year, and young people account for nearly half of all new HIV infections. While the U.N. Research Institute estimates that the richest 2 percent of adults in the world own more than half of all household wealth, a report from the World Institute for Development Economics Research at the United Nations University says that the poorer half of the world's population owns barely 1 percent of global wealth. What are these teenagers going to have to say about these things when they get the chance?

One thing is certain: they will get that chance. The Internet was great news for those of us with high-speed connections, but didn't mean much to the half of the world's population that has never used a telephone. Efforts are being made to close the digital divide between the developed and the developing worlds. Open-source education, $100 laptops, and free, decentralized WiFi networks are a great start. A report on Internet readiness rankings by the Economist Intelligence Unit in April 2007 shows that Asian and African nations are catching up with big Net users in the West. According to the report, broadband is becoming cheap and affordable in almost every nation on Earth. "Technology leadership in the world is becoming a fast-moving target," said Robin Bew, editorial director of the Economist Intelligence Unit (EIU). "Those at the top of today's league table cannot be complacent—changing technologies, and attitudes to technology usage, mean that hard-won advantages can be quickly eroded by nimble-footed rivals."

It's likely the new systems the teenagers of the past fifty years fought for will help alleviate the frustrations of the teenagers of the next fifty years. Since the industrial revolution, argues Craig O'Hara in *The Philosophy of Punk*, the rise of mass production has created "a feeling in modern society of an alienation so powerful and widespread that it has become commonplace and accepted. Repeatedly, however, a group of the alienated will recognize what is happening to themselves." There is clearly a revolution going on, but it is not yet apparent to all. It was a hundred years after the industrial revolution that someone first called it the "industrial revolution." Of course, these days we are much more obsessed with branding things.

Looking at the differences previous generations made with simple things such as hairstyles, turntables, and spray cans, it's difficult to comprehend just how much new generations and youth movements are capable of, despite the relentless pursuit from corporate cool hunters. A change is gonna come. Technology will give the teens of the future some new options to frighten their parents with. One of the first parts of the human genome biologists are predicting we will be able to hack is our own skin pigment—our color. Punks used to shock their parents by coming home with green hair. What are you gonna do when your kids come home with green skin?

Just as it was with hippies, house DJs, and hip-hop artists, it will take awhile before we take these new revolutionaries seriously. Gandhi told the story best: "First they ignore you, then they laugh at you, then they fight you, then you win." Whoever is coming next, they are out there somewhere doing something they believe in, probably being ignored and laughed at right now.

Just you wait.

One Last Thing

From old brands to new bands to the 1.5 billion teenage pirates, everyone now has access to the same spaces and is jostling for their fifteen minutes of fame. The trouble is these days it lasts only fifteen nanoseconds. It's easier than ever to get out there, but "there" is a lot more crowded. The effect of all this is that old ideas, companies, and movements can be dislodged in an instant by a new upstart. The U.K. garage crown was commandeered by grime. Parkour was tripped up by marketing pirates. Any movement, person, or company can have their thunder stolen in an instant by pirates of all stripes looking to upend an old business model, co-opt and copy an idea, or create space for a new one. There is no going back. The Pirate's Dilemma is real and it's not going away. There is only one question left to answer:

How, exactly, do we respond to this?

The Pirate's Dilemma

Changing the Game Theory

The game has changed.

Youth movements that might have seemed like fads planted some radical ideas into the heads of those who grew up under their influence, and nothing has been quite the same since.

Punk made it very clear that we could do everything ourselves, and purpose should be at least as important as profit. Pirates, like offshore radio DJs, create periods of chaos and anarchy, but improve things for the rest of us by doing so. The millions of us who remix video games, music, films, and fashion designs are expanding and improving on those industries, forcing those who make the laws to reexamine how we treat intellectual property. The new breed of street artists seeking to enhance our surroundings as opposed to vandalizing them act in the public interest, if only unintentionally, by counteracting the advertising cluttering public spaces. Thanks to the influence of 1960s and '70s counterculture, and the rave revolutionaries of the '80s and '90s, the dream of creating an all-powerful social machine has been realized in the personal computer. Open-source technology has proved to be just as effective as—and in many cases more effective than—free-market competition or government regulation when it comes to generating money, efficiency, creativity, and social progress. Hip-hop was born out of a desire to improve society for a marginalized few, but because of its ability to communicate so effectively, now has the potential to improve it for the marginalized many. And just as mass culture thought it had figured out how to control and use youth cultures, they evolved again. Mass culture needs to learn from the ways youth cultures behave and think, not just use them for their good looks.

Because all these ideas are coming together in the wider world at the same time, a new period of chaos has ensued as the Information Age has grown into a petulant teenager itself. Now we are all capable of acting like pirates, or being devoured by them. Now we all have to consider what the new conditions of this difficult adolescence mean, and how we should approach them. Now that the game has changed so much, we need to reexamine the theory behind the game.

The answer to the Pirate's Dilemma lies in something economists call game theory. Game theory examines situations where multiple players in a game make decisions based on what the other players will do, like an academic version of poker. It is used to model social situations in which decision makers interact with other agents, and often assumes individuals will act only in their own self-interest.

A game called the Prisoner's Dilemma is a simple, well-known game used to illustrate this point. Developed in the 1950s by the RAND corporation (a global policy think tank which advises the U.S. armed forces, among other things), the game goes like this: two suspects, Prisoner A and Prisoner B, are caught with stolen goods and arrested under suspicion of burglary. But the police don't have enough evidence to convict either prisoner unless one, or both of them, confesses. The police separate the two prisoners so they cannot communicate, and offer them both the same deal: if both of them confess, each will receive a two-year sentence. If neither of them confesses, the cops can't prove they were the burglars, and each prisoner will instead be sentenced to only six months in jail for possession of stolen goods. But if Prisoner A confesses and Prisoner B keeps his mouth shut, Prisoner A will walk free and Prisoner B will receive the full five-year sentence for the crime, on the strength of Prisoner A's testimony. The same holds true if Prisoner B confesses and Prisoner A does not. Neither Prisoner A nor Prisoner B knows for sure what choice the other will make. Each has two options, and there are four possible outcomes.

Each prisoner can either stay silent and hope the other prisoner does the same, or betray the other in return for a lighter sentence. The outcome of each choice depends on the choice of the other prisoner, but each prisoner must choose without knowing what his accomplice will do.

The Prisoner's Dilemma

	Prisoner B stays silent	Prisoner B confesses
Prisoner A stays silent	Each serves 6 months (6 months, 6 months)	Prisoner A serves 5 years Prisoner B goes free (5, 0)
Prisoner A confesses	Prisoner A goes free Prisoner B serves 5 years (0, 5)	Each serves 2 years (2, 2)

Assuming each will act in his own self-interest, the only logical outcome is that both prisoners will always confess. Even if Prisoner A thinks Prisoner B will not talk, his best move is still to rat him out and try to go free rather than risk the five-year sentence. If Prisoner A suspects Prisoner B will talk, his best move is to snitch as well and receive two years instead of five. Prisoner B will always reason the same way about Prisoner A, too, so betraying the other prisoner and confessing is always the dominant strategy. Both prisoners would get lower sentences if they cooperated with each other and remained silent, but assuming the other will most likely snitch out of self-interest, their best choice is always to do the same. Playing the game using self-interest will always result in each prisoner being worse off than if they had cooperated with each other. Yet when faced with this dilemma, each prisoner will choose to betray the other every time, because of their uncertainty about what the other prisoner might do.

As a society we often subscribe—in theory, at least—to the idea that we will exclusively act in our own self-interest. This theory has been a dominant force in economics, political science, military strategy, psychology, and many other disciplines since the 1950s. It has informed some of the most important decisions the human race has ever made, from the nuclear arms race of the Cold War to the way we share all kinds of resources today. This simple game of two paranoid prisoners trying to cut a shady deal helped shape the structure behind the supposedly dog-eat-dog world we live in.

Game theory is an incredibly useful tool, and more advanced versions of the game allow for cooperation between players, but according to the most basic Prisoner's Dilemma game outlined here, the idea of people acting in the interests of one another is naive. But in practice, it is obvious the game is flawed. The most basic assumption—that we all act only in our own self-interest—is simply not true. When economists test this theory, real people do not always act this way. In real life, in every corner of society, people cooperate with one another in the interest of both the public good and their own private interest. That's why we have nonprofits, nurses, and teachers. As Muhammad Yunus, founder of the Grameen Bank and winner of the 2006 Nobel Peace Prize put it, "A human being can do many other things, but economics doesn't leave any room for expressing them."

When the market won't express something, pirates will. Pirates acting in their own self-interest and in the interests of their communities are today some of the most ruthless innovators on the planet.

Solving the Pirate's Dilemma

From struggling musicians to movie executives, people in many industries already feel that their future is under fire from piracy. But there are answers. Solving the Pirate's Dilemma can also be expressed as a simple game illustrating how people, businesses, and markets facing a threat from piracy should respond. It shows us how to compete when copyright protections are no longer keeping pirates at bay, or when we are faced with the dilemma of whether to share products with competitors and consumers.

In the Pirate's Dilemma, Players A and B are not burglars but individuals or companies selling competing products. The players are not being threatened by police, but by pirates: those creating a new space outside of the traditional, legitimate market.

Pirates create a gap outside of the market.

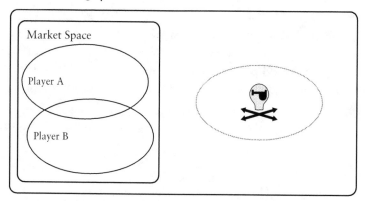

Let's assume our definition of "pirates" also includes those providing free substitute products powered by altruism, such as open-source software, for example. These pirates can add value to society, but in doing so take value from companies or individuals such as Players A and B. When people switch to Linux, for example, that takes market share away from Microsoft.

As we saw in chapter 2, when pirates create value for society, society supports them. If the pirates grow and take a larger chunk out of the traditional market space, Players A and B soon find they face a Pirate's Dilemma. Do they try to fight piracy with the law, at the risk of alienating the public, the way the record business did, or do they do what iTunes did, and compete with the pirates in the new market space?

If piracy grows, Players A and B will face a Pirate's Dilemma.

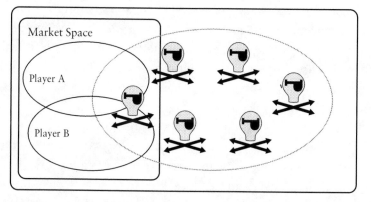

If both decide to fight piracy, and if that piracy is providing no real value to society, then Players A and B may be able to quash the threat the pirates pose, and the marketplace will return to the way it was in Figure 1. If we imagine Players A and B were in the luxury handbag business, they would be unwise to compete with pirates selling $25 knockoffs of their $2,000 handbags. If you're a consumer in the market for a $2,000 handbag, a $25 imitation is probably of no value to you, and there is no value to be gained by the luxury handbag producer by lowering their prices—in this instance it would hurt their brand to compete. The strong arm of the law will, in many cases, be the best option.

But if Players A and B, or the market space they inhabit, is inefficient—if there is a better way for society to gain the value that Players A and B provide—there will always be a threat from pirates. If a large amount of consumers will always prefer a $5 pirate copy of a movie in its opening week to a $12 box office ticket and overpriced popcorn, demand for pirated movies will persist. If a developing nation can't afford name-brand, life-saving drugs, those brands will always have to deal with pill pirates in those markets. Prohibition is unlikely to work in these cases, and inefficient industries will continue to have a problem until they react in the marketplace instead of the courts.

The decision each player makes about how to respond also poses a threat to the other player, as it does in a Prisoner's Dilemma. If pirates begin to have a serious effect on their market share, both Players A and B will (or at least, should) be tempted to compete with them. If either decides to compete with pirates by moving into the new market space, they can also cut into the market share of their competitor.

Imagine Players A and B are drug companies, and the pirates are those producing generic pills in a developing country. By fighting the pill pirates in this case, neither player stands to make a great deal of money, because the new market doesn't have much. But not allowing people access to life-saving drugs means people will die needlessly, piracy will be inevitable, and the company's image will be tarnished. But if Player B starts producing drugs in this market and competing with the pill pirates, they will gain market share (which could become profitable in time), save lives, and improve their reputation as a brand. In a world where advertising isn't working quite so well anymore, creating value for society like this is a great way to make an authentic connection to consumers. Player B's actions will also undermine Player A's position in the market. If Player B competes and Player A doesn't, B will cut into A's market share, and the share taken by the pirates.

If Player B competes, society gains, but the pirates and Player A lose out.

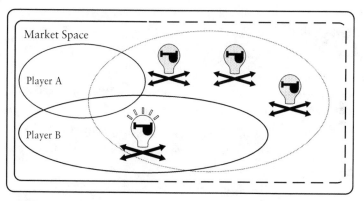

Once a player decides to compete, the new market space the pirates inhabit becomes legitimized. This adds value to society, creating a greater market space in which players can pursue profits. In this instance, Player A will also be forced to compete the same way in the long term, or risk going out of business altogether.

The new market space becomes legitimized, and Player A must compete.

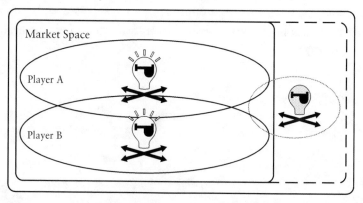

Imagine Player B is an open-source software company, such as Linux, operating in a market where there is widespread piracy, such as China. Linux gains market share by competing with the pirates—giving away its products for free and selling customized products and support to make a profit. Linux becomes more efficient (by sharing this product with outside contributors who improve it), creates value for society (as much as 12 billion Euros worth, according to the E.U. study mentioned in chapter 5), and takes market share away from Player A as well the pirates.

Now imagine Player A is Microsoft—its market share in China is under fire from both pirates and free substitutes like Linux. What is Microsoft supposed to do? In this situation, competing seems to be the only choice, other than being forced out of the market altogether. Microsoft's official position on piracy has traditionally been one of zero tolerance, but Bill Gates acknowledged this reality to a group of students in 1998. "Although about 3 million computers get sold every year in China, people don't pay for the software," said Gates to an audience at the University of Washington. "Someday they will, though, and as long as they're going to steal it, we want them to steal ours. They'll get sort of addicted, and then we'll somehow figure out how to collect sometime in the next decade."

In this model, whenever pirates are adding value to society, society will always demand that the players compete with them in the long term. In this case, the player who competes first will stand a better chance of gaining the advantage. In the simple version of the Prisoner's Dilemma, only self-interest rules. But in a Pirate's Dilemma, what's best for society as a whole is also an important factor. Because players and pirates alike can be motivated by both self-interest *and* what's best for society, the game has changed.

The Pirate's Dilemma

	Player B competes like a pirate:	Player B does not compete, fights piracy instead:
Player A competes like a pirate:	• Both gain new profits from moving into new market space. • Each becomes as efficient as possible. • Society gains maximum amount of added value.	• Player A gains share of pirate's market, becomes more efficient. • Player B loses market share, stays inefficient, loses profits. • Society gains moderate amount of added value.
Player A does not compete, fights piracy instead:	• Player B gains share of pirate's market, becomes more efficient. • Player A loses market share, stays inefficient, loses profits. • Society gains moderate amount of added value.	• Both make profits in existing market space only, but lose money to pirates. • Each stays inefficient. • Society gains the minimum amount of added value.

What is emerging from the ideas youth culture pushed on the world is a more democratic strain of capitalism. People, firms, and governments are being forced to do the right thing by a new breed of rebels using a cutthroat style of competition, which combines both their self-interest and the good of the community to beat traditional business models. We are starting to see a very different picture of how the world might work. A world of competitive pirates, it seems, is a better place to be than one full of paranoid prisoners.

Free at Last

Pirates are taking over the good ship capitalism, but they're not here to sink it. Instead they will plug the holes, keep it afloat, and propel it forward. The mass market will still be here for a long while. This book you are holding—static words printed on thin slices of dead tree brought to you by a large media company—is living proof of that. The book industry has been fortunate: books are some of the easiest things to pirate, yet the majority of book readers still choose the treeware versions rather than downloading software-based substitutes. Not everything can be replaced by an electronically transmitted copy, for now, at least.

As we learn to pirate more of the things we buy and sell, many industries will face short-term uncertainties. But looking at the history of youth movements, the social experiments that took hold by figuring out new ways to share, remix, and produce culture, in the long term, the benefits of this new, more democratic system seem clear. It is down to every one of us to approach the Pirate's Dilemma from our own unique perspective and to apply the best option to our particular situation.

Over the past few decades in the West, we have entered a period of hyperindividualism, which has its pros and cons. But the power of billions of connected individuals, now flexing more power than markets, governments, and corporations using new ideas our economic model cannot yet comprehend, should be welcomed. Punk capitalists mix altruism with self-interest to compete on new levels the free market by itself cannot reach.

The early years of the twenty-first century have conjured a new worldview, one imagined by radicals and subversives who used youth cultures to prove there were better ways of doing things. In the future, loose-knit networks and open-source communities may sit side by side as equal powers with both governments and the free market. Punk Capitalism isn't about big government or big markets but about a new breed of incredibly efficient networks. This is not digital communism, this isn't central planning. It is in fact quite the opposite: a new kind of decentralized democracy made possible by changes in technology. Piracy isn't just another business model, it's one of the greatest business models we have.

Acting like a pirate—taking value from the market, or creating new spaces outside of the market and giving it back to the community, whether it's with free open-source software or selling cheap Starbury sneakers—is a great way to serve public interests and a great way to make an authentic connection to a new audience.

Many industries and markets have not yet felt the effects of pirates and the forces of change we have discussed here. But with new technologies such as self-replicating 3-D printers lurking on the horizon, nobody is safe. The Pirate's Dilemma needs to be taken seriously by all of us, because tomorrow pirates could be coming to an industry near you.

ACKNOWLEDGMENTS

The Pirate's Dilemma would never have come to be without a little help, guidance, and inspiration from a few exceptional people. First, I need to thank Mr. Frans Johansson, author of *The Medici Effect*. It was Frans who got me thinking about innovation within the context of youth culture. It was also Frans who suggested the title *The Pirate's Dilemma*, which got me thinking about game theory in relation to piracy. His advice and encouragement throughout the writing process was invaluable. He is one of the most brilliant people I have ever met, and one of my greatest friends.

Dan Lazar at Writers House took a gamble on my idea and helped transform it into a sharp proposal, going over and above the call of duty, contributing to the project at every stage. Every author needs a superagent like Dan.

I was lucky enough to have three amazing editors. At Free Press in New York, Maris Kreizman was the first to champion the idea and greatly improved the manuscript along the way. Amber Qureshi saw it through its final stages, and the idea became better. At Penguin in London, Helen Conford's passion and enthusiasm for this idea were critical to its success. The time and effort put in by copy editor William Drennan sharpened the idea. Without them, this idea would still be just that.

If it wasn't for a long conversation I had with Dominick Anfuso at Free Press about how media companies should respond to piracy, *The*

Pirate's Dilemma might never have come out quite the way it did. At Penguin I must also thank Robert Williams and Jeremy Ettinghausen, and Editorial Director Stefan McGrath for his unwavering support. When he told me that the remix chapter of *The Pirate's Dilemma* changed the way he thought about the book business, I thought he was just being nice. When Penguin released a range of classics a few months later with blank covers for readers to remix themselves, I realized he meant it. For all the support and hard work from everyone at Free Press, Penguin, and Writers House, and the hard work of Dorie Simmonds in London, I am indebted.

I am eternally grateful to my father, Richard; my mother, Sue; my sister, Ruth; and my stepmother, Letizia, for cheering me on from the sidelines throughout this project, not to mention supporting every harebrained scheme I've ever had. I would like to thank my niece, Mir, for showing me it was possible to get a book published. Before I'd finished this book, she'd already been published in two different books. She was eight years old at the time. Watch out for her.

I need to acknowledge those who took the time to critique my work and give me the advice and support that helped this book take shape, in particular Rick and Lynn Cozart, Betty Cozart-Roy, Joe Roy and the rest of the Cozart family, my chief economic adviser, Dr. David Pinch, Jamie-James Medina, Seth Godin, Tom Curry, Susan Arciero and Milos Bang, Ryan Senser (for his idea of using a Venn diagram to illustrate the Pirate's Dilemma), Sweet Joy Hachuela-Johansson, Corey Tatarczuk, Jacques DeJardin, Phoebe Eng and Zubin Schroff (for letting me hide out at their place in the Hamptons and get some serious writing done), my uncle Stephen Boyd, my uncle Graham Brown, Esther Gold, Chris Campion, Alex Donne Johnson, Fabio Scianna, Alicia Hansen, Mr. Richard Antwi, Kirk Vallis, Anthony Mouskoundi, Tim Cooke, Graeme Pretty, Jit Shergill, Dave McConachie, Rob Moore, Spencer Giles, Rob Marciano, Jon Allen, Gaby Marciano, Laura Sunley, Laurie Basannavar, Jeff Chang, Harold Anthony at jumpoff.tv, James Barrett, Dilia Baille, Shane Tomlinson, Marvin Lutrell, everyone at dissensus.com, all the staff at the Brooklyn Public Library, and Lynne D. Johnson, who first put the idea of writing a book in my head.

The interviews, illustrations, and photographs I was given make *The Pirate's Dilemma* what it is. For these contributions, I'm obligated to an incredible cast of players, namely (in order of appearance) Art Jaz at rokstuf.com, Richard Hell, Shane Smith (not to mention Gavin McInnes, Suroosh Alvi, Jesse Pearson, Andy Capper, and everyone at *VICE* magazine), Adrian Bowyer and his team at Reprap.org, Mr. Bob Le-Roi of www.bobleroi.co.uk, the Principality of Sealand Bureau of Internal Affairs, John Ousby at the BBC, Andy Johnson and Preston Nevins of Dead Smurf Software, Duncan Marshall at Droga5, LADY PINK, SMITH, RΔMM:ΣLL:ZΣΣ, Ad and Droo of Skewville, Mark Jenkins, Kalle Lasn, Ji Lee (who also designed the book's brilliant logo), Sister Alicia Donohoe, Mr. David Mancuso, Jimmy Wales at Wikipedia, DJ Jazzy Jeff, Daymond John, Leslie Short and everyone at FUBU, 50 Cent, Russell Simmons, Pharrell Williams, Rozan Ahmed, Rolando Brown at the Hip-Hop Association, Scott Beale at Laughing Squid, Dizzee Rascal, Rana Reeves, Carl Christopher and Richard Russell at XL Recordings.

Without some inspiration earlier in life, I would have never pursued this idea at all. For this must I thank Vreni Oleram, my economics teacher at Esher College, and Tony McMahon, Wesley Jay, Ricky D, Bradley M, and all the DJs and MCs at MAC 92.7 FM and ICE 88.4 FM in London, two of the city's finest pirate stations, which I was proud to have been a part of.

Last and most important, I want to thank my wife, Emily. Without her patience, love, and support, this book would never have been finished. Without her comments, insights, and suggestions, it probably wouldn't have made any sense. Without her none of this would have been possible. Because she is next to me, every day is a little better than the one before.

NOTES

This original composition contains samples and elements from the following original compositions:

Page v
   Dr. Dre quote from the album *Straight Outta Compton* by N.W.A. (Ruthless/Priority Records, 1988).

INTRO
Enter the Lollipop

Page 4
   John Perry Barlow, "The Economy of Ideas," *Wired* no. 2.03 (March 1994). www.wired.com/wired/archive/2.03/economy.ideas.html.

Page 5
   E. F. Schumacher, *Small Is Beautiful* (Point Roberts, WA: Hartley & Marks Publishers, 1999), p. 33.

Page 6
   "Marc Ecko," interview by David Gensler, *Royal Magazine* 2, no. 9 (Winter 2006). http://www.theroyalmagazine.com.

Page 7
   Lucile Scott, "Attention Shoppers: RED Presents 'Punk Capitalism'," *Poz.com* (October 18, 2006). www.poz.com/articles/401_10713.shtml.

CHAPTER 1: PUNK CAPITALISM
From D.I.Y. to Downloading Sneakers

Pages 10–13

Richard Hell, interview by author, May 17, 2006 (other quotes from Hell that appear throughout this chapter are taken from the same interview).

Stephen Colegrave and Chris Sullivan, *Punk* (New York: Thunder's Mouth Press, 2001), p. 103.

Ian Youngs, "A Brief History of Punk," *BBC News Online*, December 23, 2002. http://news.bbc.co.uk/2/hi/entertainment/2601493.stm.

The Sex Pistols, *The Filth and the Fury* (New York: St. Martin's Griffin, 2000), p. 26.

As quoted by Stephen Colegrave and Chris Sullivan in *Punk: The Definitive Record of a Revolution.*

Page 14

Stephen Colegrave and Chris Sullivan, *Punk* (New York: Thunder's Mouth Press, 2001), p. 92.

Page 14

Dick Hebdige, *Subculture: The Meaning of Style* (Boca Raton, FL: Routledge, 1979), p. 112.

Joseph A. Schumpeter, *Capitalism, Socialism and Democracy* (New York: Harper & Row, 1942), pp. 82–85.

Page 15

For a good summary of the Situationist movement, see: Simon Ford, *The Situationist International* (London: Black Dog, 2005).

Kalle Lasn, *Culture Jam* (New York: William Morrow & Company, 1999). http://books.guardian.co.uk/extracts/story/0,,157939,00.html.

Page 16

A good, brisk synopsis of how all the major 1970s punk bands were linked can be found in: *The Rough Guide to Rock, 3rd Edition* (London, England: Rough Guides/Penguin, 2003) by Peter Buckley.

Jon Savage, *England's Dreaming* (New York: St. Martin's Press, 1992), p. 141.

Page 19

Frans Johansson, *The Medici Effect* (Boston: Harvard Business School Press, 2004), p. 40.

Page 19

Shane Smith, interview by author, May 15, 2006 (other quotes from Smith that appear throughout this chapter are taken from the same interview).

Page 21
Jon Fine, "The Rewards Of Spreading *Vice*," *BusinessWeek*, October 10, 2005.

Page 21
Ian Youngs, "Reunion fever sweeps rock world," *BBC News Online*, January 26, 2007.

The Associated Press, "Johnny Rotten to appear in reality show," *CNN.com*, January 20, 2004. www.cnn.com/2004/SHOWBIZ/Music/01/20/johnny.rotten .ap/index.html.

Page 22
Lee Gomes, "Apple's 30 Years Of Selling Cool Stuff With Uncool Message," *The Wall Street Journal Online*, April 5, 2006. http://online.wsj.com/public/article /SB114419429783417125-H_iZ_Sz2pwRy2PJR5QsU5sdafkw_20060412.html ?mod=blogs.

Page 24
Richard Siklos, "Death by Smiley Face," *New York Times*, April 2, 2006.

Page 25
American Apparel, *Mission*. www.americanapparel.net/mission.

Christopher Palmeri, "Living On the Edge at American Apparel," *BusinessWeek*, June 27, 2005.

Josh Dean, "Dov Charney, Like It or Not," *Inc.com*, September 2005. www .inc.com/magazine/20050901/american-apparel.html.

Josh Mankiewicz, "Sexy marketing or sexual harassment?" *Dateline NBC*, July 28, 2006. www.msnbc.msn.com/id/14082498/.

Page 25
"Worldwide sales of Fairtrade products rise by a third as Fairtrade sales in the UK reach £200m," press release from *Fairtrade.org*, June 28, 2006. www.fair trade.org.uk/pr280606.htm.

Green Car Congress, "January 2006 US Hybrid Sales Almost Double from Prior Year," *Greencarcongress.com*, February 23, 2006. www.greencarcongress.com/ 2006/02/january_2006_us.html.

Page 26
Lynn A. Karoly and Constantijn W. A. Panis, The 21st Century at Work (Monograph, RAND Corporation, Santa Monica, CA, 2004).

Page 27
Tamara Schweitzer, "U.S. Workers Hate Their Jobs More Than Ever," *Inc.com*, March 6, 2007. www.inc.com/criticalnews/articles/200703/work_Printer_Friendly .html.

For a great overview of why we are being driven by creativity above all else, see Richard Florida, *The Rise of the Creative Class* (New York: Basic Books, 2002).

Page 27

Lulu.com, *The Life Expectancy of Bestsellers Plummets, Finds Study*, May 19, 2006. www.lulu.com/static/pr/05_19_06.php.

Page 28

Adrian Bowyer, interview by author, June 10, 2006 (all quotes from Bowyer used in this chapter are from this interview).

Peter Wayner, "How It Works," *New York Times*, May 29, 2003.

Page 29

"On the Job," *Cadalyst.com*, February 10, 2006. http://manufacturing.cadalyst .com/manufacturing/article/articleDetail.jsp?id=306953.

Page 32

Clinton Heylin, *Bootleg: The Secret History of the Other Recording Industry* (New York: St. Martin's Griffin, 1996), p. 165.

CHAPTER 2: THE TAO OF PIRATES
Sea Forts, Patent Trolls, and Why We Need Piracy

Pages 33–35

The Principality of Sealand Bureau of Internal Affairs. www.sealandgov.org/his tory.html.

George Pendle, "New Foundlands," *Cabinet Magazine*, no. 18 (Summer 2005).

Simson Garfinkel, "Welcome to Sealand. Now Bugger Off," *Wired*, no. 8.07 (July 2000).

Steven Mathieson, "Prince Michael of Sealand cries freedom," *Vnunet.com*, October 20, 2000. www.vnunet.com/vnunet/analysis/2132036/prince-michael-sealand-cries-freedom?vnu_lt=vnu_art_related_articles.

Declan McCullagh, "Has 'haven' for questionable sites sunk?" *CNET News.com*, August 4, 2003. http://news.com.com/2100-1028_3-5059676.html.

Page 36

Doron S. Ben-Atar, *Trade Secrets* (New Haven and London: Yale University Press, 2004). www.theglobalist.com/DBWeb/StoryId.aspx?StoryId=4222.

Page 37

For an extensive discussion of the history of pirates in the media, see Lawrence Lessig's excellent book *Free Culture* (New York: Penguin, 2004) or visit www.free-culture.cc/.

Pages 37–38

Anders Bylund, "Mark Cuban on the tiered Internet," *Arstechnica.com*, February 8, 2006. http://arstechnica.com/articles/culture/cuban.ars.

Xeni Jardin, "Thinking Outside the Box Office," *Wired*, no. 13.12 (December 2005). www.wired.com/wired/archive/13.12/soderbergh.html.

Jonathan Watts, "Pirates and bloggers beat China's great wall of propaganda," *Guardian*, February 14, 2006. http://technology.guardian.co.uk/online/weblogs/story/0,,1732466,00.html.

Pages 39–44

Ormond Raby, *Radio's First Voice* (Toronto: MacMillan of Canada, 1970).

"The First Radio Broadcast." www.wfn.org/story.html.

Thomas Yocum, "Reginald Fessenden, Pioneer Of Wireless Radio." *Coastalguide.com* www.coastalguide.com/bearings/outer-banks-radio.shtml.

Dwight A. Johnson, "The Radio Legacy of the R.M.S. Titanic," *Avsia.com* (March 28, 1998). www.avsia.com/djohnson/titanic.html.

Jesse Walker, *Rebels on the Air* (New York: New York University Press, 2001).

Possibly the greatest book on the history of dance music and DJing is Bill Brewster and Frank Broughton's *Last Night a DJ Saved My Life* (London: Headline, 1999). The story of Tom Moulton is told on pp. 378–80.

For a broader discussion of the history of pirate radio around the world, see Andrew Yoder's exhaustive work *Pirate Radio Stations* (New York: McGraw-Hill, 2002).

Page 45

Simon Long, interview by author, July 2003 (this interview originally appeared as part of the cover story for the August 2003 issue of *RWD* magazine).

Pages 48–49

Rupert Murdoch, "The Dawn of A New Age of Discovery" (speech, Annual Livery Lecture at The Worshipful Company of Stationers and Newspaper Makers, London, March 13, 2006. www.newscorp.com/news/news_285.html.

Page 49

Declan McCullagh and Anne Broache, "Blogs turn 10—who's the father?" *CNET News.com* (March 20, 2007). news.com.com/Blogs+turn+10—whos+the+father/2100-1025_3-6168681.html.

Justin's Home Page, as it appeared on January 27, 1994 can still be seen here: www.links.net/vita/web/original.html.

Pages 50–51

These data are from a report released by the Genocide Intervention Fund and the American Progress Action Fund, tracking June 2005 news coverage.

Transcript of Madeleine Holt's item: "Is truth a victim?" *BBC News: Newsnight,* May 16, 2002. http://news.bbc.co.uk/2/hi/programmes/newsnight/archive/2029 634.stm.

Paul Reynolds, "Bloggers: an army of irregulars," *BBC News,* February 9, 2006. http://news.bbc.co.uk/2/hi/4696668.stm.

Katharine Q. Seelye, "White House Approves Pass For Blogger," *New York Times,* March 7, 2005. http://query.nytimes.com/gst/fullpage.html?res=9C03 E2DD1E3DF934A35750C0A9639C8B63.

Page 51
Oh Yeon Ho, "Korean Netizens Change Journalism and Politics," *OhmyNews .com,* December 14, 2004. http://english.ohmynews.com/articleview/article_view .asp?article_class=8&no=201423&rel_no=1.

Page 52
Victor Foo, "My Reflections on Roh Moo-hyun," *OhmyNews.com,* November 26, 2006. http://english.ohmynews.com/articleview/article_print.asp?menu=c104 00&no=331144&rel_no=1&isPrint=print.

Page 53
Clive Thompson, "Blogs to Riches," *New York* magazine, February 20, 2006. http://nymag.com/news/media/15967/mdex5.html.

Pages 53–54
Alan Bellows, "Remember, Remember the 22nd of November," *Damninteresting.com,* January 9, 2007. www.damninteresting.com/?p=776.

Bill Keveney, "How 'Andy' Stacks Up," *USA Today,* June 23, 2005. www.usa today.com/life/television/news/2005-06-23-andy-milonakis-show-x.htm.

Page 54
Brad Stone, "Right to the Top," *Newsweek,* January 9, 2006. www.msnbc.msn .com/id/10663353/site/newsweek/from/RSS.

Pages 55–56
Ann Harrison, "The Pirate Bay?" *Wired,* March 13, 2006. www.wired.com/ science/discoveries/news/2006/03/70358.

Gwladys Fouché, "Pirates pursue a political point," *Guardian,* February 9, 2006.

The Pirate Party, "Declaration of Principles 3.0." http://docs.piratpartiet.se/ Principles%203.0.pdf.

Page 57
The League of Noble Peers, *Steal This Film,* August 21, 2006. www.stealthisfilm .com.

The Pirate Bay, "Buy Sealand? Is it possible?" *Buysealand.com,* January 9, 2007. http://buysealand.com/?cat=1.

Tim Berners-Lee, "Net Neutrality," *Dig.csail.mit.edu*, June 21, 2006. http://dig.csail.mit.edu/breadcrumbs/node/144.

Page 58

Cory Doctorow, "Big Cable's ridiculous Net Neutrality smear video," *Boing Boing*, October 27, 2006. www.boingboing.net/2006/10/27/big_cables_ridiculou.html.

Anders Bylund, "Mark Cuban on the tiered Internet," *Arstechnica.com*, February 8, 2006. http://arstechnica.com/articles/culture/cuban.ars.

Page 59

Nicol Wistreich, "Disney Co-Chair recognises 'piracy is a business model'," *Netribution.co.uk*, October 10, 2006. www.netribution.co.uk/2/content/view/972/182/.

Steven Levy, "Q&A: Jobs on iPod's Cultural Impact," *Newsweek*, October 15, 2006. www.msnbc.msn.com/id/15262121/site/newsweek/print/1/displaymode/1098/.

Page 59

Associated Press, "'Patent trolling' firms sue their way to profits," *MSNBC*, March 18, 2006. www.msnbc.msn.com/id/11860819/.

Page 60

Kristen Philipkoski, "Monsanto Prevails in Patent Fight," *Wired*, May 21, 2004. www.wired.com/science/discoveries/news/2004/05/63555.

Pages 61–63

Joseph E. Stiglitz, "Prizes, Not Patents," *Project Syndicate*. www.projectsyndicate.org/commentary/stiglitz81.

Martin Flynn, "The Battle for Generic HIV Drugs," *Positive Nation*, no. 91 (June 2003). www.positivenation.co.uk/issue91/features/feature4/feature4.htm.

Amy Kazmin and Andrew Jack, "Thailand overrides patents to buy generic drugs," *Financial Times*, January 30, 2007.

Gary Hull, "Breaking Pharma Patents a Good Idea?" *Barron's/Dow Jones Reuters Business Interactive LLC*, June 2, 2003.

Chuck Muth, "Pirates of the Brazilian," *The Free Liberal*, June 12, 2005. www.freeliberal.com/archives/001120.html.

Don McNeil Jr., "Selling cheap 'generic' drugs, India's copycats irk industry," *New York Times*, December 1, 2000.

Page 64

Professor Benjamin R. Barber, "Overselling capitalism," *Los Angeles Times*, April 4, 2007.

Joseph E. Stiglitz, "Dying in the Name of Monopoly," *Global Envision*, March 12, 2007. www.globalenvision.org/library/9/1508/.

Noam Chomsky, "Unsustainable Non Development," *Zmag.org*, May 30, 2000. http://zmag.org/ZSustainers/ZDaily/2000-05/30chomsky.htm.

Page 65

Scott Woolley, "Prizes Not Patents," *Forbes*, April 18, 2006. www.forbes .com/2006/04/15/drug-patents-prizes_cx_sw_06slate_0418drugpatents.html.

CHAPTER 3: WE INVENTED THE REMIX
Cut-'n'-Paste Culture Creates Some New Common Ground

Pages 68–70

John von Seggern and iriXx, "The Madonna Manifesto" *IriXx.org*. www.irixx .org/madonna/madonnamanifesto.html.

Miriam Rainsford (aka iriXx), "The Madonna Remix Project," *IriXx.org*, April 30, 2003. www.irixx.org/madonna/pressrelease.txt.

Bill Evans, "Madonna WTF Remix Contest-UPDATE," *Dmusic*, April 27, 2003. http://news.dmusic.com/article/6532.

Ashlee Vance, "Like a virgin—Madonna hacked for the very first time," *The Register*, April 22, 2003. http://www.theregister.co.uk/2003/04/22/like_a_virgin _madonna_hacked/.

Chris Marlowe, "Hackers Have Field Day with Madonna Decoy," *Hollywood Reporter*, April 27, 2003.

Page 70

Susannah Cullinane, "The old new," *BBC News*, September 21, 2005. http:// news.bbc.co.uk/2/hi/uk_news/magazine/4265374.stm.

Page 71

Mary Bellis, "The First Flight of the Frisbee," *About: Inventors*. http:// inventors.about.com/library/weekly/aa980218.htm.

Nelson George, *Hip Hop America* (New York: Penguin, 1998), p. ix.

Pages 73–75

Jeff Chang, *Can't Stop Won't Stop* (New York: St. Martin's, 2005), p.31.

Bill Brewster and Frank Broughton, *Last Night a DJ Saved My Life* (London: Headline, 1999), pp. 108–122.

Steve Barrow and Peter Dalton, *The Rough Guide to Reggae* (London: Rough Guides, 2001), p. 158.

Piero Scaruffi, *A History of Rock Music: 1951–2000* (iUniverse, October 2003). http://www.scaruffi.com/history/long.html.

Jah Floyd, "Treasure Isle In Dub Rare Dubs 1970–1978," *Jamaican Recordings*. http://www.jamaicanrecordings.com/jr_pages/019_treasureisle.htm.

George Austen, "Duke Reid," *Ska2soul.net*. http://www.georgwa.demon.co.uk/duke_reid.htm.

Rubenxela, "Duke Reid," *Jahmusik.net*, March 2004. http://www.jahmusik.net/dukereid.htm.

Pages 76–77

Bill Brewster and Frank Broughton, *Last Night a DJ Saved My Life*: (London: Headline, 1999), pp. 174–179.

"Tom Moulton," *Andwedanced.com*, http://www.andwedanced.com/producers/moulton.htm.

Monica Lynch, "An interview with disco mix master Tom Moulton," The Monica Lynch Show, WFMU, September 27, 2002. rtsp://archive.wfmu.org/archive/ML/m1020927.rm?start=0:12:34.

Kai Fikentscher, "The club DJ," *The UNESCO Courier*, July 2000. http://findarticles.com/p/articles/mi_ml310/is_2000_July/ai_63845108.

Pages 78–80

For the definitive history of the birth of hip-hop, see Jeff Chang, *Can't Stop Won't Stop* (New York: St. Martin's, 2005).

Bill Brewster and Frank Broughton, *Last Night a DJ Saved My Life* (London: Headline, 1999), pp. 204–220.

Ben Williams, "The Remixmasters," *Slate.com*, July 29, 2002. http://www.slate.com/id/2068368.

Patrick Di Justo, "A Genome Shop Near You," *Wired*, no. 13.12 (December 2005). http://www.wired.com/wired/archive/13.12/start.html?pg=16.

Chris Isidore, "Attack of the movie sequels II," *CNN/Money*, May 6, 2003. http://money.cnn.com/2003/05/06/news/companies/sequels/.

Page 85

"Spike Lee slates US movie sequels," *BBC News*, September 2, 2005. http://news.bbc.co.uk/2/hi/entertainment/4207314.stm.

Scott Bowles, "Hollywood needs a good year in 2006," *Gannett News Service*, January 24, 2006. http://findarticles.com/p/articles/mi_kmusa/is_200601/ai_nl6013425.

Pages 86–87

Peter Rojas, "Hollywood: the people's cut," *Guardian*, July 25, 2002.

Daniel Kraus, "The Phantom Edit," *Salon.com*, November 5, 2001. http://archive.salon.com/ent/movies/feature/2001/11/05/phantom_edit/.

Andrew Rodgers, "New 'Star Wars' Re-Edit Skirts Law," *Zap2it.com*, June 5, 2001. http://movies.zap2it.com/movies/news/story/0,1259,—6917,00.html.

Page 88

Jim Gilliam, "Outfoxed interviews available for remixing," *JimGilliam.com*, September 14, 2004. http://www.jimgilliam.com/2004/09/outfoxed_interviews _available_for_remixing.php.

Pages 88–91

Reuters, "Myers, DreamWorks Ink Deal for Film Sampling," *Hollywood Reporter*, February 14, 2003.

Lawrence Lessig, *Free Culture* (New York: Penguin, 2004), p. 107.

Andy Johnston, formerly of Dead Smurf Software, interview by author, February 1, 2006.

Preston Nevins, formerly of Dead Smurf Software, interview by author, February 21, 2006.

Wagner James Au, "Triumph of the mod," *Salon.com*, April 16, 2002. http://archive.salon.com/tech/feature/2002/04/16/modding/index.html.

Julian Kücklich, "Precarious Playbour" *Fibre Culture*, no. 5. http://journal .fibreculture.org/issue5/kucklich.html.

Tor Thorsen, "Id Software turned down Activision takeover bid," *Gamespot.com*, September 27, 2005. http://www.gamespot.com/news/2005/ 09/27/news_6134536.html.

Stevie Case, "Women in Gaming," *Microsoft.com*, January 12, 2004. www .microsoft.com/windowsxp/using/games/learnmore/womeningames.mspx.

Page 92

Dr. Henry Jenkins, *Convergence Culture* (New York: New York University Press, 2006), p. 152.

Page 93

Stanley Holmes, "All the Rage Since Reagan," *BusinessWeek*, July 25, 2005, p.68.

Page 94

Lola Ogunnaike, "SoHo Runs for Blue and Yellow Sneakers," *New York Times*, December 19, 2004. http://www.nytimes.com/2004/12/19/fashion/19NIGO .html?ex=1261198800&en=d92dad69fcb6cb3b&ei=5088&.

Pages 95–96

Kal Raustiala and Chris Sprigman, "The Piracy Paradox," *Virginia Law Review* (August 2006).

Page 97

Reinier Evers, "Customer Made," *Trendwatching.com*, no. 21 (November 2004). http://www.trendwatching.com/newsletter/previous_21.html.

Pages 97–98

Katie Dean, "Grey Album Fans Protest Clampdown," *Wired*, February 24, 2004. http://www.wired.com/entertainment/music/news/2004/02/62372.

Bill Werde, "Defiant Downloads Rise From Underground," *New York Times*, February 25, 2004. http://www.nytimes.com/2004/02/25/arts/music/25REMI .html?ex=1179979200&en=dcc32bdb1403b769&ei=5070.

Stetsasonic, "Talkin' All That Jazz," performed by Daddy-O, Frukwan, Wise, and Delite, from the album *In Full Gear* (New York: Tommy Boy Records, 1988).

Page 99

Tim Wu, "Jay-Z Versus the Sample Troll," *Slate.com*, November 16, 2006. http://www.slate.com/id/2153961/.

Page 100

Philip Webster, "Brown will go into battle against film and music pirates," *London Times*, December 6, 2006. http://business.timesonline.co.uk/tol/business/ industry_sectors/media/article661265.ece.

Sean Garrett, "Perhaps the Coolest Moment in the History of Congress and Why It Matters," *The 463: Inside Tech Policy*, March 11, 2007. http://463 .blogs.com/the_463/2007/03/perhaps_the_coo.html.

Page 101

For more on Creative Commons, visit creativecommons.org.

CHAPTER 4: THE ART OF WAR
Street Art, Branding, and the Battle for Public Space

Pages 103–106

"Taki 183 Spawns Pen Pals," *New York Times*, July 21, 1971, p. 37.

To view the Marc Ecko/Air Force One stunt, visit www.stillfree.com.

Page 107

Joe Austin, *Taking the Train* (New York: Columbia University Press, 2002), p. 50.

James Barron, "Off the Train, Onto the Block; Auction House to Put Vintage Graffiti on Sale," *New York Times*, June 10, 2000. http://select.nytimes.com/gst/ abstract.html?res=F30A17F9345B0C738DDDAF0894D8404482.

Joel Siegel, "When TAKI Ruled Magik Kingdom," *Daily News*, April 9, 1989.

Page 108

Duncan Marshall, partner at Droga5, interview by author, September 15, 2006 (other quotes from Marshall that appear throughout this chapter are taken from the same interview).

Marc Ecko's Bio can be viewed at http://www.marceckoenterprises.com/bios/ bios1.shtml.

Rob Walker, "Cul-de-Sac Cred," *New York Times,* July 10, 2005. http://www .nytimes.com/2005/07/10/magazine/10ECKO.html?ex=1278734400&en=7849 b81705b1a0f0&ei=5088&partner=rssnyt&emc=rss.

Page 109

Ted Bridis, "Air Force One Subject of Internet Hoax," *Associated Press,* April 21, 2006. http://www.usatoday.com/news/nation/2006-04-22-air-force-one-hoax_x .htm?csp=34.

Page 110

Nelson George, *Hip Hop America* (New York: Penguin, 1998), p. 12.

Julie Andrijeski, "Bomb the City," *New York Press.* http://www.nypress.com/ 19/18/news&columns/feature2.cfm.

Page 110

"The Last Public Space," *The Thistle* 13, no. 4 (June/July 2001). http://mit.edu/ thistle/www/v13/4/graffiti.html.

Page 111

Christopher Gray, "Streetscapes/Gracie Mansion," *New York Times,* May 26, 2002. http://query.nytimes.com/gst/fullpage.html?res=9F02E2D71E38F935A15 756C0A9649C8B63.

Page 112

Shankar Vedantam, "In Boardrooms and in Courtrooms, Diversity Makes a Difference," *Washington Post,* January 15, 2007. http://www.washingtonpost.com/ wp-dyn/content/article/2007/01/14/AR2007011400720_pf.html.

Best Practices for Diversity, Thought Leadership Publication, Korn/Ferry International, December, 2001. http://www.kornferry.com/Library/Process.asp?P= Pubs_Detail&CID=297&LID=1.

Page 113

Sandra "LADY PINK" Fabara, interview by author, July 12, 2006 (other quotes from LADY PINK that appear throughout this chapter are taken from the same interview).

For good summaries of the history of graffiti, see the following:

Martha Cooper and Henry Chalfont, *Subway Art* (New York: Henry Holt and Company, 1984).

Ivor L. Miller, *Aerosol Kingdom* (Jackson, MS: University Press of Mississippi/, 2002).

Dimitri Ehrlich and Gregor Ehrlich, "Graffiti in Its Own Words," *New York: Summer Guide 2006.* http://nymag.com/guides/summer/17406/.

Peter Sutherland and Revs, *Autograf* (New York: powerHouse Books, 2004).

Roger Gastman, Darin Rowland, and Ian Sattler, *Freight Train Graffiti* (New York: Abrams, 2006).

PAUL 107, *All City: The Book About Taking Space* (Toronto: ECW Press, 2003).

Page 114
RΔMM:ƩLL:ZƩƩ, interview by author, July 27, 2006 (other quotes from RΔMM:ƩLL:ZƩƩ that appear throughout this chapter are taken from the same interview).

Pages 115–116
Emmanuelle Fauchart and Eric von Hippel, "Norms-based intellectual property systems: the case of French chefs Emmanuelle Fauchart and Eric von Hippel," *MIT Sloan School of Management Working Paper 4576-06*, January 2006.

Page 117
SMITH, interview by author, July 12, 2006 (other quotes from SMITH that appear throughout this chapter are taken from the same interview).

Page 119
Ad and Droo of Skewville, interview by author, June 29, 2006 (other quotes from Ad and Droo that appear throughout this chapter are taken from the same interview).

Page 120
Mark Jenkins, interview by author, June 21, 2006 (other quotes from Jenkins that appear throughout this chapter are taken from the same interview).

Page 121
Richard Morgan, "Reverse Graffiti," *New York Times*, December 10, 2006. http://www.nytimes.com/2006/12/10/magazine/10section3a.t-7.html?ex=13234 06800&en=d7e5ea986bc8c7e6&el=5090&partner=rssuserland&emc=rss.

Page 121
Richard Lacayo, "Takin' It To The Streets," *Time*, October 16, 2005. http://www.time.com/time/magazine/article/0,9171,1118377,00.html.

Colby Buzzell, "I am Banksy," *Esquire*, November 2005. http://www.esquire.com/features/best-n-brightest-2005/ESQ1205BANKSY_198?printable=true.

"'Naked man' mural allowed to stay," *BBC News*, July 19, 2006. http://news.bbc.co.uk/2/hi/uk_news/england/bristol/somerset/5193552.stm.

Banksy, *Banging Your Head Against A Brick Wall* (London: Weapons of Mass Distraction, 2001).

Banksy, *Wall and Piece* (London: Century, 2005).

Page 123
James Niccolai, "IBM's graffiti ads run afoul of city officials," *CNN.com/ IDG.net*, April 19, 2001. http://archives.cnn.com/2001/TECH/industry/04/19/ ibm.guerilla.idg/.

Page 123
James Curtis, "What's under the hood?" *Marketing*, October 18, 2006, p. 28.

Suzanne Smalley and Raja Mishra, "Froth, fear, and fury," *Boston Globe*, February 1, 2007. http://www.boston.com/news/local/articles/2007/02/01/froth _fear_and_fury/.

Page 125
"KFC enters the space race," *Guardian Unlimited*, November 14, 2006. http://business.guardian.co.uk/story/0,, 1947364,00.html?gusrc=rss&feed=1.

Katie Haegele, "No Rooftop Was Safe," *Philadelphia Weekly*, October 24, 2001. http://www.philadelphiaweekly.com/view.php?id=730.

David Bollier, "Protect the Night Sky from Space Advertising," *OntheCommons .org*, May 25, 2005. http://onthecommons.org/node/575/print?PHPSESSID= eac07e43054facfd4c25b6bdb49c604c.

Page 125
BBDO Energy, "Consumers are no longer buying what everyone else is selling," *Energybbdo.com*. http://www.energybbdo.com/agency_approach.php.

Page 126
Timothy L. O'Brien, "Madison Avenue's 30-Second Spot Remover," *New York Times*, February 12, 2006. http://www.nytimes.com/2006/02/12/business/ yourmoney/12adman.html?ex=1297400400&en=b2d526eaeef07853&ei=508 8&partner=rssnyt&emc=rss.

Spyros Andreopoulos, "A nation of hypochondriacs?" *San Francisco Chronicle*, November 29, 2004. http://www.sfgate.com/cgi-bin/article.cgi?file=/chronicle/ archive/2004/11/29/EDGD99EP1V1.DTL.

James Banks, PhD; Michael Marmot, MD; Zoe Oldfield, MSc; James P. Smith, PhD, "Disease and Disadvantage in the United States and in England," *Journal of American Medical Association* 295, no. 17 (May 3, 2006).

Dr. Nancy Etcoff, Dr. Susie Orbach, Dr. Jennifer Scott, Heidi D'Agostino, *"Beyond Stereotypes,"* findings of the 2005 Dove Global study, Dove Campaign For Real Beauty, February 2006. http://www.campaignforrealbeauty.com/ DoveBeyondStereotypesWhitePaper.pdf.

American Psychological Association, "Television Advertising Leads to Unhealthy Habits in Children; Says Apa Task Force," February 23, 2004. http://www.apa .org/releases/childrenads.html.

Page 126
Naomi Klein, *No Logo* (New York: Picador, 2000), p. 178.

Donella H. Meadows, "The Global Citizen," *Alertnet.org*, May 15, 2000. http://www.sustainabilityinstitute.org/dhm_archive/index.php?display_article= vn8491asned.

Page 127
Kalle Lasn, interview by author, May 24, 2006 (other quotes from Lasn that appear throughout this chapter are taken from the same interview).

Pages 128–129
Ji Lee, interview by author, June 29, 2006 (other quotes from Lee that appear throughout this chapter are taken from the same interview).

Ji Lee, *Talk Back: The Bubble Project* (New York: Mark Batty Publisher, 2006).

Page 130
Howard Rheingold, *Smart Mobs* (New York: Basic Books, 2006), p. 88.

Page 131
Elizabeth Biddlecombe, "UN predicts 'Internet of things'," *BBC News*, November 17, 2005. http://news.bbc.co.uk/2/hi/technology/4440334.stm.

Elliott Malkin, "Cemetery 2.0," *We Make Money Not Art*, November 17, 2006. http://www.we-make-money-not-art.com/archives/009130.php.

CHAPTER 5: BOUNDARIES
Disco Nuns, the Death of the Record Industry, and Our Open-Source Future

Page 134–141
Sister Alicia Donohoe, interview by author, January 10, 2007.

David Mancuso, interview by author, September 9 and 13, 2006 (other quotes from Mancuso that appear throughout this chapter are taken from the same interview).

For those who want a more detailed account of the history of the Loft and how disco evolved, I would recommend:

Tim Lawrence, *Love Saves the Day* (Durham, NC: Duke University Press, 2003).

Bill Brewster and Frank Broughton, *Last Night a DJ Saved My Life* (London: Headline, 1999).

Page 143
R. U. Sirius (aka Ken Goffman), *True Mutations* (San Francisco: Pollinator Press, 2006), p. 15.

John Markoff, *What the Dormouse Said* (New York: Penguin, reprint edition 2006).

Page 145

Bill Gates, "An Open Letter to Hobbyists," February 3, 1976. http://www
.blinkenlights.com/classiccmp/gateswhine.html.

Page 146

R. U. Sirius (aka Ken Goffman) and Dan Joy, *Counterculture Through the Ages* (New York: Villard, 2004), p. 353.

Page 147

Richard Stallman, "The Free Software Definition," Free Software Foundation. http://www.gnu.org/philosophy/free-sw.html.

For more on Vores Ø1 and other free beers, visit freebeer.org.

Page 149

Brian Bergstein, "Microsoft Offers Cash for Wikipedia Edit," *Newsvine.com*, January 23, 2007. http://www.newsvine.com/_news/2007/01/23/534218 -microsoft-offers-cash-for-wikipedia-edit.

Stacy Schiff, "Know It All: Can Wikipedia conquer expertise?" *The New Yorker,* July 31, 2006. http://www.newyorker.com/archive/2006/07/31/060731fa_fact.

Chris Anderson, *The Long Tail* (New York: Hyperion, 2006), p. 69.

Jimmy Wales, interview by author, November 14, 2006 (other quotes from Wales that appear throughout this chapter are taken from the same interview).

Page 150

Gregg Keizer, "Linux To Ring Up $35 Billion By 2008," *Tech Web*, December 16, 2004. http://www.techweb.com/wire/showArticle.jhtml?articleID=55800522.

Martha Lagace, "Open Source Science," *Harvard Business School, Working Knowledge,* November 20, 2006. http://hbswk.hbs.edu/item/5544.html.

Don Tapscott and Anthony D. Williams, *Wikinomics* (New York: Portfolio Hardcover, 2006), p. 25.

Page 151

"Open source gets European boost," *BBC News*, January 17, 2007. http:// news.bbc.co.uk/2/hi/technology/6270657.stm.

Page 154

Courtney Love, "Courtney Love does the math" (speech, *Digital Hollywood* conference, Hollywood, CA, May 16, 2000), posted on *Salon.com* on June 14, 2000. http://archive.salon.com/tech/feature/2000/06/14/love/.

DJ Jazzy Jeff, interview by author, November 2004 (this interview was first published in the January 2005 issue of *RWD* magazine).

Mary Madden, *Artists, Musicians and the Internet* (Washington, D.C.: Pew Internet & American Life Project, 2004).

Page 156

Lorraine Woellert, "Sony's Copyright Overreach," *BusinessWeek*, November 17, 2005. http://www.businessweek.com/technology/content/nov2005/tc20051117_444162.htm.

Page 157

Samuel Craig Watkins, *Hip Hop Matters* (Boston: Beacon Press, 2005), p. 112.

Felix Oberholzer and Koleman Strumpf, *The Effect of File Sharing on Record Sales*. (UNC/HBS, March 2004). http://www.unc.edu/~cigar/papers/FileSharing_March2004.pdf.

Page 158

Gabriel Alatorre, Christina Huang, Ethan Rigel, *Copyright Infringement due to Online File Sharing* (Boston: MIT, 2004–2005) via MIT OpenCourseWare. http://ocw.mit.edu/NR/rdonlyres/Electrical-Engineering-and-Computer-Science/6-901Fall-2005/B28F8F46-AE8B-4323-ACB0D99937779637/0/online_fileshrng.pdf.

Thomas C Greene, "Piracy losses fabricated—Aussie study," *The Register*, November 9, 2006. http://www.theregister.co.uk/2006/11/09/my_study_beats_your_study/.

Page 159

Kevin Maney, "If pirating grows, it may not be the end of music world," *USA Today*, May 3, 2005. http://www.usatoday.com/money/industries/technology/maney/2005-05-03-music-piracy-china_x.htm.

Page 159

"Legal music download figures ahead of pirated versions," *Newsfox*, July 25, 2005. http://www.newsfox.com/pte.mc?pte=050725044.

Bruce Houghton, "Could Nokia Be The Real iPod Killer?" *Hypebot*, August 10, 2006. http://hypebot.typepad.com/hypebot/2006/week32/index.html.

Frank Rose, "Phoning It In," *Wired*, no. 14.09 (September 2006). http://www.wired.com/wired/archive/14.09/phoning.html.

Page 160

Alain Levy, "Digital music and how the consumer became king" (speech, London, LBS London Media Summit, October 2006). For the full transcript of the speech, visit http://hypebot.typepad.com/hypebot/2006/10/emi_ceo_levy_vi.html#more.

Andrew Orlowski, "Big labels are f*cked, and DRM is dead—Peter Jenner," *The Register*, November 3, 2006. http://www.theregister.co.uk/2006/11/03/peter_jenner/.

Peter Jenner, As quoted in *Beyond the Soundbytes*, The MusicTank Report (Executive Summary) (London: MusicTank, August 2006).

Steve Jobs, "Thoughts on Music," *Apple.com*, February 6, 2007. http://www .apple.com/hotnews/thoughtsonmusic/.

Richard Hillesley, "Internet Killed the Video Star?" *Tuxdeluxe.org*, April 27, 2007. http://www.tuxdeluxe.org/node/170.

Pages 161–162
Adrian Bowyer, interview by author, June 10, 2006.

Page 163
Stephanie Dunnewind, "Teachers are reaching out to students with a new class of blogs," *Seattle Times*, October 14, 2006. http://seattletimes.nwsource.com/ html/living/2003303937_teachblog14.html.

Page 164
Don Tapscott and Anthony D. Williams, *Wikinomics* (New York: Portfolio Hardcover, 2006), p. 157.

Page 165
Andy Patrizio, "PlayStation 3 Users Power on to Cure Disease," *InternetNews .com*, April 5, 2007. http://www.internetnews.com/bus-news/article.php/ 3670066.

Page 165
Pekka Himanen, *The Hacker Ethic and the Spirit of the Information Age* (New York: Random House, 2002). This book is a fantastic read; the quote from Linus Torvalds can be found on p. xv.

Page 166
Don Tapscott and Anthony D. Williams, *Wikinomics* (New York: Portfolio Hardcover, 2006), front flap.

CHAPTER 6: REAL TALK
How Hip-Hop Makes Billions
and Could Bring About World Peace

Page 177
The Diddy and Burger King clip (which has since been posted back up) can be viewed at http://www.youtube.com/watch?v=XLcPIo1G_8E.

Page 173
James Montgomery, "YouTubers Protest Diddy TV With Parody Videos, Angry Comments," *MTV News*, October 11, 2006. http://www.mtv.com/news/arti cles/1542825/10102006/puff_daddy.jhtml.

The Lisa Nova clip can be viewed at http://www.youtube.com/watch?v=ES6kSKGv7dA.

Page 175
Saul Alinsky, *Rules for Radicals* (New York: Vintage, 1971), p. 98.

Pages 177–180
Daymond John, CEO of FUBU, interview by author, October 4, 2006.

Sloane Lucas, "For Us, Forever—marketing of urban apparel maker FUBU—Statistical Data Included—Interview," *Brandweek*, October 11, 1999. http://findarticles.com/p/articles/mi_m0BDW/is_38_40/ai_56752658.

Samuel Craig Watkins, *Hip Hop Matters* (Boston Beacon Press, 2005), p. 70.

Page 181
Douglas B. Holt, *How Brands Become Icons* (Boston: HBS, 2004), pp. 39–56.

Pages 182–183
Rapper 50 Cent, interview by author, April 23, 2005 (this interview first appeared in the May 2005 issue of *RWD* magazine).

Theresa Howard, "Rapper 50 Cent sings a song of business success," *USA Today*, July 5, 2005. http://www.usatoday.com/money/advertising/2005-07-04-fifty-cent-usat_x.htm.

Becky Aikman, "Trendy, successful Vitaminwater has LI roots," *Newsday*, October 1, 2006.

Amy Johannes, "In the Game," *Promo*, February 1, 2006.

Oren Yaniv, "Drink gets hip voice," *Daily News*, January 8, 2005.

"Demand for Beverages Bubbles Up on U.S. Heat Wave," *Reuters*, August 4, 2006.

Manasvi Mehta, "Hot or Cold?" *Business Standard*, September 18, 2006.

Page 185
Jeff Chang, *Constant Elevation*, p. 3. http://www.cantstopwontstop.com/pdfs/monographfinal.pdf.

Global Noise, Tony Mitchell, ed. (Middletown, CT: Wesleyan University Press, 2001).

Pages 186–187
Russell Simmons, interview by author, June 2004 (this interview first appeared in the July 2004 issue of *RWD* magazine).

Alex Ogg, *The Men Behind Def Jam* (London: Omnibus Press, 2002).

Stacy Gueraseva, *Def Jam Inc.* (New York: One World Books, 2005).

Page 188

Dr. Richard Oliver and Tim Leffel, *Hip-Hop Inc.* (New York: Avalon, 2006), pp. 123–128.

Ibid, p. 171.

Pharrell Williams, interview by author, March 2004 (this interview first appeared in the March 2004 issue of *RWD* magazine).

Page 190

Lola Ogunnaike, "Jay-Z, From Superstar to Suit," *New York Times*, August 28, 2005. http://www.nytimes.com/2005/08/28/arts/music/28ogun.html?ex=128288 1600&en=6c0d8de3a3fa301b&ei=5090&partner=rssuserland&emc=rss.

Carl Wilkinson, "I'm with the brand," *FT Weekend Magazine*, November 3, 2006. http://www.ft.com/cms/s/3589db72-6a42-11db-8ae5-0000779e2340.html.

Vanessa Grigoriadis, "Smooth Operator?" *New York* magazine, January 24, 2005. http://nymag.com/nymetro/arts/music/pop/10869/.

Page 191

Jeff Chang, "Change It All," *POV Borders, PBS.org*, June 29, 2006. http://www.pbs.org/pov/borders/2006/talk/jeff_chang/000311.html.

Jeff Chang, "Hip-Hop?" *POV Borders, PBS.org*, July 14, 2006. http://www.pbs .org/pov/borders/2006/talk/jeff_chang/000337.html.

Page 192

Daniel Gross, "Marbury vs. Madison Avenue," *Slate.com*, August 31, 2006. http://www.slate.com/id/2148808/.

To see Stephon Marbury's promotional video and find out more about the shoes, visit Starbury.com.

Linyee Yuan, "X-Pollination of Streetwear," *Theme,* no. 8 (Winter 2007). http://www.thememagazine.com/index.php?option=com_content&Itemid=11& task=view&id=60.

Page 193

Rolando Brown, Executive Director of the Hip-Hop Association, interview by author, October 4, 2006.

Chuck "Jigsaw" Creekmur, "Sean 'Diddy' Combs," *AllHipHop.com*, September 2006. http://www.allhiphop.com/features/?ID=1577.

Page 194

Kenny Rodriguez, "Russell Simmons Becomes a Goodwill Ambassador," *NobodySmiling.com*, July 26, 2006. http://www.nobodysmiling.com/hiphop/ news/86495.php.

Shaheem Reid, "Jay-Z Teams With U.N., MTV To Bring Attention To World's Water Crisis," *MTV News*, August 9, 2006. http://www.mtv.com/news/articles/1538213/20060809/story.jhtml.

Page 194

Samuel Craig Watkins, *Hip Hop Matters* (Boston: Beacon Press Books, 2005).

Kofi Annan, "There Is No Civilizational Clash—The Clash Is One of Closed Minds" (speech made to graduates of United Nations International School, New York, June 12, 2006). http://www.un.org/News/Press/docs/2006/sgsm10508.doc.htm.

Nolan Strong, "UN Backs South African Hip-Hop Summit, Guru Headlining Concert," *AllHipHop.com*, October 19, 2005. http://allhiphop.com/hiphop news/?ID=4957.

Patrick Neate, *Where You're At* (New York: Riverhead Books, 2003).

Pages 195–196

Rozan Ahmed, interview by author, October 2006.

Pages 196–197

Missy Elliott and Jay-Z, "Wake Up," from the album *This Is Not A Test!* (London: Elektra/WEA, 2003).

"Has rap music hit a wall?" *Associated Press*, March 5, 2007.

Geoff Boucher and Chris Lee, "In major awards, rap gets no love," *Los Angeles Times*, December 8, 2006.

Page 197

Deborah Campbell, "Post-Autistic Economics." http://www.adbusters.org/metas/eco/truecosteconomics/post-autistic.html.

Deborah Campbell, "Kick it Over!—The Rise of PostAutistic Economics," *Adbusters.org*, #55 Sept–Oct 2004. http://adbusters.org/the_magazine/55/Kick_it_Over_The_Rise_of_PostAutistic_Economics.html.

Page 198

Dart Adams, "Cause And Effect AKA What's Wrong With Hip Hop In 2007?" *Poisonous Paragraphs*, March 12, 2007. http://poisonousparagraphs.blogspot.com/2007/03/cause-and-effect-aka-whats-wrong-with.html.

Page 200

DJ Premier and Haze, *Haze Presents New York Reality Check 101* (New York: Payday/ffrr, 1997).

CHAPTER 7: ETHERNOMICS
Pillow Fights, Happy Slaps, and Other Memes That Leave a Mark

Pages 202–206

William Gibson, *All Tomorrow's Parties* (New York: Penguin, 1999), p. 173.

Patrick Hoge, "Pillow fight erupts amid shrieks, giggles," *San Francisco Chronicle,* February 15, 2006. http://www.sfgate.com/cgi-bin/article.cgi?f=/c/a/2006/02/15/BAGCJH8EI11.DTL.

"'Flashmob' of 12 Proposed to One Girl in Beijing," *CriEnglish.com,* September 3, 2006. http://english.cri.cn/3100/2006/09/03/202@134346.htm.

Pru Vincent, "Flash mob disco," *thelondonpaper,* December 20, 2006. Check out a video of the flash mob disco here: http://www.thelondonpaper.com/cs/Satellite/london/lcsearch/article/1157140552745?packedargs=suffix%3DArticle Controller.

"Colombian musicians organise online," *BBC News,* June 1, 2006. http://news.bbc.co.uk/2/hi/technology/5033626.stm.

"FARC blamed for Colombia club blast," *BBC News,* February 9, 2003. http://news.bbc.co.uk/2/hi/americas/2741105.stm.

Page 207

Seth Godin, *Unleashing the Ideavirus* (Dobbs Ferry, NY: Do You Zoom, 2001), pp. 23–24.

Stephen Hawking quote from "Life in the Universe," 1994 (lecture given by Stephen Hawking and Roger Penrose at the Isaac Newton Institute in Cambridge, the transcript of which can be viewed here: http://www.hawking.org.uk/pdf/life.pdf).

Page 211

Dizzee Rascal, interview by author, July 2002 (this interview originally appeared in the August 2002 edition of *RWD* magazine).

Page 211

Chris Campion, "Inside Grime," *Observer Music Monthly,* May 23, 2004. http://observer.guardian.co.uk/omm/story/0,,1219493,00.html.

Dizzee Rascal, interview by author, April 2003 (this interview originally appeared in the May 2003 edition of *RWD* magazine).

Page 212

Kelefa Sanneh, "If It's Grime, It Rhymes," *New York Times,* March 14, 2005.

Page 213

Dizzee Rascal, interview by author, August 2004 (this interview originally appeared in the September 2004 edition of *RWD* magazine).

Page 219

Malcolm Gladwell, *The Tipping Point* (New York: Little, Brown & Co, 2000) pp. 30–89.

Page 221

Catherine Holahan, "Raising the Bar on Viral Web Ads," *BusinessWeek*, July 23, 2006. http://www.businessweek.com/bwdaily/dnflash/content/jul2006/db2006072 4_535865.htm.

"I Sold It Through The Grapevine," *BusinessWeek*, May 29, 2006. http://www.businessweek.com/magazine/content/06_22/b3986060.htm?campaign_id=search.

Page 222

Michael Tchong, "Why Fast Is in Retail Fashion," *FastCompany.com*. http://www.fastcompany.com/resources/innovation/tchong/072604.html.

Page 222

For a thorough and brilliant analysis of how physical capital is losing its meaning, see Jeremy Rifkin, *The Age of Access* (London: Tarcher/Putnam, 2000).

Page 224

Matt Mason, "Slap Out of It," *RWD*, April 2005.

Page 224

Joseph Brean, "Happy Slapping," *National Post*, December 17, 2005. http://www.fradical.com/Assaults_recorded_on_cellphones.htm.

Page 225

Carl Christopher, UK Manager of Content and Sponsorship, Sony Entertainment UK, interview by author, August 8, 2006.

Page 226

Rana Reeves of Shine Communications, interview by author, August 8, 2006.

Richard Russell of XL Recordings, interview by author, August 8, 2006.

Pages 227–229

"Global net use makes rapid rise," *BBC News*, April 27, 2007. http://news.bbc.co.uk/2/hi/technology/6583141.stm.

Craig O'Hara, *The Philosophy of Punk* (Oakland, CA: AK Press, 1999), p. 21.

OUTRO
The Pirate's Dilemma: Changing the Game Theory

Page 232

The version of the simple prisoner's dilemma game used here is from: John Eatwell, Murray Millgate, Peter Newman (eds), *New Palgrave Series: Game Theory* (New York: W. W. Norton, 1989).

Page 234

Muhammad Yunus, "Seek Big Rewards in Small Ideas," from the article "How to Succeed in 2007," *Business 2.0.* http://money.cnn.com/popups/2006/biz2/howtosucceed/16.html.

Page 238

Charles Piller, "Bill Gates on Piracy: 'They'll Get Addicted, and Then We'll Collect,'" *Los Angeles Times*, April 9, 2006.

INDEX

ABOUT THE AUTHOR

Matt Mason is an award-winning writer, consultant, and entrepreneur based in New York City. He was the founding editor in chief of the underground fanzine *RWD*, which he helped grow into the U.K.'s number one urban music magazine and one of the world's leading urban music websites.

Printed in the United States
By Bookmasters